About the editor

Alex de Waal is executive director of the World
Peace Foundation and a research professor
at the Fletcher School, Tufts University. He
is considered one of the foremost experts on
Sudan and the Horn of Africa, and his scholarship and practice have also probed humanitarian
crisis and response, human rights, HIV/AIDS
and governance in Africa, and conflict and
peace-building. He was a member of the African
Union mediation team for Darfur (2005–06) and
senior adviser to the African Union High-Level
Implementation Panel for Sudan (2009–11). He
was on the list of *Foreign Policy*'s 100 most influential public intellectuals in 2008 and *Atlantic
Monthly*'s 27 'brave thinkers' in 2009.

ADVOCACY IN CONFLICT

CRITICAL PERSPECTIVES ON TRANSNATIONAL ACTIVISM

edited by Alex de Waal

with Jennifer Ambrose, Casey Hogle,
Trisha Taneja and Keren Yohannes

Zed Books
LONDON

Advocacy in Conflict: Critical perspectives on transnational activism was first published in 2015 by Zed Books Ltd, 7 Cynthia Street, London N1 9JF, UK

www.zedbooks.co.uk

Editorial copyright © Alex de Waal 2015
Copyright in this collection © Zed Books 2015

The right of Alex de Waal to be identified as the editor of this work has been asserted by him in accordance with the Copyright, Designs and Patents Act, 1988

Set in Monotype Plantin and FFKievit by Ewan Smith, London
Index: ed.emery@thefreeuniversity.net
Cover designed by www.alice-marwick.co.uk
Printed and bound in Great Britain by 4edge Limited, Essex

A catalogue record for this book is available from the British Library

ISBN 978-1-78360-273-5 hb
ISBN 978-1-78360-272-8 pb
ISBN 978-1-78360-274-2 eb
ISBN 978-1-78360-275-9 epub
ISBN 978-1-78360-276-6 mobi

CONTENTS

PREFACE

The start of this book was, unexpectedly, a quiet discussion between four students, over coffee and in between classes, at the Fletcher School of Law and Diplomacy at Tufts University. A discussion about various work experiences in the development and humanitarian aid sector quickly turned into a dialogue about the misrepresentations and inadequacies of advocacy campaigns seen in our work, centring on the last and most visible of them all – *Kony2012*. Eventually, this discussion was turned into a proposal for the World Peace Foundation Student Seminar Competition, which is an annual competition that gives students the opportunity to host a research seminar with renowned academics and practitioners on a topic of their choice. Our proposal was chosen, and over the next few months we worked with the wonderful staff of the World Peace Foundation to refine the topic, choose cases similar to Uganda and *Kony2012* from around the world, and invite academics and practitioners to contribute their own research and opinions. The research seminar was held at the Fletcher School on 28 February and 1 March 2013. At the end of the seminar, we realized that our conversations – though fruitful – were still incomplete, and moreover that these debates could benefit from a wider audience and added perspectives. And so the idea of a book developed, one that could encompass not only the discussions from the seminar and its participants, but also views from others working to promote a similar understanding of 'reclaimed activism'.

We would like to thank Lisa Avery and Bridget Conley-Zilkic at the World Peace Foundation, and all the seminar participants, including Rony Brauman, Holly Fisher, Kate Cronin-Furman, Mvemba Dizolele, Elliot Prasse-Freeman, Sara Roy, Amanda Taub and Kennedy Tumutegyereize, in addition to those who contributed to this volume.

1 | INTRODUCTION: TRANSNATIONAL ADVOCACY IN CONTENTION

Jennifer Ambrose, Casey Hogle, Trisha Taneja and Keren Yohannes

'Nothing for us without us'

Activists across time zones, decades and topics have used variations of the slogan 'nothing for us without us' to express a key tenet of responsible advocacy: people affected by conflict, rights abuses and other injustices should play the leading role in movements that advocate on their behalf. When repression, silencing or dispersal leaves those people disadvantaged, it places particular responsibilities on Western advocates to act in a way that allows the substantive agenda, targets and goals, media portrayal, and methods to be set in accordance with the articulated priorities of the affected population. Most recently associated with the international disability rights movement of the 1990s, 'Nothing for us without us' demands that audiences listen to the self-expressed interests and goals of oppressed people. In the wake of recent advocacy campaigns, such as Invisible Children's *Kony2012* film and the US Campaign for Burma's 'It Can't Wait' videos – both of which became international sensations more for their tactics and messaging than for the issues they promote – the slogan encourages reflection on the extent to which recent trends in transnational advocacy have deviated from core principles of responsible activism. Hence, the impetus for this book is our recognition of the need to reclaim international advocacy movements to make them more self-reflective and accountable to the people and the evolving situations they represent.

Our focus is on a particular subset of transnational activism, itself a subset of activism more generally, namely professionalized Western advocacy concerned with particular conflicts in other parts of the world. While there is a rich literature on global society and activism (Kaldor 2003; Feher 2007; Reydams 2011), Western-led campaigns that focus on particular conflict-affected countries are dealt with only in passing. While individual campaigns such as Save Darfur have generated both controversy and research (Mamdani 2009; Hamilton 2011), there is little comparative analysis on how these movements fit with broader issues of global civil society. This book targets that gap, and our central argument is that the development of these specific forms of activism, in which advocates have shaped strategies to fit the requirements of marketing their cause to Western publics, and adapted them to score tactical successes with Western governments (especially that of the USA), has led to the weakening or even abandonment of key principles. This is akin to what Mary Kaldor (2003) calls the 'taming' of civil society, as social movements transform into professionalized NGOs. The key principles we identify as needing to be asserted or reclaimed include receptivity to the perspectives of affected people and their diverse narratives and attention to deeper, underlying causes, and therefore a focus on strategic change rather than superficial victories.

In March 2012, Invisible Children unveiled its *Kony2012* campaign, based on sparse and ill-constructed logic, designed to 'make Kony famous'. What soon became one of the most viral YouTube videos in history sparked a mad dash by the organization's target audience of American high school and college students to purchase advocacy kits. With these kits, student activists purportedly possessed the tools needed to pressure the US Congress to take on the responsibility of stopping Joseph Kony (or, to be precise, not ending its support for efforts to stop him). However, the student activists and organizers ignored their obligation to represent the priorities of the affected population, a central tenet of responsible international advocacy. While students stepped up to the task of 'saving' the people of central Africa from the terror of the Lord's Resistance Army (LRA) – without being invited to consider the marginal role Africans themselves were allowed to play – the video's misleading portrayal of the situation on the ground sparked a widespread counter-movement and hearty discourse in the blogosphere. The Tumblr site most critical of *Kony2012*, Visible Children, gained thousands of followers, and major television networks began calling on academic experts to articulate their concerns over the campaign.

The *Kony2012* video succeeded in propelling Joseph Kony to international stardom. The seemingly black-and-white, for-or-against

Kony2012 debate that immediately followed the video's release provided a platform for everyone opposed to the campaign to name a plethora of reasons why it was bad. Few critics, however, could fully articulate how an international advocacy campaign in the twenty-first century should be conducted in an ethical, responsible and effective way. While *Kony2012* made it clear that, with skilful use of media, a mass public campaign on an international issue can make a big splash, it reinforced the need for local leadership and for being conscientious regarding the intricacies of a situation. As *Kony2012* began to outshine home-grown advocacy movements and their objectives for Uganda, it also brought up the necessity of ensuring enough space for indigenous and international movements to work together, with local movements setting the agenda and Western groups offering resources, scale and solidarity.

Two years later, in April 2014, a leading instance of 'hashtag activism' – the #BringBackOurGirls campaign – demanded the return of the over two hundred Nigerian girls kidnapped from the Chibok girls' school by the Islamic extremist group Boko Haram. This has interesting echoes of the activism against the LRA, beginning with the way the LRA's mass abduction of pupils from the Aboke girls' school in 1996 suddenly provided a focal point for wider awareness and campaigning across Uganda. Similarly, Boko Haram had been killing, abducting and terrorizing for more than two years before Nigeria's elite or Western actors began to take notice: it took the girls' kidnapping for this to happen.

The kidnapping sparked the origination of #BringBackOurGirls locally before the campaign was amplified internationally. The Nigerian campaign focused equally on Boko Haram and on the Nigerian government, and its ineptitude, corruption and brutality. It criticizes not only Boko Haram's devastating actions, but also the environment that has given the group its *raison d'être* and the ability to conduct such a major attack. Nigerians asked for the return of the Chibok girls, of course, but also for better governance, more security and less corruption. The activist message simplified a complicated story, but it did break through that domestic barrier.

The American narrative, though, diverged significantly from the original Nigerian campaign. Its focus is exclusively on Boko Haram. The Western campaign was not organized around a specific 'ask', but some Nigerians worried it would transmute into lobbying for American military action – as that is the default option for US foreign policy and American popular culture (Balogun 2014). However, despite the fact that Boko Haram is identified as a terrorist organization associated with al-Qaeda, the USA has not dispatched its own troops, at the time of writing. It provided surveillance aircraft to assist the Nigerian military, but US government spokespeople were openly critical of the Nigerian army's record on corruption and human rights (Schmidt and Knowlton 2014).

What accounts for this less interventionist message and outcome? A large part of the reason is likely to be reluctance in the US Department of Defense, translating into a policy decision in the White House not to intervene (ibid.). Insofar as the leading Washington lobbyists on African human rights issues pick up this signal, they are unlikely to advocate for an intervention that would be strongly resisted. A second, related reason is that none of the American 'advocacy superpowers' (Carpenter 2014: 40) have taken up the cause, leaving the agenda-setting – by default – to the Nigerians. As a result, the #BringBackOurGirls campaign failed to create a lasting international publicity blitz; its presence on social media platforms rapidly dwindled. The campaign left its Western audience with a short and savvy glimpse into a complicated Nigerian story, having diluted the message and having had almost no international impact (Fisher 2014). Cognizant of the lessons of *Kony2012*, Nigerian activists may be grateful for this neglect.

Key questions

With these two examples in mind, many questions demand further reflection regarding the future of international activism and how to more closely align efforts with the 'nothing for us without us' adage.

The first set of questions is about the legitimacy and accountability of Westerners advocating for geographically and culturally distant issues. If these advocates' legitimacy is not derived from the people on whose behalf they are advocating, what gives them the right to propose solutions? To whom are advocates accountable, and how are advocates accountable when they do harm?

A closely related question is: how are different advocacy groups to be involved? One of the recurrent themes of this volume is the overlapping cast that is involved in different campaigns: some focused on campaigning through publicity; others through using international organizations, including the platforms and instruments (such as treaties) they provide; others through the mobilization of mass constituencies; and still others through the intellectual labour of defining the issues and narratives. Among all these groups, the people immediately affected may struggle to find their voice, or – a less appreciated but equally significant challenge – to be able to reflect on the issues and define an agenda. Inclusivity means taking to heart the perspective of the affected people, and listening to different voices.

A third recurrent question concerns singularity versus multiplicity of narratives, and the related element of openness to new perspectives and voices. Part of what makes for superficial and easily co-opted advocacy is the singular narrative, which defines the story in a plausible and compelling manner, but prescribes a simplistic solution – which is almost invariably wrong. Inclusivity allows for multiple voices and a complex debate. On the other hand, the narratives with the most resonance are those that allow the faraway individual to make an emotional connection. This is one reason actors are often enrolled as spokespeople for international causes, because they specialize in such vicarious connectivity. *New York Times* columnist Nicholas Kristof labels and heavily employs such 'bridge characters', who are easily relatable to Western audiences, but define the issue through a single lens. A local 'bridge character' may also have a 'Janus face': she may say one thing to foreign sponsors, and another to her own constituents.

Following from this, more specifically, is a set of questions about the role of academics in activism. Should scholars with an in-depth knowledge of local issues have a say in setting the agenda for activist movements? How should we reconcile academic knowledge with the more practical demands of activism?

A fifth set of questions concerns the targets of activism and the relationship between the local and global. Given that activists cannot hope to change everything at once, how should they prioritize their targets? Should they enlist global power to change local conditions? And if so, on what basis should advocates engage with powerful governments, such as that of the USA, knowing that the governmental agenda will invariably prevail over the activists' at the end of the day? Should they target global inequities and enlist local power structures in that struggle, knowing that whatever their emancipatory rhetoric, politicians in conflict-affected countries tend towards the venal and brutal? Or should they target both levels of power, aware that activists have limited capacity for enacting real change? These questions recur throughout the case studies in this volume.

Those critical of campaigns like *Kony2012* should outline an alternative way forward, creating a model for responsible activism while drawing lessons from successful transnational advocacy movements.

However, it would not be appropriate to suggest a single unchanging model. Each activist campaign unfolds in a different local and international context. As Alex de Waal's historical overview in Chapter 2 makes clear, today's transnational advocates operate in very different historical conditions to those that confronted activists a generation ago. The heyday of radical transnational activism was in the 1970s and 1980s. The Cold War was on, the remnants of colonialism were fighting on in southern Africa, and the US government was struggling to assert its legitimacy in the wake of the Vietnam War and Watergate. The gold standard for activism was a mass movement that spanned different countries, even continents, and which could press governments for change using a range of tools including the media, public demonstrations, practical action in support of oppressed peoples, and legal and legislative measures. Veterans of those movements, when they observe today's *Kony2012* or Enough campaigns, feel the label 'activist' has been misappropriated by people more interested in celebrity profile and insider politics than in real change.

The world has changed: it is not possible to return to what De Waal calls the 'anti-colonial solidarity model' at a time when colonialism is history and the Western democracies' enemy is terrorism, not communism. For example, in the 1980s, the anti-apartheid campaign made Nelson Mandela its icon: he was a guerrilla commander whom the South African government labelled a 'terrorist', but the campaigners burnished his image while also making the irrefutable case that apartheid was wrong. Recent and ongoing occupations, such as those of the USA in Iraq and Israel in the Palestinian Territories, are the focus for more convoluted activism, especially in the USA, in part because the line between 'terrorist' and 'freedom fighter' has now become much more problematic. We are cautious about specifying any political or normative agenda that constitutes 'genuine' activism. Our concern is more with the process than the issues themselves. Instead of looking at the complete cloth of a successful activist movement and trying to replicate that, it is better to examine those elements that are positive and durable, and those that are problematic or transient. This challenge recurs throughout the volume and is taken up in the concluding chapter.

Outline of the book

The chapters examine various dimensions of the relationship between Western advocacy and local movements through six regional and three thematic case studies. With the goal of fostering dialogue, readers will have the space to reflect upon how to realize principles of responsible advocacy within their own contexts and roles. Although we primarily focus on conflict-affected countries, we include chapters on transnational issues that reveal different challenges of advocacy around issues that transcend borders.

In Chapter 2, Alex de Waal outlines the historical roots of Western advocacy and examines how current Western activist practices have evolved through particular global circumstances. He frames activism with reference to three abiding impulses: the personal salvation or fulfilment of the activist her- or himself; protection of the social order through charitable assistance to those in need, who might otherwise be subversive of that order; and an ethic of solidarity in support of radical political change. Transnational advocacy is a subset of broader activism, in which the tension between these three principles is often particularly acute, because of the remoteness of the subjects of the activism – in a faraway country, unable to add their voices in a straightforward manner. Drawing upon the 'boomerang model' of how local and transnational advocates interact (Keck and Sikkink 1998), De Waal shows how trajectories of initiating and guiding campaigns have changed in response to changing international political circumstance. In particular, he examines the way in which the model of professionalized adversarial advocacy, 'mobilizing shame', was utilized by human rights organizations in the

nd 1980s, and how this combined with humanitarian organiza-
advocacy for intervention in crisis in the 1990s to generate a
new form of specialized Western policy lobbying in Washington, DC,
and to a lesser extent in European capitals. This coincided with the
US government regaining its own sense of moral authority in world
affairs and resulted in a series of campaigns for Western military
intervention in humanitarian and human rights crises. He argues
that with the growth of these 'advocacy superpowers' that have close
links to policy-makers inside government, the ability of activists
in affected countries to set the agenda and determine priorities,
including definitions of success, has been undermined. The task
of reclaiming activism therefore consists of returning that primacy
to national actors, with Western activists obliged to act in a spirit
of self-critical solidarity. While recognizing that it is impossible to
return to the heyday of anti-colonial and anti-racist activism, De
Waal calls for scrutiny of the basic principles that made for effective
and ethical advocacy.

This chapter also situates the volume in the current debates on
transnational activism, drawing upon and critiquing the leading
current theories, including the work of Sydney Tarrow, Mary Kaldor,
Clifford Bob, Katharine Sikkink and her colleagues, and others. The
particular element that distinguishes the contribution from other
current literature is that it focuses on transnational activism in a
historical and comparative perspective.

The next three chapters – on Burma, Guatemala and Gaza – represent cases in which Western activism has linked with social movements and local activists pushing for democracy and human rights,
with mixed outcomes.

In his account of the democracy movement in Burma (Myanmar)
and its international supporters, Maung Zarni and Trisha Taneja
highlight the tensions that emerge when evolving national political
movements become linked to a one-dimensional strategy, deriving
from the priorities of Western advocates. In this case, the international campaign elevated Aung San Suu Kyi to be the singular icon
of democratic resistance and human rights. While this gave a Burmese face and Burmese leadership to the international campaign, it
undermined and disenfranchised the broader democracy movement
in Burma. When the USA and European countries decided to move

towards normalization of relations with Burma, they were able to do so on the basis of relatively modest domestic political reforms, because they required only the assent of Suu Kyi. The role of Suu Kyi has since turned out to be a disappointment, with fundamental issues of human rights and democratization shunted aside in the Western rush to embrace Burma as a political and commercial partner. This case illustrates the difficult political challenges inherent in any campaign for change and shows that the solutions required go much deeper than simply identifying a local leader to support.

The Burma case also highlights challenges of inclusivity. What should be the role of the diaspora in shaping a campaign? Burmese exiles and refugees played an important role in raising consciousness and setting an activist agenda, but they often had an incomplete view and were not united. A related question is the balance between the Burmese who advocated for democratic liberalization and those who campaigned for the rights of ethnic minorities – two groups whose agendas have not always converged.

The iconic role of Suu Kyi in the Burmese democracy campaign invites a comparison with Nelson Mandela within the anti-apartheid movement. The transnational campaign against apartheid in South Africa is a paradigmatic case of a successful activist movement, and Mandela was at its centre. The similarities and contrasts demand closer attention.

The international anti-apartheid movement was closely engaged with the South African community and the leadership of the African National Congress (ANC). Although the transnational movement had its origins with a British organization mobilizing consumer boycotts to oppose the apartheid regime, the anti-apartheid movement had strong local ties to, and support for, the ANC. The decision to choose one individual – Nelson Mandela – to become the international face of the anti-apartheid struggle was made at the insistence of the British movement. Its demand was based on the need to develop a stronger international image, and was initially resisted by the ANC, which opposed the development of a personality cult. Committed to strict party discipline and collective leadership, the ANC leadership nonetheless submitted to the wishes of their international counterparts, but it made the concession only as a tactical decision. Undoubtedly, the creation of Mandela as a personalized symbol of resistance was an important part of the struggle against apartheid. However, Mandela himself was deeply aware of how and why this decision was made, and that he remained subject to the discipline of the party and its strategic goals. For him, his celebrity status was an asset to be utilized for the collective good, not a personal entitlement (De Waal 2013).

Zarni and Taneja describe how the Burmese activist campaign elevated Suu Kyi to a similar status, but found that their icon was not grounded in a disciplined democratic movement in the same way.

Roddy Brett's case study on Guatemala exposes the two-faced nature of Western assistance to a national movement. It focuses on indigenous activism in support of the rights of the Maya people, who were the main victims of the genocidal counter-insurgency conducted by the Guatemalan junta in the early 1980s, and it broadens the cast to include those involved in promoting the 'Liberal Peace' agenda, a set of actors closely associated with multilateral institutions.

The Guatemala case includes neither a national icon nor the kinds of celebrity activists who have become familiar from contemporary African causes. According to Brett, in part this is because the campaign was developed before the rise of celebrity activism, and in part it reflects the strength of Latin American civil society advocacy, which did not leave room for such people to enter. International activists vigorously campaigned against US support for the genocidal government of General Rios Montt, but they did not share a common analysis of the underlying political causes of the conflict and repression. While local civil society was strong enough to put some issues on the agenda for peace talks, it was not strong enough to ensure that its definition of the issue prevailed over the 'Liberal Peace' framework promoted by international actors, including Western governments and multilateral organizations. The resulting peace agreement enshrines the rights of indigenous people, but it also consolidates a political system that limits the ability of the Maya people to pursue their core agenda, including land reform and territorial autonomy. After the peace agreement of 1996, Maya leaders were required to compete within a political system in which they remained at a severe structural disadvantage.

The Guatemalan case therefore illustrates how a deep agenda

can be set by international actors, ostensibly to the benefit of their national subjects of concern and solidarity, but informed by ideological structures that are at odds with how those national actors define their predicament.

Anat Biletzki analyses the case of activism for the people of Gaza, in which transnational advocates speak out against Israel's actions and call for policy changes by Israel and the USA. The Gazan case is unique and complex, and Biletzki delves into the practical, political and philosophical issues it raises. Israel is both a Western country closely associated with the USA and also an occupying power itself, and therefore the distinction between domestic and transnational advocacy is blurred.

Those advocating for the rights of Palestinians in Gaza face several profound difficulties, most particularly a very powerful and effective advocacy apparatus that works on behalf of the Israeli state. This skilfully and persistently uses a claim of Jewish-Israeli victimhood as the basis for a narrative that portrays the Palestinians as aggressors. The Israeli government and its friends also argue that Israel is the only democracy in the region and its adversaries in Gaza are terrorists. In the international arena, especially in the USA, Israeli state definitions and goals are dominant and serve to deny pro-Palestinian activism a space in the public debate. Biletzki concludes by noting that 'ironic' Israeli activism remains dominant and the fundamental challenge for activism in genuine solidarity with the Gazan people requires a careful deconstruction of claims to victimhood.

Biletzki documents the breadth of forms of activism in support of the 'abandoned people of the Israeli regime' but notes the fundamental problem, which is that advocacy *for* Gazans is identified as advocacy *against* Israel, making advocacy into a taking of sides. Compare for a moment the anti-apartheid movement, which campaigned to dismantle the regime precisely for a better future for all South Africans, irrespective of race. The fundamental challenge for activists for Gazan Palestinians is how to change the basic political calculus so they stand for something positive for all.

The next three case studies – on the Democratic Republic of Congo (DRC), Uganda and its neighbours, and South Sudan – are those in which Western activism has focused on armed conflicts in Africa, and are all instances in which there has been a marked divergence between national and local priorities on one hand and Western advocacy strategies on the other.

Laura Seay examines the case of the 'conflict minerals' campaign in the DRC, one of the highest-profile campaigns of the Washington DC-based advocacy group the Enough Project. It has the objective of pressuring international companies that purchase minerals from eastern DRC to certify that their minerals are 'conflict free' and thereby contribute to an end to the illicit financing of armed groups in that area, thus reducing violence. Enough trumpets this as a success. Seay deconstructs each part of this chain of argument, both analytically and empirically, and questions the claims of the campaign. There is, she argues, powerful evidence that the 'conflict minerals' campaign has had adverse effects on the economy and politics of DRC. She also points out that Congolese activists have never made the arguments or claims put forward by Enough: their focus has been very different, on national processes of democratization. This case study is a stark illustration of the perils of defining a campaign, and setting its goals and methods, around the requirements of a Western advocacy group, rather than a local constituency.

The conflict minerals campaign has interesting parallels with contemporary labour rights activism. Gay Seidman (2007) has criticized the way Western activists have focused their methods on consumer boycotts of goods produced in sweatshops or using child workers, using images that demand sympathy, rather than on building up trade unions in the affected countries, which would emphasize the strength and dignity of workers and enable them to articulate their own grievances. She writes, 'Examples of transnational campaigns that have successfully strengthened local unions are hard to find. Around the world, local trade unionists express strong suspicions of transnational campaigns ... [which] find it difficult to construct viable channels for workers' voices' (p. 35).

No book on contemporary international advocacy would be complete without a discussion of the Lord's Resistance Army (LRA) and the *Kony2012* campaign mounted by Invisible Children. Mareike Schomerus provides an analysis of this, based on her deep involvement in northern Uganda and the adjoining areas of DRC, South Sudan and Central African Republic, in which the LRA was active after it was removed from Uganda in 2006–08. She challenges the simplistic portrayal of the LRA by the *Kony2012* campaigners and argues that those Western campaigners have unknowingly colluded with the LRA leadership in constructing a 'singular narrative' that emphasizes the special, irrational and spiritual power of the LRA, and in playing up the military dimension of the conflict and playing down its politics. Schomerus shows how the arming of local militia to combat the LRA and broadcasts by a radio station set up by Invisible Children have had the effect of amplifying villagers' fears about the LRA, both of which generate greater insecurity for local people.

One of the most striking elements of the *Kony2012* campaign is that it called for US military intervention in a Third World country. It would have been unthinkable for transnational activists in an earlier era to campaign to dispatch American troops on combat missions to developing countries. It is testament to the success of the post-Cold War US administrations in shedding the moral opprobrium of the Vietnam War era that American advocates can look so favourably on the use of American military force. Another element that emerges from the story is that Invisible Children was campaigning in support of an existing US government policy – the troops it was calling for had already been deployed – although the casual observer would not realize this.

Until the eruption of civil war in December 2013, South Sudan was proclaimed as a Western activists' success story. Alex de Waal challenges this. In a case study that has a number of interesting echoes of Zarni's account of Burma, he highlights how a group of Washington, DC policy lobbyists, rotating in and out of government and campaigning organizations, set out to support the leadership of the Sudan People's Liberation Army (SPLA). In contrast to the tradition of solidarity with liberation movements, which had followed the ethos that an organization campaigning against oppression should hold itself to higher ethical standards than its adversary, the Western advocates for the SPLA preferred to explain away or justify the human rights abuses, corruption and anti-democratic behaviour of their South Sudanese counterparts. The particular tragedy of this choice was that Sudan did indeed possess a vibrant democratic movement, which the most prominent Western activists chose not to support. When the war broke out in South Sudan, and the pretence that the SPLA was promoting a progressive agenda could no longer be sustained, its apologists in Washington, DC were thrown into confusion. However, this represents an important opportunity for reappraising the principles of activism more broadly.

The South Sudanese case highlights the way in which the US administration set the policy and the advocates followed. The key decision to support the SPLA was taken by the Clinton administration in 1997, and widespread American campaigning on the cause of southern Sudan followed. Until the outbreak of civil war in South Sudan in 2013 the advocates' criticism of the US government was that it was not doing enough to support the South Sudanese, and ironically the administration took the lead in criticizing the SPLA's human rights record.

Three chapters on issue-based activism conclude the book, concerned with disability rights, the arms business and land rights. These are issues more central to the broader debates on global civil society, and are included here in part because of the light they shed on the country-specific campaigns. All have connections with conflict. The twentieth-century movement for the rights of disabled people began during the First World War, with René Cassin and the Conférence internationale des associations de mutilés de guerre et anciens combattants (Cabanes 2014), and groups such as Handicap International and the Landmine Survivors' Network were instrumental in the International Campaign to Ban Landmines. There is an interesting parallel evolution, between the 'old social movements' focused on transforming states and the 'new' ones, focused on individual autonomy and resisting governmental intrusion (see Kaldor 2003), and the shift from anti-colonial activism to anti-atrocity advocacy. But what is perhaps most striking is the tenuous connections between country-specific advocacy and broader campaigns on arms and land grabbing – issues that often lie at the heart of armed conflict.

Chapter 8 delves into a thematic case in which tensions between a group demanding rights and representation and a transnational advocacy campaign have been evident: disability rights. Tsitsi Chataika, Maria Berghs, Abraham Mateta and Kudzai Shava consider how the intricacies of representation are simplified when Western activists are directing the narratives. Drawing upon the experiences of African disability rights activists and their struggles to set the agenda, goals and methods of campaigning and policy, the authors reflect upon how the structures and operations of NGOs can end up reproducing the marginalization of the concerns of local activists. This chapter distinguishes between superficial advocacy that targets only the immediate issues and activism that addresses the deeper political and economic structures that disempower people with disabilities. In order to pursue the latter, the authors argue that it is essential to challenge the power structures associated with global neoliberalism.

The second thematic case is the global arms business and campaigns over the last hundred years to restrict arms and to make the arms trade more transparent and less corrupt. Andrew Feinstein and Alex de Waal consider the reasons for the lack of international activism on the broader issue of the global arms business, looking first at how efforts in the period after the First World War made significant progress but were then stalled – and discredited – by the rise of fascist militarism and the Second World War. They then consider how, in the shadow of nuclear weapons and the Vietnam War, the business of conventional weaponry was largely neglected. The chapter details the campaigns that have made headway in the last twenty years, including the International Campaign to Ban Landmines (ICBL), the Cluster Munitions Coalition and the campaign for an Arms Trade Treaty, identifying the tensions within these campaigns. In each case, a well-organized and influential elite advocacy group has set a limited agenda, framed around achieving progress in international legislation, but at the cost of addressing deeper challenges of tackling the structural issues in the arms business.

The ICBL is an important case study. It is widely heralded as a success and an exemplar to be emulated. Feinstein and De Waal question this. Analysis of the ICBL allows us to understand how an international campaign can be inclusive, by engaging with all groups in all countries around the world where landmines posed a significant problem. The ICBL was centred on a coalition of NGOs lobbying for both local and international action, and it also involved grassroots organizations for far-reaching impact. It was strengthened by the fact that its founders were well grounded in the complexity of their campaign and understood the technicalities of landmines. The strengths of the campaign lay in this inclusiveness and in its agenda, which was both focused on a particular weapon and broad, in that it encompassed all manner of action against these weapons. Its weakness lay in the readiness of some of its leaders to rush for a premature declaration of victory based on a narrow definition of the issue and the priorities of just a small segment of the campaign. Feinstein and De Waal argue that the Ottawa Convention that banned anti-personnel landmines was both premature and incomplete, and served to demobilize the campaign when there was still much work to be done. They also suggest that subsequent arms campaigns, such as the campaign against cluster munitions, have failed to learn the right lessons, and as a result have taken arms advocacy in the wrong direction. This chapter concludes by noting that the strongest campaigns in this field are those that are the most inclusive and which target the underlying issues of militarism.

We conclude by examining a thematic case study that has, perhaps, taken a step forward in reclaiming activism through complementary interactions between local and Western activists. Rachel Ibreck's chapter on land rights explores how local campaigns have led the movement against land grabs in Africa and Latin America with the support of international organizations and Western advocacy campaigns. She identifies how the question of land rights is itself in contention among scholars and campaigners, and how academics – including those in affected countries – have taken a leading role in defining the issues and linking communities with various kinds of activists, national and international, policy-focused and public campaigners. Diverse groups have been engaged in exposing and campaigning against land grabbing. Even though they do not agree on the fundamental definition of the problem, specifically whether it is a rights issue and, if so, what kinds of rights are involved, they have managed to cooperate on a common platform. Ibreck's analysis highlights the difficulties activists face in identifying underlying structural issues and reaching agreement on a deep agenda. On the basis of this deliberately untheorized consensus, the campaign has put this issue on the international agenda, itself an important success.

Reflecting on the campaign against land grabbing in the wider context outlined in this volume, the success is perhaps related to the way in which land rights have yet to become a major focus for the Western 'advocacy superpowers', which has allowed space for a creative debate among a range of practitioners, activists and academics. However, the success of this disparate coalition in actually changing global policies and practices is yet to be tested.

References

Balogun, J. (2014) 'Dear world, your hashtags won't #BringBackOurGirls', *Guardian*, 9 May, www.theguardian. com/world/2014/may/09/nigeria-hashtags-wont-bring-back-our-girls-bringbackourgirls, accessed 23 June 2014.

Cabanes, B. (2014) *The Great War and the Origins of Humanitarianism, 1918–1924*, Cambridge: Cambridge University Press.

Carpenter, C. (2014) *'Lost' Causes: Agenda vetting in global issue networks and the shaping of human security*, Ithaca, NY: Cornell University Press.

De Waal, A. (2013) 'Recognizing Nelson Mandela', World Peace Foundation, 10 December, sites.tufts.edu/reinventingpeace/2013/12/10/recognizing-nelson-mandela/, accessed 26 June 2014.

Feher, M. (ed.) (2007) *Nongovernmental Politics*, New York: Zone Books.

Fisher, M. (2014) 'Forgetting Nigeria's girls', *Vox*, 14 June, www.vox. com/ 2014/6/24/5837836/forgetting-nigerias-girls?utm_medium=social&utm_source=

twitter&utm_name=staff &utm_campaign= voxdotcom&utm_content=tuesday, accessed 25 June 2014.

Hamilton, R. (2011) *Fighting for Darfur: Public Action and the Struggle to Stop Genocide*, New York: Palgrave.

Kaldor, M. (2003) *Global Civil Society: An answer to war*, London: Polity.

Keck, M. and K. Sikkink (1998) *Activists beyond Borders: Advocacy networks in international politics*, Ithaca, NY: Cornell University Press.

Mamdani, M. (2009) *Saviors and Survivors: Darfur, Politics and the War on Terror*, New York: Pantheon.

Reydams, L. (ed.) (2011) *Global Activism Reader*, New York: Continuum.

Schmidt, E. and B. Knowlton (2014) 'U.S. officials question ability of Nigeria to rescue hostages', *New York Times*, 15 May, www.nytimes. com/2014/05/16/world/africa/nigerian-military-schoolgirl-hunt. html?_r=0>, accessed 23 June 2014.

Seidman, G. W. (2007) *Beyond the Boycott: Labor Rights, Human Rights, and Transnational Activism*, New York: Russell Sage Foundation.

2 | GENEALOGIES OF TRANSNATIONAL ACTIVISM

Alex de Waal

Introduction

The *Kony2012* video produced by Jason Russell of Invisible Children caused a shudder of dismay among scholars – because of its success in generating an extraordinary level of public attention in the USA and Europe, because of its simplistic and misleading message, and because it claimed the mantle of anti-atrocity activism for what appeared to be military adventurism. Directed with a skill that evoked comparison with Leni Riefenstahl, these twenty-nine minutes became, nearly instantaneously, both famous and the target of scorn. *Kony2012* became a touchstone for Western advocates, dividing them into a camp that believed in the legitimacy of viewers' emotional awakening, and an opposing camp that believed in the authenticity of a resolution of the conflict in that unhappy part of central Africa, derived from the political realities and experiences of the people who actually live there.

The video was endorsed by celebrities who applauded Russell's manifest skill in video production. The performer's task is to make the audience feel vicarious emotion, and the performer-activist focuses on the emotions of outrage and/or pity at a current state of affairs, and satisfaction or fulfilment at doing something that, it is promised, will mitigate it. This is a well-established element in philanthropy and social advocacy, occasionally so strikingly narcissistic that it has excited cultural critics to identify a 'post-humanitarian' sensibility, which is all about the subjective feeling of authenticity of the consumer, and very little to do with recognizing the objective suffering of a distant person (Chouliaraki 2013).[1]

There would be no activism without emotion, and no humanitarianism or progressive politics without the emotions of outrage, sympathy, empathy and the personal fulfilment that comes through acts of kindness and solidarity. Peter Benenson, the founder of Amnesty

International, wrote candidly that he hoped 'to find a common base upon which the idealists of the world can cooperate ... Those whom the Amnesty Appeal primarily aims to free are the men and women imprisoned by cynicism and doubt' (quoted in Buchanan 2002: 593). Transnational advocacy occurs where humanitarian action meets social and political activism. But when the emotions that propel humanitarianism are projected on to silent faraway strangers and are indifferent to evidence, they are ripe for co-option by the powerful.

In the case of *Kony2012*, the Ugandan government and the US Department of Defense Africa Command (AFRICOM) were the immediate beneficiaries. If the Ugandan president, Yoweri Museveni, did not already have Kony as an enemy, he would most likely invent him, so helpful is the LRA commander to the Ugandan leader's agenda of maintaining a high defence budget (beyond the scrutiny of parliament and international donor auditors) and projecting military power beyond his frontiers (Mwenda 2010).

After being appointed as US Permanent Representative to the United Nations, Samantha Power gave her first speech to a meeting attended by the Invisible Children group: 'You're not just activists. You're leaders. You're diplomats. And we who have the privilege to serve in government can learn a lot from watching you' (Power 2013). Among the young Americans who supported the *Kony2012* video there are many who would consider themselves social liberals and (in the USA) likely Obama voters, and this is no doubt one of the reasons why Power was eager to connect with them. But it is interesting to note contiguities with right-wing transnational activism. For example, Invisible Children is aligned with evangelical Christian groups that have aggressively promoted a homophobic agenda. A deeper connection is the isomorphism between the interventionist agenda of Invisible Children, Enough and their ilk, and the neoconservative militarism that led to the invasion of Iraq. This is not a phenomenon that easily lends itself to placement on a left–right political spectrum: it can be progressive at home and regressive abroad.

Kony2012 is a paean to power – especially arms – as symbolized by a photograph of Russell and two other founders of Invisible Children posing with guns in the company of South Sudanese soldiers.[2] Russell and his friends seem cheerfully oblivious to the implications of their posing in this way, regarding it as a bit of a joke to tease their friends back home. They show a lack of empathetic imagination bordering on narcissism.

Invisible Children received an endorsement from Bono, albeit with the proviso that he hoped that the video would generate enough interest to help 'lasting meaningful solutions' (Browne 2013: 110). Bono's humanitarianism is of the variety that does not challenge power. It is action in a venerable tradition of Christian charity that (in the English-speaking world) dates back to the Elizabethan Poor Laws, intended to protect the realm from disturbances wrought by hungry vagrants. This is a second organizing principle for humanitarian principle and action – using resources and expertise to mitigate suffering, so as better to preserve existing power.

Both Russell and Bono have some ardent supporters in Uganda. This is not surprising: they come with a package that offers a kind of material-moral cargo cult, promising both riches and salvation at an unspecified but not-too-distant future date, and sufficient immediate down payment to make a living now. In Malawi, Harri Englund (2006) has described a similar phenomenon in which local human rights activists/entrepreneurs pursue what might be called a 'hunter-gatherer' strategy of picking off those fruits that are within reach, offered by human rights donors. Such phenomena are familiar to historians of missionary and colonial penetration of Africa. From desperate circumstance or personal ambition, people readily try to associate with and benefit from the power and resources of international campaigns, and will use one language when speaking to foreign patrons and another when dealing with their peers and constituents.[3]

There is a third tradition of humanitarian sensibility and action, which is the project of collective action for social justice and socio-political change. Historically this has been rooted in social movements that make claims on the national state (Kaldor 2003; Tarrow 2011). There appears to be little sign of this in northern Uganda and across its borders, despite the proliferation of highly visible NGOs, national and international, around the main towns of this region. But closer inspection reveals several vibrant traditions of social movements for progressive or democratic political change in those countries, even under the least auspicious circumstances (Monga 1996; De Waal and Ibreck 2013).

This chapter outlines a genealogy of transnational advocacy for humanitarian issues and political emancipation. This exists at the intersection of social and political activism (typically in the form of a domestically rooted social movement aimed at political change) and humanitarian solidarity (typically action to support suffering people in a distant country). The ideational and practical space for such advocacy is defined by the three approaches mentioned above: personal salvation or fulfilment; preserving social order and power relations; and collective action for transforming society in pursuit of a more just order.

An identifiably modern form of each of the three elements emerged in the late eighteenth century. Subsequently, the centres of gravity of these different forms of social action have shifted. Today's transnational advocacy was shaped by the anti-colonial and civil rights struggles of the mid-twentieth century: movements that shared important precepts but also diverged on key principles. During the 1970s this evolved into a dominant model of adversarial advocacy headed by Western human rights organizations. In the 1990s, these models changed again with the post-Cold War atrocities in former Yugoslavia and sub-Saharan Africa and calls for intervention, and yet again with the war on terror and a parallel liberal anti-genocide interventionism. In parallel to the shift from 'old' social movements at national level that sought to organize governmental power for the benefit of broader constituencies, to 'new' ones concerned with freedom from such governmental intrusions (Kaldor 2003), we can see an evolution from movements for national self-determination from imperial rule, to anti-atrocity campaigning that extends intrusive forms of global governance into former colonies. Western governments – notably the Obama administration – have found mechanisms for managing today's transnational advocacy lobbies. In part, they co-opt the advocates, and in part they make sufficient superficial adjustments to what the advocates demand to give a plausible illusion of influence.

Ambassador Power put the Obama administration's approach cogently, speaking to Invisible Children: 'what matters to us in government is our partnership with you. We need your voices and energy. We need your ideas and your sense of mission. We need your activism and your action. And since the most sustainable and effective policies are those with public support, *your activism enables us to do more*' (Power 2013, emphasis added). What she generously credits the *Kony2012* video with achieving was already in fact determined as policy by the White House and the Pentagon. By contrast, Vali Nasr, who served in Richard Holbrooke's team, and witnessed the marginalization of diplomatic strategy in the Obama administration, has a different perspective. He writes:

> In the cocoon of our public debate, Obama gets high marks on foreign policy. That is because his policies' principal aim is not to make strategic choices but to satisfy public opinion – he has done more of the things that people want and fewer of the things that we have to do that may be unpopular. (Nasr 2013: 12)

Power's passion may be genuine, but her government's strategy boils down to co-opting the campaigners as voters. The concern of this chapter is what this episode tells us about the state of European and American transnational activism.

The evolution of transnational advocacy

Thomas Davies has warned against linear narratives that celebrate the advance of global civil society, noting for example that while the *number of NGOs* may have risen to unprecedented levels in recent decades, the *numbers of people* participating in these organizations today may not match those of a century ago.

> Contrary to conventional opinion, it can be argued that in some respects transnational civil society has failed fully to recover from the mid-century shocks of the Great Depression, Second World War and Cold War. For example, popular participation in post-Cold War campaigns such as Jubilee 2000 and the Global Call to Action against Poverty has arguably been less substantial as a proportion of the world's population than was participation in the campaign for disarmament of the 1920s and 1930s. (2011: 41)

Measuring activism is at best imprecise, and Davies' caution is in order. We can instead chart how social movements – especially metro-colonial and transnational campaigns – have changed. Mary Kaldor (2003) has identified 'old' social movements as those that 'aimed at persuading states to act and in the process helped to strengthen them', whereas 'the "new" movements are much more concerned about individual autonomy, about resisting the state's intrusion into everyday life'. Sydney Tarrow (2011) analyses the trajectories of social movement organization, which, depending on the kinds of participation and the orientation towards the authorities, can become radicalized, institutionalized or commercialized, or can suffer involution. I have described how African liberation struggles made common cause with the American civil rights movement, but 'second generation' Western human rights organizations diverged sharply from the political agendas of Africa's liberators once the latter were in power (De Waal 2003). We also need to be alert to how terms such as activist, social movement and transnational civil society can attach equally to emancipatory, apolitical and reactionary projects (cf. Chappell 2006; Bob 2011).

Most scholarly attention has focused either on national social movements or international issue-based movements. Our concern here is a specific subset: the coalition between a domestically rooted movement in a colony (or post-colony) and solidarity from a campaign in the metropolis (or elsewhere in the developed world). There is no shortage of political histories of the independence movements in Latin America, Asia and Africa, and their close brethren such as the anti-apartheid movement and advocacy for the Palestinians and Eritreans, but these tend to be individual case studies rather than chapters in the story of global civil society.

Metro-colonial and transnational advocacy is rooted in the broader social movements of the era. Thus European solidarity for the American Revolution was an offshoot of domestic political agitation. The international workers' movement of the nineteenth century was truly international, but consisted of a coalition of equals – social and political groups organizing to promote their own interests (albeit with a dose of idealism and allies in other social classes). The post-Great War transnational humanitarian rights campaigns, for the war-disabled, to create the International Labour Office, for famine relief in Russia, were either European affairs or run by Americans on behalf of Europeans with strategic intent (Cabanes 2014). The distinct element in transnational activism is that the metropolitan advocates are motivated by principle or sentiment, and do not have a material interest in the issue. But it is, of course, political nonetheless.

Anti-colonial solidarity and its variants The history of metro-colonial activism begins in the second half of the eighteenth century with the Quaker-led transatlantic anti-slavery campaign (David 2007), followed by English radicals' support for American revolutionaries. A century later, Edmund Morel's campaign against the Belgian king Leopold's misrule in Congo – a land that neither of the two men ever saw for themselves – provides another famous humanitarian campaign. Non-violent resistance by Mohandas Gandhi, first in South Africa and subsequently in India, probably constitutes the largest such movement in history, and it enjoyed solidarity among metropolitan radicals, notably including Irish nationalists who played an important bridging role.

The transnational campaign against the Fascist invasion of Ethiopia linked a 'Southern' cause to a pressing European issue. This case is a revealing anomaly. It flagged philosophical tensions that were to persist throughout the colonial era: the Ethiopian emperor Haile Selassie was an articulate exponent of anti-racism and multilateralism on the international stage, but a feudal autocrat at home, and the anti-Fascist Sylvia Pankhurst became an ardent admirer of a ruler who presided over repression and famine in his domain.

The leaders of mid-twentieth-century African independence movements – many of which also count as exemplars of non-violent political action – worked closely with one another in the global Pan African Movement, with the Asian and Latin American anti-colonialists, and with the American civil rights movement. They gained state power, fulfilling (in the words of Kwame Nkrumah) the aim of 'winning the political kingdom first'. Prioritizing national self-determination over individual human rights, these movements were contributors to state-building, in much the same way as the eighteenth- and nineteenth-century struggles for political liberties in Europe and America helped build modern institutionalized states.

In the era of 'old' social movements and associated transnational advocacy campaigns, we therefore have two models. One is humanitarian: a 'parallel campaign', comprising Western advocates who pressure their own governments on behalf of faraway oppressed and unheard people such as slaves. The second is advocacy in support of a national social and political movement. This 'anti-colonial solidarity' model has three particular features. First, the initiative lies with the

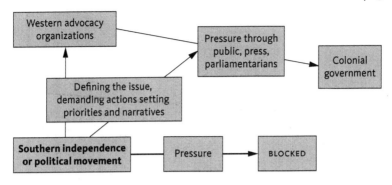

2.1 Anti-colonial solidarity model

Southern movement, which defines the issues (primarily: decolonization). Secondly, the Southern movement enlists like-minded Western advocates, who may assist with tactics, but cannot define the goals. Thirdly, the two sets of players have the same target: the imperial government.

The victories of anti-colonial struggles – armed and unarmed – were won as much in the metropolis as in the colonies. These movements had ambivalent links to Western human rights movements. On one hand, the right of self-determination was juxtaposed with universal human rights, in such a manner that the achievement of collective freedom from colonial subjugation was a distinct struggle to that of achieving individual rights (Moyn 2010), and on the other, a generation of African liberation leaders was closely associated with the civil rights leaders in the USA, creating a remarkable transcontinental solidarity and shared ownership (Sutherland and Meyer 2000; De Waal 2003; Bartkowski 2013). For transnational activists, the tensions at the United Nations between the right of self-determination and human rights mattered less than the ethos of shared struggle for human dignity. These struggles also had a clear political aim, articulated by their African leaders: national independence, and in the case of South Africa, a democratic non-racial country. In these movements, the main target of Western mobilization and pressure was the metropolitan sponsor of the local regime. Thus, Britain was targeted in order to press the Rhodesian settler regime to surrender to majority rule, and Western countries that supported South Africa were targeted by the anti-apartheid movement.

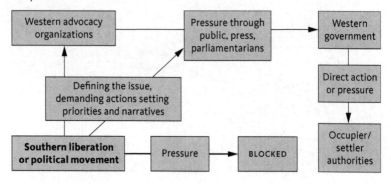

2.2 Anti-neocolonial solidarity model

When the anti-colonial struggle had been won – signified by the independence of the Portuguese colonies in 1974 – space was opened for transnational solidarity movements that focused on individual human rights. Self-determination struggles continued too, but with a different character: Western solidarity with post-colonial independence struggles in Tibet, Bangladesh, Biafra, East Timor, Western Sahara, South Sudan and Eritrea targeted Asian and African governments, not European imperial powers or white settler regimes. As the target shifted, the discourse of genocide and a focus on famine relief became more prominent, and advocacy became dominated by specialized advocacy groups.

Solidarity with Palestine is a special case. As discussed by Anat Biletzki in this volume, divergent narratives clashed with the creation of Israel and, especially, the Israeli occupation of Palestinian territories following the 1967 war. For many anti-colonial activists, this was nothing other than latter-day colonial occupation, but such advocacy ran into an exceptionally well-organized publicity and propaganda campaign by the Israeli government and its supporters, especially in the USA. Unlike other liberation movements, the Palestine Liberation Organization was never able to set the international agenda and claim the moral high ground.

Biafra occupies another special place in the story. The basic political issue – Biafran secessionism in response to repression and atrocity by the Nigerian Federal Government – was defined by the Biafran political elite. But, assisted by a public relations firm in London, Markpress, and by sympathetic Western journalists, missionaries and aid workers, the Biafrans turned a humanitarian crisis to political effect. The Biafrans identified the humanitarian issue in an opportunistic manner for its utilitarian benefits, not because that defined the Biafran cause. Hence we have a variant: the 'anti-neocolonial' solidarity model. As with anti-colonial struggles, post-colonial liberation struggles were won or lost as much in Western capitals as on the streets and battlefields of southern Africa, South-East Asia, Latin America and the Middle East.

The human rights revolution of the 1970s An importantly different form of transnational advocacy developed in Latin America in the 1970s, which, together with near-contemporaneous developments in Greece and eastern Europe, created a new form of linkage between Western advocacy organizations and non-violent social movements elsewhere in the world. The focus was civil and political rights, and from this emerged a new focus, notably in America, on human rights. This represented a decisive shift from promoting the state sovereignty of oppressed peoples, to challenging the sovereignty exercised over these people by their rulers (see Moyn 2010: 116–17). Right-wing dictatorships and communist regimes suppressed dissent and blocked opportunities for mobilization in pursuit of rights. Western organizations – paradigmatically, Americas Watch and Helsinki Watch, later to become Human Rights Watch (HRW) – campaigned on their behalf. Initially human rights solidarity was a matter of principle, of lighting a candle in the dark, as it were. But over fifteen years, the effects were spectacular. It is worth dwelling on this particular historical development, because the resulting method and model came to dominate the field of international rights activism. All current methods are variants of the 'mobilizing shame' or 'leveraging hypocrisy' approach developed by the two watch committees in the 1970s and perfected in the 1980s.

The 1970s saw a remarkable turnaround in US public discourse on human rights. At the beginning of the decade, the government was mired in the Vietnam War and then Watergate, and the country was divided as never before, but by the end, the concept of human rights had crystallized as a central aspiration of national self-image and foreign policy (Keys 2014). Although the election of Jimmy Carter as president marked the zenith of this, perhaps a more striking index of this transformation was the fact that the politician who mentioned human rights more than any other in his 1976 campaign speeches was Henry Kissinger. As Barbara Keys notes, 'It was testament to how deeply the concept had infiltrated U.S. diplomacy that a secretary of state who raged against it in private felt obliged to embrace it, within limits, in public' (ibid.: 221–2). The immediate post-Vietnam turmoil and self-reflection had led to a spate of initiatives to generate moral probity in government, at home and in foreign policy. Notable among these was the 1973 decision by Congress to condition foreign assistance on recipients' performance on human rights, which later became an important point of leverage for HRW. Critique of US actions was not regarded as treasonable, and indeed had increasing numbers of influential friends inside government.

The HRW model worked so well partly because the organization placed itself precisely on the fault line of the internal contradictions in both the Eastern Bloc and the USA. It was perfectly balanced: Helsinki Watch dealt with the communist countries and the Turkish generals, while Americas Watch focused on the USA's allies plus Fidel Castro and the Sandinistas. Therefore, HRW could fend off accusations of partiality by citing its stand against regimes of both left and right. More fundamentally, HRW could exploit both sides' desire for respectability in the court of international public opinion. Each side avowed an enlightenment project: vulnerability to shame was the tribute that they paid for their claims to legitimacy.

Although the official target of Americas Watch reports were the governments concerned, it always included an assessment, usually critical, of the US administration too. In fact, Congress, the State Department and the National Security Council may be seen as the main audience for its recommendations. During Ronald Reagan's presidency, HRW exploited the hypocrisy of US foreign policy: the USA claimed to be fighting a global moral crusade, for – among other things – human rights and democracy, and against the Soviet 'evil empire'. This meant that the administration was required to be interested in every corner of the world, however remote. Avoiding HRW's criticisms became an important task for US officials, and its reports (and anticipated reports), and the possible censure of Congressional committees, became instruments for internal struggles within the administration. Over time the practice, and then the principle, of human rights became domesticated within government, a shift that was consolidated when many of the people who joined the Clinton administration were veterans of human rights policy advocacy groups. Helsinki Watch was even more successful in confronting the Soviet bloc. It was founded after the signing of the Helsinki Accords in 1975, which included a 'final basket' concerned with human rights. According to activists, this was 'more important than UDHR [Universal Declaration of Human Rights]' (Korey 1998: 232), because it opened the door for a *practice* of human rights, using the repertoire of rhetoric and shaming. Ultimately, and to the total surprise of both superpowers, citizens' mobilization in eastern Europe to defend human rights became the lever that brought down the Berlin Wall. The internal contradictions in the communist bloc proved more life-threatening to the Soviet rulers than were double standards to the Americans, because the Soviet system was unable to acknowledge them, respond to them and accommodate them. The peaceful end of European communism was one of the great victories of social movements led by Solidarity in Poland, the churches and organizations such as Helsinki Citizens' Assemblies in various countries. The dissident movement was also a cultural movement, claiming the right to watch contemporary films and listen to rock music. Charter 77 in Czechoslovakia was more a movement of intellectuals and artists than a popular mobilization, but at the key moment in 1989, its leaders were ready to take to the streets themselves: not only did they help organize the demonstrations that brought down communist rule, but they put themselves at the forefront of those protests. People, as well as shame, were mobilized.

It is instructive that the two next watch committees to be formed – Asia Watch (1985) and Africa Watch (1988) – were rarely able to use the same repertoire of leveraging hypocrisy and mobilizing shame to similar effect. Political and historical circumstances were different. Governments had more diverse projects or were less susceptible to shaming – or were collapsing altogether. But the HRW model adapted to a more generic one of promoting rights claims and norms on behalf of national activists who were unable to do the task themselves. A rapidly expanding and diverse range of international human rights organizations became engaged in this enterprise, many of them linked to the United Nations and other international mechanisms.

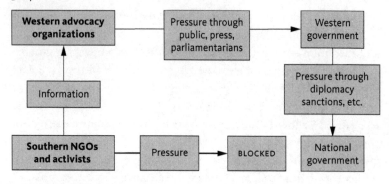

2.3 Boomerang model

The most influential theorists of these linkages are Thomas Risse, Stephen Ropp and Kathryn Sikkink (1999, 2013). Based upon comparisons of cases across the world, they argue that, first, national social movements, blocked from direct access to or engagement with national authorities, can turn to international allies, which will indirectly pursue their case, through demanding that their own governments put pressure on the offending government, and secondly, national governments have an incentive to sign up to international norms or adopt reforms, initially in bad faith, but then may over time find that they have unwittingly domesticated those norms and consolidated those reforms through sustained governmental engagement, the education of public and civil servants, and the accretion of minor or symbolic concessions. This works through a combination of sustained governmental concessions, opening space for domestic actors and international pressure. This has become known as the 'spiral model' or, following its first codification (Keck and Sikkink 1998), the 'boomerang effect'. The implication is that, in the short term, the issue is exposed and some redress may be found. In the medium and longer term, the norms are domesticated and the blockage is lifted.

We should note that the model does not specify the *content* of the information and does not question what happens as that information proceeds on its circuitous route. But the outcome of the circuit is not just potential unblocking: the substance of the issue changes as it moves. Certain issues of concern to Southern NGOs are likely to make the circuit unscathed, while others are filtered out or changed en route. The process of vetting, selecting and repackaging issues by Western gatekeepers is the ambiguous key to this cycle, and has subsequently become a focus for study (Bob 2011; Carpenter 2014).

Institutionalizing advocacy and broadening the agenda Power over agenda-setting and defining issues of concern and action lies at the centre of our concern. The foundational issues for the first professional international human rights organizations – Amnesty International (AI) and HRW – were sharply defined. They were the demands for basic civil and political rights by individual dissenters, including in particular lawyers, journalists, writers, artists and scientists. For these cases to be taken up, publicized and campaigned upon was an authentic realization of the demands of the affected individuals and their supporters. Having started as a mass-membership prisoners' advocacy campaign, AI evolved into a broad-remit human rights organization. HRW focused on publishing and advocacy. It is not a membership organization and was financed by philanthropic organizations such as the Ford Foundation. Its more specialist form of advocacy became a more readily replicable organizational model.

Initially, AI and HRW focused on civil and political rights. However, in the 1990s the question of economic, social and cultural (ESC) rights emerged. For many Southern activists, rights to land, language, food and employment were the most important, the grist of their struggles. Western human rights organizations debated whether ESC rights should be taken on. Some purists in AI and HRW argued not, as a matter of basic principle: ESC rights were secondary to civil and political rights, or not even rights at all. Others considered the practical and organizational constraints on expanding the remit of their work.

After the departure of its founding director, Aryeh Neier, HRW took the latter route. Its justification reflects HRW's trademark adversarial method. When it first moved into ESC activism, its website explained, 'We focus particularly on situations in which our methodology of investigating and reporting is most effective, such as when arbitrary or discriminatory governmental conduct lies behind an ESC right violation.' Here we see a hint that what makes HRW special is less its advocacy of a set of human rights, but more its adherence to a particular brand of human rights practice. Neier's successor as executive director of HRW, Ken Roth, laid this out explicitly when he wrote,

> many who urge international groups to take on ESC rights have a fairly simplistic sense of *how this is done*. Human Rights Watch's experience has led me to believe that there are certain types of ESC issues for which our methodology works well and others for which it does not. In my view, understanding this distinction is key for an international human rights organization such as Human Rights Watch to address ESC rights effectively. Other approaches may work for other types of human rights groups, but organizations such as Human Rights Watch that rely foremost on shaming and the generation of public pressure to defend rights should remain attentive to this distinction. (2004: 64, emphasis added)

This is a significant admission of the priority of method – located within a certain political culture – over principle. As a key gatekeeper – or 'advocacy superpower' (see Carpenter 2014: 40) – HRW filters issues so as to pursue selectively those that fit its method. Sociologically, therefore, human rights organizations should be defined by *what they actually do*. The method also implies a means of governance of the issue: the substantive matter of concern, initially voiced by the Southern activist, becomes translated into a question of what *the transnational advocate can do*.

An interesting example of issue selection and reframing, from the formative period of debate on ESC rights, is the question of human rights and famine. This formed a chapter in the HRW report 'Indivisible human rights', written in advance of the World Conference on Human Rights in Vienna, at which the Asian critique of the universality of human rights norms was anticipated (Human Rights Watch 1992). Building upon Amartya Sen's famous observation that famines rarely if ever occur in a country marked by democratic institutions and a free press (Sen 1990), this report drew a strong link between deprivations of those civil and political rights elsewhere (for example, in China, Ethiopia and Sudan) and the occurrence of famine. In this vein, Roth characterizes the debate over how a human rights organization should approach the question of famine:

People are hungry; therefore, we should say that their right to food has been violated. Such 'analysis,' of course, wholly ignores such key issues as who is responsible for the impoverished state of a population, whether the government in question is taking steps to progressively realize the relevant rights, and what the remedy should be for any violation that is found. More to the point, for our purposes, it also ignores which issues can effectively be taken up by international human rights organizations that rely on shaming and public pressure and which cannot. (2004: 65)

Roth is correct but limited. He ignores the processes of social mobilization and political contestation whereby the right to food – to be precise, the right to be free from famine – is achieved (De Waal 1997: ch. 1). The irony is that Indian farmers, trade unionists and journalists campaign on famine on the basis of the right to food, but their success is celebrated by HRW as a victory for their right to campaign, not the issue to which they devote their passion. He also downplays the extent to which it is not national governments but former colonial powers, transnational corporations and international financial institutions which may be responsible for the impoverished state of a population.

During the 1990s, a succession of international conferences on human rights defined a new agenda (Nelson and Dorsey 2008), integrating ESC rights, and promoting women's rights, in a broader human rights agenda. During these years, advocacy organizations such as HRW for the first time began to identify private sector corporations as duty-bearers with respect to human rights in relatively restricted cases, such as with respect to oil companies' responsibilities for violations in places such as the Niger Delta. The decade also saw the emergence of a new consensus on international development and poverty reduction, leading to two parallel approaches, namely a rights-based approach to development, and the adoption of the Millennium Development Goals (MDGs) by the UN in 2000. As both Southern and international advocacy organizations embraced ESC rights, they identified a range of new targets of pressure including transnational corporations and multilateral organizations.

A second key issue that defined international human rights organizations during the 1990s was humanitarian intervention in response to mass atrocity. The elections of Bill Clinton and Tony

Blair marked the ascendancy of a new generation, with closer links to domestic social movements and a deeper commitment to human rights (in the case of the USA, including many who had been in government under President Jimmy Carter). The post-Cold War years witnessed mass atrocities in former Yugoslavia and Rwanda, and calls for military-humanitarian intervention in both. These instances became the definitive contemporary chapters in a human rights narrative that focused on an American obligation to intervene to prevent genocide (Power 2002). This narrative turns a complex debate on political violence into a one-dimensional controversy on when to use external military force.

The replacement of an agenda of anti-colonial self-determination by the objective of stopping mass atrocities can symbolically be dated to April 1994, the month when Nelson Mandela became president of South Africa, and the Rwandese *génocidaires* unleashed their carnage. This shift is parallel to the way in which domestic social movements moved from an older agenda of strengthening states and redirecting their power, to a new priority of limiting the power of states in former colonies – except that transnational anti-atrocity advocates also campaigned to enhance the authority of metropolitan powers to intervene.

Amnesty International and HRW were sparingly engaged in issues of peace and peacemaking, other than arguing that internationally mediated peace agreements should not include impunity for war criminals. However, the formula of the 'Liberal Peace' crystallized at this time, prescribing a capitalist economy and a liberal democratic political order (Richmond 2005; Mac Ginty 2008). Social and economic injustices that may have underpinned armed conflict are marginalized within the Liberal Peace, often to be treated as a humanitarian assistance or reconstruction issue. Specialist NGOs help set such peace agendas and gain a seat at the peace talks, and may also benefit from a donor-funded peace dividend. Members of wider social movements which sought to articulate other agendas would be obliged to join a belligerent party or a recognized NGO to have their voices heard.

The 'boomerang model' therefore needs to be adjusted to take into account how the content of the *issue* in contention may change, as it moves from local to international actors, and also as it moves from a social movement to a structured NGO.

Insider policy advocacy The shift from wider social movement to specialist NGOs is replete with friction (Kaldor 2003; De Waal 2003; Tarrow 2011; Lang 2013). As Tarrow observes, many NGO advocates 'come from social movement backgrounds and continue to think of themselves as movement activists, even as they lobby in the corridors of power or offer services to underprivileged groups' (2011: 242). They bring coordination, power to amplify messages, and resources – in short, institutionalization and professionalization. But the relationship is fraught because hierarchies of power emerge. Charli Carpenter has analysed how members of the North American and European professional activist community choose human rights issues for advocacy. She observes that 'my research shows that ... a human security network exists as an empirical fact' (2014: 5) and goes on to detail the links between issues, how those issues are framed, the 'gatekeepers' who 'vet' issues, funders, and the 'advocacy superpowers' that determine which issues become the focus for organized policy lobbying.

This network extends into government. Here we can observe the feedback loop between the former social movement activist who has become a broker between policy-makers in government, and his or her erstwhile comrades who are still active in a social movement. Sabine Lang (2013: 8) describes how, as more venues for institutional advocacy open up, it 'might lead to NGOs becoming experts in institutional advocacy and lobbying at the expense of generating broader public debates', and how, in turn, governments utilize NGOs as 'proxy publics', substitutes for broader consultation that are 'just one phone call away'. The former activist becomes an insider lobbyist, seeking specific policy changes, and persuading activists to adjust their demands to what can be achieved within the policy process. Insiders in government – both executive and legislature – quickly learn to use this brokerage process to their own advantage. To be effective, the specialist NGO must become literate in the substance and process of policy, and focused on the dual tasks of developing expert analysis and critique that is useful for the policy-maker, and identifying the maximally effective methods of exerting leverage in pursuit of these incremental policy goals. Its public language must be in two dialects: messages sufficiently simple and moralized to maintain a public constituency, but sufficiently coded for real intent to be clear to policy-makers. The lobbyist must balance effective leverage – enough pressure to be salient – while not overstepping the bounds of decorum to embarrass the policy-maker. In this triangle, professional expertise and institutional power win out: the agenda, issues and methods are set between the lobbyist and the policy-maker. The original activists in a social movement are either co-opted or marginalized.

These power relations are amplified in the case of a poor social movement using a vernacular in a Southern country, and a better-funded lobbying NGO in a Western capital. The Western NGO has enormous freedom of action. This begins with its selection of the issue and its choice of partner or client organization, a process that automatically relegates causes that fit less well with the institutional, political and fund-raising priorities of the sponsor. The issue in question is thus either the winner of the competition for attention in a competitive buyer's market of causes (see Bob 2006) or one crafted by a local NGO precisely to gain the best chance of adoption in this market, following the example set by the Biafrans more than forty years ago. This power relationship continues such that the Western organization's definition of the issue, preference for method, and relationship with its own government become the dominant set of factors in the circuit. The consequence is that the Southern NGO is principally a client of the Western lobby NGO, its funds and profile dependent on its foreign sponsor, or is left without profile and support.

Transnational campaigns framed by ESC rights have generated a different character to those concerned with specific countries. The former include campaigns on issues such as debt relief, the MDGs, HIV/AIDS and land rights. They are characterized by very broad coalitions, a focus on cross-cutting issues, and targeting a combination of Western governments, multilateral organizations and transnational companies. A paradigmatic example is the campaign to reduce the cost of anti-retroviral drugs and to extend access to HIV/AIDS programmes throughout sub-Saharan Africa. This involved local organizations (most famously South Africa's Treatment Action Campaign), international service delivery NGOs (such as Médecins Sans Frontières) and activist physicians within international organizations such as UNAIDS. The result was that mechanisms for liberal global

governance became embedded within the international res
to HIV/AIDS, so that – uniquely – an incurable sexually transm.
infection was not the occasion for a clampdown on human righ
but rather the occasion for advancing rights (De Waal 2006).

By contrast, the 'conflict minerals' campaign spearheaded by
Enough, while similarly targeting an intersection between ESC and
civil and political rights, showed a very different character. As detailed by Laura Seay (in this volume), 'conflict minerals' advocacy
was constructed from the top down and designed for impact in
Washington, DC. Contrasting these campaigns highlights the question of who defines the issue.

Such power dynamics drive radical critiques of the international
human rights project, such as those of Issa Shivji (1989) and Tony
Evans (1998). These critiques have mostly focused on the substance of
the rights (e.g. the neglect of ESC and the right of national political
autonomy) rather than on the sociological process whereby human
rights are produced, prioritized and deployed (see Freeman 2001).
Theorists of how diverse political and cultural groups can agree
on the concept of rights, and on the substance of many specific
human rights, emphasize how consensus on such matters can –
indeed must – be achieved without agreement on theory (Sunstein
1999; Taylor 1999). Rachel Ibreck's analysis of the campaign against
land grabbing (this volume) is an excellent example. However, an
untheorized consensus is fertile ground for the quiet assertion of
hegemonic ideas and the rooting of such ideas, as argued by Roddy
Brett (this volume). As Mary Kaldor (2003) observes, by such processes
are social movements 'tamed'.

Thus we have a new model. Advocacy is driven by a dominant
Western NGO or network, run by specialized lobbyists who act as
brokers with policy-makers, adapting their agenda and methods to
accord with the practicalities of that lobbying process. Under these
conditions, the boomerang model at once gains enhanced efficacy
vis-à-vis the target Western government, and is likely to neglect or
distort the Southern movement's issues and framings.

The Western advocacy/lobby organization can take different
forms. Some become institutionalized, focusing on providing expert policy analysis. Others become commercialized, catering to the
consumerism of their national constituents. Others become, in part,

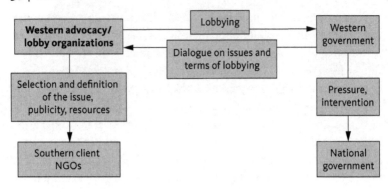

2.4 Insider policy lobby model

a transmission belt of ideas and policies generated *within* government to a broader public. A striking case, which I describe (in this volume), is the way in which the US government took the lead in human rights and conflict resolution lobbying on South Sudan in 2012, cajoling and compelling advocacy organizations to follow.

The principal impacts of this brand of advocacy/lobby organization are *within* Western societies. Indeed, even if it is not the initial stated intent for such organizations, enacting such change soon becomes their primary objective. Thus the US campaign on Darfur began as an effort to end violations in Darfur but, after a short while, member organizations began to shift to objectives such as 'building a permanent anti-genocide constituency in the U.S.' or 'raising awareness' (Hamilton and Hazlett 2007). The international campaign to increase women's involvement in government went through a process of involution in which it fastened on to a potential measure for this participation (the quota of women in legislature), and then came to focus exclusively on this indicator as the objective of the campaign rather than as a means, despite the lack of evidence connecting the achievement of the latter with progress on the former (Klot and Seckinelgin 2011). It is a fine example of 'policy-based evidence making' (Boden and Epstein 2006) in which the activities of the lobby groups and their target policy-makers become a self-referential and self-reinforcing cycle.

In America, the Save Darfur campaign for international intervention in Sudan emerged alongside the escalation of the civil war

DE WAAL | 39

in Iraq following the US invasion (Mamdani 2009). Exemplified by the protesters' banner 'Out of Iraq and into Darfur', the campaign was at once an unthreatening critique of President George W. Bush's 'war on terror' and a logically isomorphic case for using the same military tools for a US-led 'war on genocide'. The critique made of Bill Clinton for inaction in Bosnia and Rwanda was echoed, precisely ten years later and in the same language, in criticism of George Bush, who was modestly responsive (Hamilton 2009). The campaign's impact on Sudanese affairs may have been mixed, but the lesson of the power of mobilizing American youth was not lost on candidate Barack Obama.

Transnational advocacy groups have become absorbed into the US body politic, and we can chart their short-term effects on the foreign policy management of the Obama administration. Not only did Obama mobilize the same constituency that turned out for the Save Darfur rallies as his voters, but he brought some of those organizers into his White House as advisers. Obama drew upon individuals who had personal histories both as policy-makers and civil society advocates on African issues, especially Rwanda and Sudan. The feedback loop between policy-maker and activist became much tighter. The advocates enjoyed access and influence, and the policy-makers both helped set the agenda – often in minute detail – and also used these networks to manage public opinion. The process becomes self-referential, dedicated to an exercise in self-persuasion by the policy-makers and their erstwhile friends outside government – now more accurately termed lobbyists rather than activists.

The transnational issue lobbyists' impact is at the margins of real policy. Under both Republicans and Democrats, the major foreign policy decisions have been set by the Department of Defense – in Obama's case, partly in order for his party to steal the national security issue away from the Republicans – or to manage domestic public opinion and accommodate partisan political concerns (Nasr 2013: 2). The policy lobbyists play to the same tune: as for the administration, impacts on the faraway countries that are the subjects of campaigning are a secondary concern. Both policy-makers and lobbyists thereby find themselves in a positive-reinforcement feedback loop in which they are encouraged to believe their own rhetoric. And such is their dominant status internationally that many activists in Africa, Asia and Latin America are encouraged to believe that down this road lies the promise of real change.

A post-humanitarianism?

It is tempting, following Chouliaraki (2013), to see a transformational shift in the last decade associated with the dominance of neoliberalism and the ascendancy of social media, leading to a new 'post-humanitarianism' concerned almost entirely with self-gratification by Western consumers in their bubbles. Undoubtedly there has been a shift, but the histories sketched above and the case studies explored in this volume give us reason to question whether it is unprecedented, linear, ubiquitous and irreversible. The changes are more historically contextual, more closely aligned with the politics of advocacy, lobbying and policy-making in Western capitals, especially Washington, DC.

Histories of human rights tend to identify two key moments: the immediate post-Second World War era in which the principles of human rights were codified, and the 1970s, when post-Vietnam America and post-colonial Europe could rise above their ambivalence about the right to self-determination, and make those principles real. A third turning point occurred in the early 1990s, when the post-colonial critique of human rights, having so definitively abandoned the right of self-determination, moved to override not just the state sovereignty of poor and ill-governed countries, but the popular sovereignty of their peoples too, in the name of stopping atrocities and advancing the 'responsibility to protect'. This was the brief encounter between human rights activism, at its moment of post-Cold War triumph, and interventionist humanitarianism, which, among other things, spawned the latter-day philanthropic imperialism of a journalist in Bosnia, later to become President Obama's representative at the United Nations. Samantha Power's outrage at atrocities in Bosnia and Rwanda, and the feeble international efforts to stop them, was shared by many. But that outrage became more closely tied to US power, and unmoored from local ownership of political solutions, and the spirit of solidarity was lost.

However, the model of transnational advocacy as political solidarity has not disappeared. Awareness of the unfinished agendas of decolonization runs deep in the global South. On some issues, Southern actors continue to enjoy primacy, not just in information but also in defining the issues and the actions required. Most examples are issues that have little traction among the advocacy superpowers in Western capitals – for example, land, labour rights, and corruption in the arms business. This is not the case when Western advocates target individual countries on atrocity-related issues. Without the framing issue of decolonization that earlier enabled them to assert their primacy, activists from the global South face a struggle to set the agenda and build coalitions. There is an ever-present danger that their issues will be co-opted by their Western partners and pursued in ways not to their liking, and most often that co-option will be led by well-networked Southern advocates themselves, alert to the power and potential of their Western colleagues.

This co-option is resisted. As Southern movements grow, in the bigger non-Western countries such as Brazil, India and South Africa, they will tend to prioritize domestic pressure in their own countries, and will choose issues such as ESC rights irrespective of their efficacy with regard to Western NGO methods. They may also choose which Western partners they work with and set the terms on which they work, seek direct access to the means of pressuring Western governments, and monitor the narratives and outcomes.

If this seems radical within the human rights community, it ought not to be so. The principle of respect for the primacy of the poor and marginalized has a strong history in development studies, exemplified by Robert Chambers, whose book *Rural Development: Putting the Last First* (1983) inspired a generation of radically minded practitioners and researchers of practical development and relief. This is both a political and a methodological point: it is a sensibility and a choice, and an option for how one studies, interprets and represents the experience of those who are suffering and being repressed. The first underlying principle is that the most fundamental act of solidarity is to see the world through the eyes of those who are suffering or being repressed, and act accordingly.

The heyday of radical transnational advocacy was the latter days of the anti-colonial movements, which coincided with the anti-war movement in the USA and the emergence of specialized human rights advocacy. Many veterans of that era hark back to those transnational solidarities and the resonance of the critique of global power as

...g what should constitute an authentic activism – and criticize ...likes of *Kony2012* and Enough accordingly. But those days will not return, and comparable campaigns cannot now be reconstituted. The campaign against the invasion of Iraq was the strongest recent echo, but though large, it was not sustained, and the Obama administration's withdrawal from military adventures means that such targets of activist ire are unlikely to recur. What we have instead are more complicated excesses, some concealed (such as the total electronic surveillance of the National Security Agency), some delegated to client governments (such as the nastier operations in the war on terror), some packaged as protection against terrorism (both of the above) or even as action to protect human rights (the NATO campaign in Libya). Since 2001, the US administration has used the moral and political rhetoric of friends and enemies and has justified exceptional actions in pursuit of the latter (with echoes of Carl Schmitt), and Western advocates have at best struggled to challenge this logic, and at worst adapted it to demonize a different set of villains. The likes of Joseph Kony and Omar al-Bashir may indeed be villains, but authentic human rights activism demands holding one's friends to the same standards as one's enemies, or indeed a higher one. Those 'friends' include allies in transnational activism and personal friends and political allies in government at home. The second underlying principle is that the adage of 'speaking truth to power' should not be selective.

The challenge of reclaiming transnational advocacy as activist solidarity is to discover mechanisms whereby these twin principles and practices can be developed, seeing the world through the eyes of the powerless and resisting the magnetism of the personal salvation and power-expertise centres of gravity.

Notes

1 Chouliaraki uses ActionAid's 'happy bubble' fund-raising campaign as an exemplar of this: www.actionaid.org.uk/news-and-views/what-a-feeling-actionaid-launches-supporter-recruitment-drive, accessed 15 June 2014.

2 www.washingtonpost.com/blogs/blogpost/post/invisible-children-founders-posing-with-guns-an-interview-with-the-photographer/2012/03/08/gl

QASX68yR_blog.html, accessed 15 June 2014.

3 Their rulers do precisely the same thing (Bayart 2009).

References

Bartkowski, M. (2013) *Recovering Nonviolent History: Civil resistance in liberation struggles*, Boulder, CO: Lynne Rienner.

Bayart, J.-F. (2009) *The State in Africa: The politics of the belly*, London: Polity.

Bob, C. (2006) *The Marketing of Rebellion*, Cambridge: Cambridge University Press.

— (2011) *The Global Right Wing and the Clash of World Politics*, Cambridge: Cambridge University Press.

Boden, R. and D. Epstein (2006) 'Managing the research imagination? Globalisation and research in higher education', *Globalisation, Societies and Education*, 4(2): 223–36.

Browne, H. (2013) *The Frontman: Bono (in the name of power)*, London: Verso.

Buchanan, T. (2002) '"The truth will set you free": the making of Amnesty International', *Journal of Contemporary History*, 37: 575–97.

Cabanes, B. (2014) *The Great War and the Origins of Humanitarianism, 1918–1924*, Cambridge: Cambridge University Press.

Carpenter, C. (2014) *'Lost' Causes: Agenda vetting in global issue networks and the shaping of human security*, Ithaca, NY: Cornell University Press.

Chambers, R. (1983) *Rural Development: Putting the Last First*, London: Longman.

Chappell, L. (2006) 'Contesting women's rights: charting the emergence of a transnational conservative counter-network', *Global Society*, 20(4): 491–520.

Chouliaraki, L. (2013) *The Ironic Spectator: Solidarity in the age of post-humanitarianism*, London: Polity.

David, H. (2007) 'Transnational advocacy in the eighteenth century: transatlantic activism and the anti-slavery movement', *Global Networks*, 7(3): 367–82.

Davies, T. R. (2011) 'The rise and fall of transnational civil society: the evolution of international non-governmental organizations since the mid-nineteenth century', in

L. Reydams (ed.), *Global Activism Reader*, New York: Continuum.

De Waal, A. (1997) *Politics and the Disaster Relief Industry in Africa*, London: James Currey.

— (2003) 'Human rights and the political imagination: how the West and Africa have diverged', *Journal of Human Rights*, 2(4): 474–95.

— (2006) *AIDS and Power: Why there is no political crisis – yet*, London: Zed Books.

De Waal, A. and R. Ibreck (2013) 'Hybrid social movements in Africa', *Journal of Contemporary African Studies*, 31(2): 303–24.

Englund, H. (2006) *Prisoners of Freedom: Human rights and the African poor*, Berkeley: University of California Press.

Evans, T. (1998) 'Introduction: Power, hegemony and the universalization of human rights', in T. Evans (ed.), *Human Rights Fifty Years On: A Reappraisal*, Manchester: Manchester University Press.

Freeman, M. (2001) 'Is a political science of human rights possible?', *Netherlands Quarterly of Human Rights*, 19(2).

Hamilton, R. (2009) *Fighting for Darfur: Public action and the struggle to stop genocide*, New York: Palgrave Macmillan.

Hamilton, R. and C. Hazlett (2007) '"Not on our watch": the emergence of the African movement for Darfur', in Alex de Waal (ed.), *War in Darfur and the Search for Peace*, Cambridge, MA: Harvard University Press.

Human Rights Watch (1992) *Indivisible Human Rights*, New York.

Kaldor, M. (2003) *Global Civil Society: An answer to war*, London: Polity.

Keck, M. and K. Sikkink (1998) *Activists beyond Borders: Advocacy networks in international politics*, Ithaca, NY: Cornell University Press.

Keys, B. (2014) *Reclaiming American*

44 | TWO

Virtue: The human rights revolution of the 1970s, Cambridge, MA: Harvard University Press.

Klot, J. and H. Seckinelgin (2011) 'Women's political participation and gender equality in fragile and conflict affected contexts', London School of Economics.

Korey, W. (1998) *A Curious Grapevine: NGOs and the Universal Declaration of Human Rights*, New York: St Martin's Press.

Lang, S. (2013) *NGOs, Civil Society and the Public Sphere*, Cambridge: Cambridge University Press.

Mac Ginty, R. (2008) 'Indigenous peacemaking versus the Liberal Peace', *Cooperation and Conflict*, 43(2): 139–63.

Mamdani, M. (2009) *Saviors and Survivors: Darfur, Politics, and the War on Terror*, New York: Pantheon.

Monga, C. (1996) *The Anthropology of Anger: Civil society and democracy in Africa*, Boulder, CO: Lynne Rienner.

Moyn, S. (2010) *The Last Utopia: Human rights in history*, Cambridge, MA: Belknap Press.

Mwenda, A. (2010) 'Uganda's politics of foreign aid and violent conflict: the political uses of the LRA rebellion', in T. Allen and K. Vlassenroot (eds), *The Lord's Resistance Army: Myth and reality*, London: Zed Books.

Nasr, V. (2013) *The Dispensable Nation: American Foreign Policy in Retreat*, New York: Doubleday.

Nelson, P. and E. Dorsey (2008) *New Rights Advocacy: Changing Strategies of Development and Human Rights NGOs*, Washington, DC: Georgetown University Press.

Power, S. (2002) *A Problem from Hell: America in the Age of Genocide*, New York: Basic Books.

— (2013) 'Remarks by Ambassador Samantha Power, U.S. Permanent Representative to the United Nations, at the Fourth Estate Leadership Summit, August 10, 2013', Los Angeles, CA, usun.state.gov/briefing/statements/213034.htm, accessed 15 August 2013.

Richmond, O. (2005) *The Transformation of Peace*, London: Palgrave Macmillan.

Risse, T., S. Ropp and K. Sikkink (eds) (1999) *The Power of Human Rights: International Norms and Domestic Change*, Cambridge: Cambridge University Press.

— (eds) (2013) *The Persistent Power of Human Rights: From commitment to compliance*, Cambridge: Cambridge University Press.

Roth, K. (2004) 'Defending economic, social and cultural rights: practical issues faced by an international human rights organization', *Human Rights Quarterly*, 26: 63–73.

Sen, A. (1990) 'Individual freedom as a social commitment', *New York Review of Books*, 14 June.

Shivji, I. (1989) *The Concept of Human Rights in Africa*, London: CODESRIA.

Sunstein, C. (1999) 'Agreement without theory', in S. Macedo (ed.), *Deliberative Politics: Essays on Democracy and Disagreement*, New York: Oxford University Press.

Sutherland, B. and M. Meyer (2000) *Guns and Gandhi in Africa: Pan African Insights on Nonviolence, Armed Struggle and Liberation in Africa*, Trenton, NJ: Africa World Press.

Tarrow, S. G. (2011) *Power in Movement: Social Movements and Contentious Politics*, 3rd edn, Cambridge: Cambridge University Press.

Taylor, C. (1999) 'Conditions of an unforced consensus on human rights', in J. Bauer and D. A. Bell (eds), *The East Asian Challenge for Human Rights*, Cambridge: Cambridge University Press.

Tilly, C. (2003) *The Politics of Collective Violence*, Cambridge: Cambridge University Press.

3 | BURMA'S STRUGGLE FOR DEMOCRACY: A CRITICAL APPRAISAL

Maung Zarni with Trisha Taneja

Introduction

This chapter draws upon the author's direct political engagement in Burma's pro-change opposition, and on his own research, to reflect critically on the struggle of the last twenty-five years between the ruling military and the opposition movements.

Aung San Suu Kyi is widely acclaimed as the face of Burmese democratic activism, as a dignified and principled exponent of non-violent resistance, and as the symbol of the aspirations of the Burmese people for a government, freely and fairly elected, that champions the rights and welfare of its people. Suu Kyi's iconic status is exemplified by the award of the 1991 Nobel Peace Prize – awarded a mere three years after she became politically active.

This chapter questions the simplified heroic narrative commonly associated with Suu Kyi, and portrays a more complex story behind the struggle for human rights and democracy in Burma. Transnational activism centred on Burma has been plagued by disunity among national actors, and has evolved to follow the Western policy lobby model outlined by De Waal in Chapter 2, with Suu Kyi acting as a national link for Western advocacy/lobby organizations. This anointing of Suu Kyi at the apex of the Burmese struggle has allowed Western policy-makers to selectively craft a singular narrative about the country that is aligned to their strategic and domestic interests, without ensuring a corresponding positive change in Burmese struggles.

Burma was renamed Myanmar by its military rulers in 1989, following a crackdown on the people-power movement that had challenged the country's military rulers. Following this crisis, the then newly minted State Law and Order Restoration Council (SLORC) hoped that the new name, derived from the Burmese word *myanma*, referring to the dominant ethnic-racial group in the country, would signal a break with the country's colonial past. The SLORC leaders liked to blame their country's woes on the colonial legacy, ignoring the decades of post-colonial misgovernment, especially after the army took power a quarter of a century earlier. Another twenty-five years on, despite the generals' oft-publicized avowals of good intention and the Western embrace of their purported democratization, the deeds, outlook and policies of the ruling elite remain consistent with the country's bloody recent past. In particular, the ongoing campaigns against the Rohingya Muslims (Zarni and Cowley 2014) show the perils of a democratization concerned more with symbols than substance.

For several decades until recently, Burma was one of two anomalies in East and South-East Asia (the other is North Korea), where societies were moving towards better governance, increased prosperity and more societal and cultural openness. Following Burma's opening to the West, signified by the November 2010 release from house arrest of Suu Kyi, the unbanning of the National League for Democracy (NLD), and the party's subsequent participation in elections, Burma at long last appeared to be moving in the right direction. However, the political status of Suu Kyi as an individual is not a good marker of substantive change, and there is good reason to fear that the democratization and liberalization are largely a charade.

It is a truism that anti-authoritarian movements and organizations tend to mirror their opponents in thinking, modes of operation and political practices, and especially to become intolerant of any view that differs from that of the leadership. And indeed, in Burma's case, the choice to elevate Aung San Suu Kyi to the status of icon for democracy has had important and potentially fatal limitations, for both the domestic and international components of the democracy campaign.

The Burmese democratic movement, drawing its support from a highly diverse set of constituents, does not possess a coherent set of views and prescriptions, and there is much to be said for uniting around a single leader. But having Suu Kyi as an undisputed leader has major drawbacks. Because she has been elevated to a position in which she can do no wrong, other approaches to political change that are not in conformity with her publicly expressed views are generally interpreted by her supporters as a direct challenge to her leadership. During her years of opposition, anyone who dared criticize Suu Kyi was denounced as an apologist for the regime, and regarded as committing an act of heresy resulting in social ostracism, condemnation, personal slander and threats. In their attempts to ensure that Burmese democrats unite under Suu Kyi's leadership, the opposition has stunted its own growth by limiting its communication with international actors to one channel and one message, even while internal and geopolitical changes demand a shift in strategies.

Analysts have criticized the Burmese democratic movement for inflexibility and failure to appreciate the need for a changing paradigm (Hlaing 2007) and for internal rivalries and factionalism (Taylor 2009). But neither of these faults, typical of exile and opposition movements, fully explains why the opposition movement continued to fight in the way that it did, and found itself at the mercy of a geopolitical shift that assumed the garb of democracy and human rights, respected neither, and co-opted the symbols of democratic resistance to a new political order, possessing fundamental continuities with its military predecessor.

The transnational advocacy movement for Burma has displayed important strengths, and in some respects is an important example of the general framework advocated in this volume, able to create positive change while remaining grounded in complex national realities. Transnational activists for Burma served as a resource, supporting a national social or political movement as the primary actor. The widespread international deference to Suu Kyi's leadership undoubtedly helped focus international policy on the domestic prerequisites and processes for democratic reform, and ultimately legitimized Suu Kyi's long-standing insistence on dialogue with the regime. However, by transforming Suu Kyi into an international celebrity and promoting her NLD as the principal agent of change, transnational activist groups became inflexible and unable to respond to changing realities. Their unconditional support for Aung San Suu Kyi allowed Western (primarily American) actors to selectively amplify a singular Burmese narrative, thus isolating other aspects of a complex Burmese political struggle. When political change did finally come, in a much-changed international context, the singular narrative impeded effective response to the challenges of peace, democracy and human rights in the country.

The campaign for Burmese democracy therefore illustrates the shift in transnational advocacy movements, exemplifying – despite its show of public solidarity with a national icon – a transfer of the power to set the agenda from national to Western actors, and has in fact further contributed to the ongoing political crisis, armed conflict and mass atrocity in the country. This chapter will critically examine the history of Burmese activism and resistance to successive military governments, and will discuss the events that led to the evolution of a Western-policy-centric model of transnational advocacy, and the implications of this model for Burmese political struggles.

Democratic resistance in Burma

Following Burma's first coup, in which General Ne Win seized power in 1962, social unrest, internal mutinies and purges within the military, armed resistance from ethnic minorities and organized political opposition were a persistent feature of the Burmese political scene. There were major protests in 1962 and in 1975–77. The roots of today's pro-democracy movement go back to the resistance to Ne Win's coup. The armed ethnic resistance organizations have even deeper roots, having emerged during or shortly after Burma's independence in 1948 (Win 2008).

General Ne Win faced recurrent protests and invariably repressed them with force. In 1987/88, a non-violent popular revolt that became known as the '8888' uprising erupted. It was a huge demonstration of people power, modelled on the challenges to President Marcos in the Philippines. The protests forced Ne Win from power, and following the collapse of his government in July 1988, for a brief moment a new democratic era looked imminent. A group of well-respected leaders emerged. The individual who emerged as the international face of the democracy movement, Aung San Suu Kyi, was a newcomer to politics who had only recently returned to Burma from her academic studies in Britain. With barely a month's record as an active politician, she owed her prominence to the fact that she is the daughter of Burma's leading nationalist, Aung San, founder of the Burmese national army and the Communist Party of Burma. Despite the presence of a few other leaders, none was able to establish a united leadership that could fill the void left by the imploding regime.

Hence, rather than ushering in democracy, the uprising prompted a coup, led by the commander-in-chief of the country's armed forces, General Saw Maung, and his intelligence chief, then brigadier Khin Nyunt. This was an attempt by second-line generals to save the 'old guards'. With the despot Ne Win officially retired, these two men established the SLORC. The authoritarian elements in the armed forces regained confidence and a younger generation of army officers rediscovered the will and energy to rule the country. Having taken power by force in the middle of a surge of popular protest, the new junta needed legitimacy. The SLORC therefore promised multiparty elections, under the rubric of 'disciplined flourishing democracy'. Although few expected the May 1990 polls to be free and fair, they did represent the only legal opportunity for the Burmese public to press for change.

The SLORC stage-managed most of the electoral process, keeping all the country's genuine democrats either in maximum-security prisons or, in the case of Suu Kyi, under house arrest. Less threatening candidates were allowed very limited broadcast time on national television, during which they were instructed to read only from regime-approved campaign speeches. Nonetheless, the election results stunned the regime. Despite the seemingly fractured nature of the electorate, which had given rise to a ridiculously high number of political parties, voters voted tactically. Suu Kyi's NLD won a landslide victory – 80 per cent of the seats – over the military-backed National Unity Party (NUP). Even some constituencies dominated by the military voted for the NLD. Initially, the regime was confused as to how to handle this situation, with its nominal leader, Senior General Saw Maung, talking about the possibility of respecting the results. Instead, officers decided to play hardball, removing General Saw and locking up hundreds of dissidents and more than one hundred successful parliamentary candidates who criticized the clampdown. The NLD leader herself was kept under house arrest and her party was stripped of its organizational infrastructure, reduced to just a single office in Rangoon.

Emboldened by its electoral victory, the NLD leadership and supporters demanded a direct transfer of power and began talking about convening a parliament. Technically, the election winners were to convene an assembly that was to draw up a new constitution, after which a new government would be formed. But the army did not permit the NLD to convene the Constitutional Convention, nor to call a Representatives' Assembly. The NLD leadership itself was divided on how to respond. One faction wanted to confront the army by calling the parliament unilaterally, while the other counselled caution. Soon afterwards, a dozen elected MPs fled to insurgent-controlled areas, where they were given refuge by the Karen National Union (KNU), which had been fighting a decades-old insurgency against the government. There, claiming a mandate from their party members, they formed a parallel government, the National Coalition for the Government of the Union of Burma.

In total, an estimated 8,000–10,000 urban dissidents, primarily university students and teachers, fled to remote areas near the borders with India, China and Thailand. In their minds, they were following in the footsteps of the colonial-era anti-imperialist student nationalists, most prominently Suu Kyi's martyred father Aung San, who had fled abroad in search of external support, formed a nationalist army with the help of Japanese Naval Intelligence, and returned clandestinely to Burma to fight the British. Having witnessed the failures of past non-violent protests by a generation of dissidents, and having witnessed military persecution first hand, they were determined to take up arms against the military regime.

The sheer number and varied backgrounds of the student dissidents proved a major problem. Overwhelmed by the volunteers and worried about the possibility of penetration by agents of the regime, the ethnic resistance organizations, with the exception of the Kachin Independence Organization in the north, were reluctant to give arms to these young men, who mostly hailed from the heartlands of the country. A small number of military officers who had joined the anti-dictatorship protests in 1988 also sought refuge in the KNU area. The KNU leadership finally decided to take a gamble and to support the setting up of a student revolutionary army, under the banner of the All Burma Students Democratic Front (ABSDF). This led to an improvement in the inter-ethnic relations between the radical students and their Karen hosts by the time the MPs elect fleeing the aftermath of the 1990 post-election crackdown arrived.

However, the lack of adequate material and financial support, and the inability of student leaders to work together for a common mission plagued the resistance. Factionalism took hold within the ranks of the ABSDF, which led to its near-collapse. Many of the members took the option of resettlement in developed countries. A small band of a few hundred revolutionary former students fought on. While their commitment was exemplary, their practical contribution to the struggle for democratic change was not significant.

The resettlement of most of the democratic student movement had a silver lining in two respects. First, the domestic Burmese opposition acquired policy advocates in major Western cities, including Washington, DC and London. The narratives of oppression and heroic resistance brought by former student revolutionaries were inspirational, and unexpectedly gave the Burmese government-in-exile a voice in international policy debates. Secondly, these newly arrived dissidents linked up with previous waves of political exiles and their Western supporters, consolidating groups of friends of a democratic Burma around the world. Initially, the advocacy in this case was similar to the 'boomerang model' described by Keck and Sikkink (1998); the exiled Burmese dissidents had a role delivering information to the West, and a stake in crafting their messages for international policy circles.

However, serious rifts developed between the government-in-exile made up of MPs elect, and the National Council of the Union of Burma (NCUB), comprised of representatives of armed resistance groups. Over the following twenty years, differences over strategies, personalities and organizational agendas were further exacerbated between those running the exiled government from Washington, DC, and those on the Thai–Burma border leading the NCUB. This undermined the credibility and effectiveness of both groups, leaving a political vacuum not only at the heart of the opposition, but also at the heart of the transnational activist model, which started lacking unified expertise and a strong vision.

The 'Free Burma' movement

For centuries, repressive rulers have relied on exiling their adversaries to remote places, confident that if political leaders are far from the home country where day-to-day struggles for change must take place, they will be ineffective. But the global dispersal of Burmese democrats coincided with a number of factors that enabled them to exercise continuing influence.

First, the end of the Cold War made the promotion of liberal values an affordable mission for Western governments. Several months before the fall of the Berlin Wall, the world witnessed televised images of China's popular uprisings and the bloody crackdown in Tiananmen Square. In response to this, the USA set up Radio Free Asia, with a target audience of China's masses, oppressed by communist rule. Burma, whose uprisings preceded the Chinese protests by a year, was similarly a target for ideological penetration, and Radio Free Asia soon began transmitting a Burmese-language programme, which became an influential source of information and an alternative to the junta's propaganda.

Secondly, in 1990 Suu Kyi was named as recipient of a Norwegian human rights award, the Thorolf Rafto Memorial Prize. This prompted the Norwegian government to set up a radio station in Oslo, the Democratic Voice of Burma. The DVB is run by Burmese dissidents in exile, in support of democracy and the spread of an independent media culture in Burma, and has proved a first-class and highly influential media outlet. The next year, Suu Kyi was awarded the Nobel Peace Prize. This award caught the tide of a growing international campaign and kept Burma in the spotlight.

The third factor transforming Burmese democratic activism was therefore the loss of an information monopoly by the junta. During the previous twenty-five years, the Burmese public was subject to the information and opinion provided by the state's broadcasters, through Burma TV and Radio Broadcasting Services. The daily broadcasts by the Burma Communist Party, which continued until its collapse in 1989, barely made a dent in the regime's propaganda wall. But from 1990 onwards, first with Radio Free Asia and then DVB, while the SLORC could control most of the physical territory of Burma, the opposition ruled the airwaves. The advent of the internet a decade later made the saturation of electronic communication by democratic voices complete (Zarni 2000). This even shaped official propaganda, and it is even possible that the members of the now defunct Directorate of Defence Services Intelligence, who were required to monitor foreign broadcasts, were gradually and positively affected in their attitudes towards democracy and human rights.

The fourth critical factor explaining the effectiveness of the international Burma movement was that satellite dishes became commercially available to the Burmese public. This meant that the citizens could view the junta's brutal crackdowns on popular protests. Following the demonstrations in 2007, images of Buddhist monks being beaten, kicked or shot in cold blood were captured on camera by citizen video journalists. Their footage was smuggled to the Thailand branch of the DVB, and was then edited and transmitted. At the same time, the traditional media beamed into living rooms narratives and images of the regime's efforts to cosy up to other pariah regimes, such as North Korea, and the opulent wedding parties of the generals' children.

These four factors, coupled with the disunity in the Burmese opposition movement, and its de facto reliance on Suu Kyi as its main voice, allowed the 'Free Burma' movement to become embedded within a liberal human rights discourse. Since liberal human rights emerged as an important theme in Western, especially US, international policies at the end of the Cold War, American activists and policy-makers actively encouraged this discourse, and responded with economic and political disengagement to push for liberal democratization. At the outset, the military crackdown following the 8888 uprising prompted the Reagan administration to stop all arms sales to the country, and suspend aid programmes and full diplomatic relations (Martin 2012). US diplomatic relations with Burma were downgraded to chargé d'affaires level, and development aid from the World Bank and other international financial institutions was denied.

The problem with this representation of the Burmese struggle was twofold. First, it neglected a more complex and realistic depiction of the Burmese political situation by ignoring the numerous ethnic insurgencies. Secondly, the over-reliance on Suu Kyi as the sole voice of Burma made it easier for American actors to co-opt campaign messages and align them with their own political interests. Eventually, activism and policy messages developed a circular nature – while some messages were crafted in Rangoon by the NLD and amplified in the West, others were formulated in key Western capitals and 'blessed' by the NLD. The activist model had in fact shifted to resemble the 'Western policy lobby' one, whereby the Western activist-lobbyist organizations played a key role in setting the agenda for Burmese political struggles.

A good example of this circular messaging is the policy of economic boycotts and sanctions, which was inspired by the anti-apartheid struggle that targeted foreign investors and campaigned for using consumer boycotts in Western countries. The Burmese junta was well aware of the role of economic hardship in triggering the protests that had brought down General Ne Win. As soon as it had taken control of the state, the new regime therefore began a process of controlled economic liberalization, modelled on the experiences of China and Vietnam. These steps, coupled with opportunities offered by untapped natural resources and a cheap labour force, were attracting Western investors.

Burmese dissidents in exile, at home and in the conflict zones along the border made common cause with their international supporters in the West on this issue as they sought to undermine the government's effort to seek 'performance legitimacy' by emulating the development model of the Asian Tigers, which – in the cases of China and Vietnam – involved maintaining single-party rule.

Economic boycotts and sanctions

The idea of an economic boycott of the Burmese regime was not new, but it caught on only when the Free Burma Coalition, coordinated by Burmese and American students at the University of Wisconsin, experimented with the internet as a new activist medium in the autumn of 1995. At that time, a split in the leadership of the ABSDF, with infighting between two rival leaders, had seriously weakened the Front. One unintended consequence of this setback was that dissidents, dismayed by the fading prospects of guerrilla warfare, turned instead to Western students and especially to left-leaning idealist groups. Representatives of ABSDF began travelling to Western countries, especially to universities, churches and labour and activist conferences, telling their stories about repression, escape and life as guerrillas in the jungle. Their message caught the imaginations of many, especially as it coincided with an 'issue vacuum' on Western university campuses.

Meanwhile, little-known local groups focusing on documenting human rights – most importantly, the pioneering Karen Human Rights Group – were also stepping up their work. In particular, these groups were publicizing evidence not just of the regime's abuses, but also of atrocities directly linked to the government's joint economic ventures to construct oil and gas pipelines, in partnership with Total of France and Union Oil Company of California (UNOCAL), as well as roads, bridges and other infrastructure. Visual and narrative evidence of these abuses was rapidly circulated. Groups in the West could not only target the faraway regime in Burma, but also companies in their own countries – much more accessible and vulnerable targets. Their main target, a company most exposed to a consumer boycott, was PepsiCo.

From this, the Free Burma Coalition emerged as a spearhead network, and in turn this sparked a global campaign to boycott the Burmese regime. This campaign had two aims: to weaken the military regime by cutting it off from foreign direct investment and trade revenues, and to strengthen Suu Kyi and the non-violent opposition movement within the country. The hope was that the campaign would both boost the morale of the internal opposition and raise its political profile internationally.

Suu Kyi was released from house arrest (for the first time) in July 1995, giving a boost to the campaigners and enabling them to legitimize and amplify their 'Boycott Pepsi, Free Burma' slogan. Through activist 'pigeons', all of whom were Western female activists funded by George Soros's Open Society Institute, the boycott campaigners were able to secure Suu Kyi's endorsement of the campaign on video and audiotape, as well as in the form of solidarity and press statements, all of which were disseminated through the Coalition's networks. A small team of representatives of the exiled government and dissidents in exile travelled extensively to spread the message, and to lend credence to the message that 'Free Burma' activist groups were promoting. Within a year the economic boycott had grown into a large and effective campaign.

Most importantly, the Coalition put the aspirations of the Burmese people on the radar, not just of young idealists in the West, but also of politicians, journalists and corporate leaders. The campaign created a small but significant pro-NLD and pro-Suu Kyi constituency where none had existed beforehand, and framed the Burma issue in the language of human rights promotion and democratization. The result was that almost all Western investors, other than those in the mining sector, began to withdraw. Notably, the Free Burma Coalition took the lead in forcing Pepsi out of several American universities, including Harvard. Pepsi eventually cut all ties with Burma in 1997 but never conceded that it had been morally wrong to invest in the country.

The Free Burma Coalition also lobbied the USA and the European Union to impose economic sanctions and a visa ban on regime officials. This element in the campaign was only a qualified success. While Washington, DC and European capitals were prepared to issue strong verbal condemnations, they were reluctant to take any measures to stop oil and gas companies doing business in Burma. The US sanctions and measures adopted in 1997 and 2003 allowed US oil corporations to continue investing, and in Europe, despite extremely negative publicity, there was no effort to compel Total, one of the biggest investors in Burma, to break its economic ties. Indeed, despite its early well-publicized victories, the boycott campaign began to lose momentum. Firstly, most Western companies divested from Burma because of the lack of a sound business environment, poor infrastructure and reputational costs among Western consumers. Secondly, the economic rise of Asian countries, whose companies were not susceptible to the campaigners' pressure, meant that there was no shortage of Eastern investors ready to fill the investment vacuum created by the withdrawal or lack of interest of Western ones. Even the regional critics of the Burmese regime, such as Indonesia and the Philippines, were keenly interested in its natural resources.

In the end, the boycott campaigners failed to anticipate two major developments. One was the rapid rise of China as a global economic power, and the second was the rivalry between India and China, which led to New Delhi withdrawing its support for Suu Kyi and the Burmese opposition in order to counter Chinese influence by building closer ties with the regime. By not taking these regional factors into account, the campaigns became much less effective.

Nonetheless, the Free Burma campaigns on economic disengagement remain powerful examples of how transnational advocacy for Burma evolved to include Western activists, NGOs and policy-makers. While the agenda in these campaigns was largely motivated by a disjointed Burmese desire to weaken the military junta's 'performance legitimacy', it was the first Burmese activist campaign to substantially include Western actors in crafting its messages, and required Western activists to push for a domestic solution to an international problem. The campaign's limited success also highlighted the fundamental Western political bias of transnational activism; the activist vision could be pursued only if it aligned with domestic political and economic interests.

A tide in the affairs of men

The most difficult decision for any democratic movement is when and how to negotiate with the enemy. If the opening is taken at the right moment and in the right way, there is a chance – never assured – of success. And if that success is achieved, those who engineered it will win the plaudits of history. This is the story of the African National Congress's first secret meetings with the emissaries of the apartheid regime, and the negotiators' subsequent efforts at facing down their respective hardliners and reaching a historic compromise. In the case of Burma, such an opportunity glimmered in the early 2000s, but the chance was missed. There was no guarantee of success, but the missed chance haunts the Burmese democracy movement to this day. In narrating this story, the role of the international activist campaign demands careful scrutiny.

The Burmese generals are deeply fearful of China, which they see as a potentially expansionist giant neighbour. The SLORC's unhappiness with China was amplified when they discovered that Beijing had sold it near-decommissioned and low-quality military hardware for a price tag of more than $1 billion. This not only reinforced suspicion of China but led some unhappy generals, among them General Khin Nyunt, the head of intelligence, to seek a rapprochement with the USA and a softening of the dictatorship. Meanwhile, in Washington, DC, some security-minded officials also began to reassess the USA's closeness to rights-focused advocacy, questioning whether it was in America's long-term interest, against the backdrop of declining US influence and the rise of China. The result was a mutual attempt to renormalize relations between the USA and Burma after 2001, and an opening towards the reformists.

Under General Khin Nyunt, the military intelligence group within the Burmese regime began to soften its stance towards Suu Kyi. Among other things, it took her around the country to show off development projects and showcase the progress made by the government.

The government also permitted the USA to use Burmese airspace for US aircraft based in Thailand to fly missions to Afghanistan, and regime officials took steps to show Washington, DC that they were serious about narcotics eradication.

This was the strategic opening that the democracy camp could have seized upon and used to good effect. Unfortunately, for various reasons, the Burma activist-lobby block, comprising campaign groups and Burma-interested members of the US Congress, derailed this nascent effort at normalization and dialogue. This was achieved by making sure that Burma failed its tests with regard to cooperation on narcotics eradication, despite the recommendation from the US Drug Enforcement Administration that Burma be removed from the list of non-cooperative countries.

This left General Khin Nyunt and his group in a precarious position, squeezed between the military hardliners at home and the pro-NLD campaigners abroad. One manifestation of this was that military intelligence was powerless to stop a well-orchestrated mob attack against Suu Kyi's motorcade on a country road in May 2003. This was an ambush planned by hardliners within the inner circle of Senior General Than Shwe, which is widely believed to have been given a green light by the general himself. The Depayin massacres, as they came to be known, after the name of the small town in which they took place, put a halt to any possibility of the outward-oriented military intelligence faction making a quiet rapprochement with the pro-democracy groups. Suu Kyi and the NLD's chair, former general Tin Oo, escaped relatively unscathed but were detained and put under house arrest.

In an attempt to salvage their initiative, Khin Nyunt and his group used the good offices of the UN Special Envoy, Razali Ismail, to arrange a meeting with Suu Kyi and announce a five-point Roadmap for Democracy, and even attempted to revive contacts with dissidents abroad. However, dissidents in the West did not want a dialogue after Depayin, which they saw as a brazen attempt to assassinate two prominent democracy leaders. Still, Khin Nyunt persisted in his attempts to engage; the military intelligence camp began a series of political initiatives, including a high-profile meeting in Bangkok in January 2004. In this 'Bangkok Process', regime representatives explained to diplomats from fifteen countries that the regime was embarking upon democratization, in which the NLD would purportedly have a meaningful role.

Led by Khin Nyunt, the regime was also reported to have reached a verbal agreement with the NLD on the latter's rejoining the regime-sponsored National Convention, which was to draft the country's new constitution. It was reported that they gave the NLD leadership, and particularly Suu Kyi, the opportunity to take issue with any draft constitutional provision that they chose. The NLD leadership decided that a verbal agreement was not sufficient, and in April 2004 sent an official letter to Senior General Than Shwe, reiterating its concerns. There was indeed much to which they could legitimately object, as the document was clearly intended to constitutionalize the army's supreme role in Burma's politics, economy and society. For example it required 'national security' (i.e. military) experience for the head of state and allocated 25 per cent of parliamentary seats to the army. After waiting a month for a reply, the NLD leadership released a public statement explaining its decision not to participate in the National Convention, due to be held in May.

The internal crisis within the regime deepened. The hardliners within the military junta were questioning Khin Nyunt's loyalty, most particularly regarding his uneasiness over their efforts to prevent Suu Kyi from mobilizing public support for her party. Than Shwe later rejected the agreement that Khin Nyunt was said to have reached with Suu Kyi, and by October 2004 tensions within the army and military intelligence had come to boiling point. The hardliners removed General Khin Nyunt and dismantled the entire institution of military intelligence. Khin Nyunt and his family were put under house arrest and most of his deputies were arrested and sentenced to prison terms ranging from seven to 135 years. The demise of this powerful intelligence service was, paradoxically, a blow to the opposition struggle, because the hardliners who now had untrammelled power saw politics through the prism of a zero-sum power struggle. The consequences of that were seen over the next few years.

The hardline faction that took over in 2004 was inept and erratic in dealing with domestic and international challenges. The economic hardships that ensued from its poor policies caused enormous public discontent and unrest. In the years that followed, a dramatic rise in food prices and a 500 per cent increase in fuel prices prompted

several large-scale protests, including the 'Saffron Revolution' organized by Buddhist monks in 2007. The military used violence and mass
arrests to crack down on these protests, proving that the regime
was not interested in the public's basic needs. In 2008, when the
worst cyclone in living memory struck the Irrawaddy Delta, killing
an estimated 140,000 people and leaving nearly two million without
shelter, drinking water and basic food items, the regime failed to
initiate or allow substantive aid for two weeks for fear of increasing
international presence during a referendum on the new constitution.

Ultimately, this opportunity to engage with the reformist movement within the military regime was more than just a missed negotiation; it was also a key turning point in the history of Burmese
politics that led to a stronger presence of the hardline regime, and
a more difficult, more brutal society for the Burmese people. The
initial blocking of dialogue that the Burma activist lobby in the USA
had facilitated in the name of human rights and democracy had
eventually worsened the situation on the ground, and increased the
hardships and human rights concerns for the people directly affected
by the regime's actions. Later, under President Obama, these human
rights concerns about engagement with a repressive regime were
promptly forgotten when US economic and geopolitical interests in
the region were deemed too important.

A new paradigm of engagement and transition to civilian government

The American regime of hardline sanctions towards Burma remained constant until 2009 and the election of President Barack
Obama. Under the umbrella of rebalancing American foreign policy
to 'pivot' towards Asia, Obama commissioned an internal review
of Burma policy and instituted a policy of 'practical engagement'
with Burma. The USA's major interest was clear: it was keen to take
the opportunity offered by Burma's pro-American position, and to
bring the former pariah nation into closer economic and political
ties to keep it out of the Chinese embrace. Burma's position as a
new market for natural gas, the direct access to the Indian Ocean its
coastlines offered the Chinese navy, and the alternative it offered to
using the Malacca Straits for Chinese energy transport all brought a
belated realization of Burma's strategic importance in Washington,

and played an important role in reversing a hardline stance towards the regime. The USA was also concerned about reports that Myanmar was developing nuclear ties with North Korea.

Through the new policy, the USA engaged in direct dialogue with representatives of the Burmese leadership, and soon after the transition to a nominally civilian government led by President Thein Sein, the USA had formally lifted most economic sanctions on Burma to demonstrate public support for the reform process (Martin 2012). In December 2011, Secretary of State Hillary Clinton visited Burma (the first such visit for more than fifty years), and met with President Thein Sein and Aung San Suu Kyi.

The decision to re-engage with Burma had already been taken well in advance of Clinton's visit, but it was important for the USA to consult – and be seen to consult – with Suu Kyi. The high-level visit was preceded by a flurry of visits by lower-level US officials to prime Suu Kyi for acceptance of the US re-engagement with the regime. Before dispatching Clinton to Burma, President Obama spoke to Suu Kyi on the phone. Unusually, the fact that Obama had made the call was made public, presumably so that the administration could make it clear to the Burma activist constituency that she had approved the trip, and thus implicitly approved the shift in US policy (Selth 2012). In actuality, the shift in US policy was brought about purely in light of the changing geopolitical context and concerns about its hegemonic power; the co-optation of Burmese advocacy to implement this foreign policy allowed Obama to use foreign policy as a tool for domestic satisfaction. Without public knowledge of Suu Kyi's endorsement, Clinton's historic visit would have been politically impossible, for purely domestic American political reasons.

Thereafter, US policy shifted decisively to economic engagement and cooperation. In keeping with the policy of pragmatic engagement, the USA also made modest efforts to engage with the Burmese military. These efforts are diverse and include workshops on promoting civilian control of the military and allowing observers during the last two Cobra Gold military exercises (Hirsch 2014). Economically, Washington also reinstated official economic and development assistance to Burma, both bilaterally and through international financial organizations (Selth 2012). It encouraged Burma to align itself with the Association of South East Asian Nations (ASEAN), and in 2014

ASEAN members approved Burma's bid for the chair of the organization (Emmerson 2008).

Throughout this change in US policy towards Burma, the official American interest in the country has been repeatedly reiterated as wanting to 'support a unified, peaceful, prosperous, and democratic Burma' (Campbell 2009). US policy-makers see economic reforms and growth as a means to induce a political shift towards democracy and human rights.

This underlying uniformity of objective has only partially been reflected in Western advocacy, which has followed suit and moved away from the 'human rights discourse' towards a more 'civil society discourse', so that advocacy is now about building a civil society, and opening up Burma as a frontier market. This shift in the framing of advocacy narratives in response to changing American interests and foreign policy is explicitly demonstrative of the current state of transnational activism. The agenda for Burmese change is being set, not in solidarity with or by the Burmese people, but in alignment with Western geopolitical and domestic interests. This model of activism is ignoring voices in opposition to the Western hegemony of market, political and ideological interests and the broader ethnic conflicts and strife in the country, and yet is propagating a narrative of 'successful' democratization and change.

In this narrative, progress was signified by the release of several political prisoners, and by the 2012 by-elections, in which the NLD was allowed to compete and to win forty-three of the forty-five seats being contested. However, democracy is permitted only within the confines of a system that is still designed to preserve military power. The constitution must still be approved by the regime's hand-picked delegates and is still framed as 'discipline-flourishing democracy', whereby the army preserves a de facto veto over any proposed legislation. As well as a quarter of the legislature, the military also appoints three ministers and one vice-president. The interior, defence and border affairs ministers must be current serving generals. There is no independent judiciary, and Suu Kyi has been barred from running for president in the 2015 elections on account of the British citizenship of her late husband and children (Holland 2014), because the 2008 constitution renders anyone whose family members enjoy the rights and privileges of a foreign country ineligible as candidates.

In 2014 the military-controlled legislature in Naypyidaw categorically rejected any call to modify this clause, known as '59 (F)'.

In the realm of human rights, violent abuses against minority groups such as the Rohingya Muslims not only continue unabated but have indeed escalated (Zarni and Cowley 2014). The military has been able to mobilize long-standing Burmese racism against Muslims and especially the Rohingya, to reshape the public discourses in Burma away from democracy, human rights and labour rights towards 'race and faith'. This resurgent identity-based discourse is powerful and politically toxic, and suits the military's goal of reinserting themselves into Burmese politics as both the literal keeper of law and order and public safety, and the ultimate defender of 'faith and race'. However, Burma is home to more than a dozen ethnic groups, including the Kachin, Karen, Lahu, Rohingya and Shan, which have long been waging insurgencies under successive governments against the central state in the hands of the majority Burmese chauvinists. Stopping massive human rights violations against the Rohingya, negotiating power- and resource-sharing agreements with the Kachin Independence Army and other insurgents, and building an inclusive society with all the diverse ethnic factions remains an ongoing (and perhaps the most important) challenge for Burma. Yet this is a challenge that is almost entirely excluded from the singular advocacy narrative.

Conclusion: consequences of a singular narrative

Transnational activism for democracy and human rights in Burma is an important case, in its own right, and because it displays a variant form of solidarity to that found elsewhere in the world. From the beginnings of the transnational campaigns for Burma in 1988, the movement had a domestic Burmese face and anointed leader: Aung San Suu Kyi. She was not only the acknowledged leader of the internal democracy movement but also the focal point of the Western activist campaign, pursued by both Burmese dissidents and Western activists. This had clear advantages, but also caused deep problems, which emerged over time.

The main problem was that Suu Kyi was not a politician with leadership qualities tested in the fire of democratic organization, but rather an accidental leader, anointed because of her parentage and because she happened to be in the right place at the right time. In the discourse wherein Big Men (and Women) make history, one often hears comparisons between Aung San Suu Kyi, Mahatma Gandhi and Nelson Mandela. These comparisons are misplaced in a number of ways. First, both Gandhi and Mandela built their own political platforms as activist and revolutionary lawyers, while Suu Kyi was parachuted on to the stage built on the corpses of student and other dissidents solely as the direct result of her family. Secondly, she has repeatedly privileged 'sincerity' and 'patriotism' over organized political strategy in dealing with a military regime that prioritizes power and strategy over all else. She has long been known to have dismissed any question about her political 'strategy' to secure power from the generals who are dead set against an Aung San Suu Kyi presidency.

Thirdly, and most importantly, while Mandela and Gandhi were organizational leaders thoroughly appreciative of the need to build a political infrastructure and adhere to its discipline, Suu Kyi has shown no appreciation for or ability to build a solid team of fellow dissidents. Having 'The Lady' as the face of Burmese and Western advocacy meant that advocacy did not include diverse voices that represented all the people of Burma. The rest of the dissident movement was marginalized, its more progressive voices were unheeded, and the dissidents became more vulnerable as the whole world focused its attention on a single beautiful woman who speaks perfect English. When opportunities arose for broadening the political base of the Burmese democratic movement, they were lost partly because of the absence of a democratic procedure and the lack of a culture of dissent within the dissident movement.

One of these opportunities was offered by the reformist camp inside the regime led by General Khin Nyunt, which failed for several reasons, including the internal political rivalries within the junta. However, an important reason for its failure was the inability of the democracy movement to seize such an opportunity owing to its singular focus on Suu Kyi and her party. Only The Lady was permitted to shift the thinking among the rank-and-file supporters, and she and her external supporters did not seize the opportunity for re-engagement with a more progressive faction of the armed forces.

This has incentivized the junta to position itself to fight on a single front: with Suu Kyi and her pro-democracy Western supporters. It has consolidated power and ushered in rapidly signed ceasefire deals with ongoing ethnic insurgencies by enticing corrupt, unrepresentative leaders with commercial opportunities. These ceasefire deals are not inclusive, and have not changed the discrimination against ethnic minorities. On the contrary, they have distracted attention from ethnic tensions and served to further promote the singular narrative.

In light of this, by giving her a veto over the strategic identity and direction of the Burmese democracy movement, both Burmese dissidents and Western activists made themselves hostage to an icon of their own creation. All proposed changes in policy and narrative had to go through the NLD and Suu Kyi (at least publicly) in order to be 'blessed' with her approval, even though she had no formal decision-making power in the Burmese system. The apogee of this was in late 2011, when Obama was obliged to let it be known that he had consulted with Suu Kyi before Clinton's trip to Burma. When Suu Kyi was finally able to join the Burmese political process that year, she did not turn out to be the paragon of human rights and democracy, or the inspired leader, that many had hoped. For example, despite the liberal vocabularies of human rights and democracy, Suu Kyi and the NLD failed to make concrete any ideals they advocated by refusing to condemn state-facilitated violence against the Muslim Rohingya, even as the regime accepted the NLD as a political player in 2012 amid an escalation of this violence.

As changes in global and national interests perpetuated the evolution of activist narratives from 'human rights' to 'civil society', Suu Kyi's iconic stature was not sufficient to keep her as a driver of policy. A small number of Burmese dissidents based in Western capitals foresaw this irreversible shift in political fortunes and were fully aware that Western support for human rights was fragile. Members of this group did not succeed in educating the broader dissident movement, both inside and outside Burma, about the perils of policy shift. Their failure was largely due to the undemocratic structure of the pro-democracy and human rights movement, which had coalesced around a singular narrative and a single channel of communication and power.

Throughout the twenty-five years of the international campaign for Burma, the strengths and weaknesses of transnational activism have been symbolized by the person of Aung San Suu Kyi. As we appraise this history of activism, it becomes clear that 'The Lady' was manufactured as an icon of democracy and human rights by both Western and Burmese activists, and that this manufacture is one of the greatest political tragedies that the country has experienced, resulting in wasted potential and lost opportunities. Meanwhile, Western engagement with Burma has closely entwined policy with advocacy, and has served the changing interests of the national elites and the international economic order instead of helping to realize the rights of all Burmese, including members of already marginalized communities. Both the undemocratic culture and the strategically indifferent leadership of a pro-democracy opposition internationalized as the singular voice of Burma help explain why a movement that has so many dedicated grassroots dissidents and constituencies has failed so miserably – at great cost to the society. Tragically, the society remains sandwiched between strategically incompetent and strategically ignorant opposition leadership and the ruling clique of sinister generals and ex-generals.

References

Campbell, K. M. (2009) 'U.S. policy towards Burma: statement before the Subcommittee on East Asian and Pacific Affairs Senate Foreign Relations Committee', US Department of State, www.state.gov/p/eap/rls/rm/2009/09/130064.htm, accessed 2 May 2014.

Emmerson, D. K. (2008) 'Asean's "Black Swans"', *Journal of Democracy*, 19(3): 70–84.

Hirsch, S. (2014) 'Cracks appear in US Myanmar rapprochement', *The Diplomat*, 30 April, thediplomat.com/2014/04/cracks-appear-in-us-myanmar-rapprochement/, accessed 3 May 2014.

Hlaing, K. Y. (2007) 'The state of the pro-democracy movement in Myanmar', Working Paper no. 11, Washington, DC: East West Center.

Holland, H. (2014) 'Is Suu Kyi eclipsing Myanmar's peace process?', *Al-Jazeera News*, 17 February, www.aljazeera.com/indepth/features/2014/02/suu-kyi-eclipsing-myanmar-peace-process-20142169443994675.html, accessed 1 March 2014.

Keck, M. and K. Sikkink (1998) *Activists beyond Borders: Advocacy networks in international politics*, Ithaca, NY: Cornell University Press.

Martin, M. F. (2012) 'U.S. sanctions on Burma', Congressional Research Services, www.fas.org/sgp/crs/row/R41336.pdf, accessed 2 May 2014.

Selth, A. (2012) 'United States relations with Burma: from hostility to hope', Griffith Asia Institute Regional Outlook Paper, www.griffith.edu.au/__data/assets/pdf_file/0004/413446/Selth-Regional-Outlook-Paper-36.pdf, accessed 29 April 2014.

Taylor, R. H. (2009) 'Myanmar: reconciliation or reconsolidation, isolation or resolution?', *Asian Affairs*, 40(2): 210–33.

Win, K. Z. (2008) 'A history of the

Burma Socialist Party (1930–1964)', Unpublished PhD thesis, University of Wollongong, Australia.

Zarni, M. (2000) 'Resistance and cybercommunities: the internet and the Free Burma movement', in A. de Vaney, S. Gance and Y. Ma (eds), *Technology and Resistance: Digital communications and new coalitions around the world*, University of California Press, pp. 71–89.

Zarni, M. and C. Cowley (2014) 'The slow burning genocide of Myanmar's Rohingya', *Pacific Rim Law and Policy Journal*, 23(1): 681–752.

4 | THE JANUS FACE OF INTERNATIONAL ACTIVISM AND GUATEMALA'S INDIGENOUS PEOPLES

Roddy Brett

Introduction

In the wake of Latin America's brutal and protracted Cold War, the visibility of the region's indigenous peoples, many of whom had been subject to systematic and egregious violence during the decade of the dictators, has spiralled. Within this context, the growing political impact of indigenous actors within both the international system and Latin American domestic politics has owed much to their adoption of and strategic engagement with the international normative framework relative to indigenous rights, as well as to strategic mobilizations articulated through the globalized politics of 'Indian resistance' (Brysk 2000). Indigenous movements across the region have been linked intimately, then, to transnational activism and social movement networks, wielding key legal instruments, such as the International Labour Organization's Convention 169 Concerning Indigenous and Tribal Peoples in Independent Countries (ILO169). Concurrently, over recent decades, indigenous organizations in Latin America have received decisive development aid from IGOs, NGOs and bilateral donors, tying their own political agendas and development to socio-political and economic processes and cultural and political paradigms established elsewhere.

This chapter addresses a central dilemma that has emerged in the above context, exploring how international assistance in Guatemala has strengthened the capacity of indigenous actors to demand their rights, while at the same time imposing irreconcilable restrictions upon the realization of those rights. The argument presented here is that the politics of international activism and assistance has stopped short of a politics of emancipation, remaining intrinsically Janus-faced. In this respect, the chapter examines how, during Guatemala's peace process, international development assistance, characterized by financial and political support from international actors to indigenous organizations, was framed within the paradigm of Liberal Peace politics. Mac Ginty argues that the Liberal Peace paradigm represents the 'dominant form of peacemaking and peacebuilding' favoured by states, international organizations and IFIs (2010, 2012a). Richmond and Franks have defined this frame as undergirded by a four-pillar approach: the guarantee of physical security (demobilization, disarmament and reintegration; marginalization of extremists; sidelining of spoilers; security sector reform); the moderation of political conflict (political democracy); economic development; and the rule of law (2011: 7–11). Critiques of the Liberal Peace posit it as an eminently state-centric, top-down peace-building practice, arguably reflecting the values of the West, as we shall see below (Richmond 2011: 2–5; Mac Ginty 2010, 2011b).

Political and financial support for indigenous movements and the Guatemalan state from a range of donors, including the Scandinavians, Holland and Spain, and political support from institutionalized naming-and-shaming NGOs such as Human Rights Watch, was focused principally upon a limited rights framework, as the Liberal Peace posits: civil and political rights and certain collective rights. Support for broader rights frameworks, such as collective right to land or political and territorial autonomy, was excluded from international assistance, ultimately illustrating how aid would undercut true emancipation.

The research presented here explores those national and international processes that were decisive in the evolution and impact of the indigenous movement in Guatemala. The political mobilization of indigenous peoples in Guatemala reflects patterns seen across Latin America. However, indigenous activism in the country was shaped initially by key endogenous particularities, in particular by the genocide against the indigenous Maya in the early 1980s. At the same time, the unprecedented political space afforded to indigenous actors that accompanied and was consolidated by the country's internationally monitored peace process that brought the country's conflict to an end between 1994 and 1996 was a second endogenous factor. Along with El Salvador and Colombia, Guatemala represents one of three cases in Latin America where Cold War internal armed conflicts/civil wars were ended through formal peace processes, rather than through conventional political transitions, as was the case with the authoritarian regimes of Argentina and Chile. However, Guatemala is the only country where indigenous rights represented a key tenet of the Liberal Peace settlement, an agenda that was arrived at through the strategic and systematic intervention of international actors. Significantly, international intervention in this regard challenged and reshaped the boundaries of sovereignty in a number of ways, as we shall see. In fact, it is precisely here where the aforementioned endogenous factors shaping indigenous activism would become codependent upon their complex and dialectical relationship with a singularly decisive exogenous factor, namely the presence and influence of heavyweight international actors in the context of Guatemala's peace process. In this respect, the role of international actors, shored up by their formal mandate to mediate and monitor the country's peace process and motivated by their interest in indigenous peoples' rights and identity in the post-Cold War conjuncture, was critical to the emergence and gradual trajectory of indigenous political mobilization and of the peace process more generally. It is this relational process that, as has been suggested, ultimately represents the Achilles heel of the Guatemalan indigenous movement.

The chapter concludes that, during the peace process and in the post-conflict conjuncture, the demands and interests of Guatemala's many indigenous organizations, and those of the international actors that have accompanied them – including the UN, the World Bank and bilateral donors, such as Norway, Sweden and the United States and international activist networks – have oscillated between concurrence and rupture. However, a constant element of the ongoing political interventions and multimillion-dollar financial support on the part of international donors and IGOs has been the imposition of a series of conditions that have at once strengthened and legitimized the indigenous movement, while imposing the parameters that have ultimately limited its impact and challenged its unity. In other words, international assistance has collaborated positively with local efforts, while, ultimately, also having a distorting and damaging effect on them. In this regard, while indigenous leaders were able to develop and assert a leadership role during the peace process, the sheer resources and power of Liberal Peace actors ultimately co-opted and distorted their impact. Given this, it is germane to identify at which moment and for what reasons the platforms, demands and strategies of indigenous peoples and those of the international community have coincided and diverged. It is thus through identifying said convergences and fractures that we are able to understand *the Janus-faced politics of international assistance* (see Brett and Santamaria 2010) and comprehend how it has ultimately restricted the capacity of indigenous activists to assert a politics of emancipation and autonomy in the wake of Guatemala's armed conflict and during the process of post-conflict reconstruction.

Theoretical considerations

Social movement networks The activism carried out by social movements in the context of Guatemala's transition and peace process can be understood as 'contentious collective action', defined by Sidney Tarrow as 'action used by people who lack regular access to institutions, act in the name of new or unaccepted claims, and behave in ways that fundamentally challenge others' (1994: 4). Sustained political mobilizations by non-elite actors targeting and challenging the state and political realms often instrumentalize symbolic politics, such as street theatre, shaming politics and other forms of non-violent resistance and, in the process, create collective identities (ibid.: 3–4; Brett 2008).

Contentious collective action emerges within what Tarrow terms a *cycle of protest*, or 'moment of madness'. Scholars characterize *cycles of protest* as phases of heightened conflict and systemic contention that likely spread rapidly throughout the entire social system (ibid.; McAdam et al. 1996). As a cycle develops, diffusion of contentious action becomes socially and geographically widespread, gradually incorporating increasing numbers of mobilized social sectors and permitting the creation of new repertoires of protest.

The focus of indigenous movements has often reflected that of the so-called *old movements* – in short, demanding access to resources, including land, and seeking to redress structural causes of conflict. However, indigenous collective action has not been tied exclusively to class interests, as its predecessors were. Consequently, indigenous movements, and Latin American social movements more generally, have more often been defined as *new social movements* (Escobar and Alvarez 1992), given their prioritization of identity politics – in short, the importance of the role of collective identity to the recognition, interpretation, attribution, social construction and framing of common interests and grievances (D'Anieri et al. 1990; Melucci 1985, 1988; Offe 1985; McAdam et al. 1996).

A further piece of the puzzle that structures our engagement with the *how* of indigenous activism and its relationship to international assistance pertains to the issue of how activists frame their demands, platforms and strategies. McClurg Mueller has argued that a social actor 'actively constructs and is constrained by a world of social meanings rooted in specific historic contexts and based in the experiences and identities of race, gender, class and nationality' (McClurg Mueller 1992: 21–2). Social movement actors will develop a repertoire through which to identify, give meaning to and voice demands and grievances according to the (material and non-material) resources available to them. This process of 'framing', or 'signification', is the process through which actors ultimately confer meaning and project this meaning into the social sphere with the aim of wielding impact: it is 'an active, process-derived phenomenon that implies agency and contention at the level of reality construction' (Snow and Benford 1992: 136). The availability of discourses, historical visions of identity, funds and legal instruments shape the framing process.

According to Tarrow, a successful movement should be able to develop symbols and discourse that resonate with the daily lives of the movement's social base, constructing frameworks with which they are able to identify and through which they may interpret and situate their own grievances – in short, to feel represented. However, if movement activists are to achieve impact, they must also develop a discursive language that 'speaks to' the official culture of the state and the international community and the norms and values that undergird it (Tarrow 1994: 122–5).

In the case of Guatemala, indigenous activists developed from a movement that initially perceived itself as constituted by victims of state-sponsored terrorism into a movement run by activists who increasingly articulated an essentialized vision of indigenous identity as the predominant frame through which they identified and claimed their grievances. Socio-political developments in Guatemala and in the broader region were key to this process. Indigenous identity politics emerged as a key terrain of struggle as the peace process developed and became the principal motor for the country's process of democratization, as Azpuru has argued (1999). While this approach, closely supported as it was by the international community, gained purchase and legitimacy for certain demands and rights, it met closure for other rights, as we shall see below.

While the concept of new social movements is useful for our understanding of *how* indigenous activism emerged in Guatemala, it tells us little about the factors that impede or precipitate activism within a specific context, placing emphasis instead on the strategic actions oriented towards or resulting in the construction of collective identity. However, in this regard, the political process model developed by Tarrow (1994) and McAdam (1996) has particular relevance. This focuses on the concept of *political opportunity structure* (POS), a concept utilized to identify how the conditions that characterize, and the changes within, a national political system may in turn restrict or precipitate mobilization. As McAdam et al. state, 'social movements and revolutions are shaped by the broader set of political constraints and opportunities unique to the national context in which they are embedded' (1996: 3). In general, scholars prioritize the following characteristics to define the parameters of the national POS: the relative openness or closure of the institutionalized political system, the stability of state-level elite alignments, the presence or absence of elite allies, and the state's capacity or propensity for repression.

In the case of Guatemala, the emergence and trajectory of the indigenous movement was framed by two key endogenous factors that determined the POS: the genocide and the subsequent protracted peace process. However, factors at the international level, including changes wrought in the aftermath of the Cold War and related shifts within the international system, played a significant role, providing instruments and discourses that indigenous actors strategically adopted and took advantage of, as we will see below.

A final concept of relevance to the research presented in this chapter is that of transnational advocacy networks (TANs), as defined by Keck and Sikkink (1998). The authors have defined TANs as networks of activists guided by the centrality of 'principled ideas or values'. TANs are composed of organizations that act at the international level, articulating their networks with political mobilizations at national and local levels in zones of conflict. In those contexts where political space is restricted, repression may be ongoing, and the impact of national activists is thus impeded and ineffective. In said contexts, actors are likely to enjoy little leverage upon their own political system, civil society or state, where domestic channels may be blocked and where they lack visibility or legitimacy. Consequently, international pressure may be the most germane form through which to exercise impact. A movement at the national level will correspondingly seek the support of a TAN; the network will subsequently pressure other more responsive governments or IGOs to exert pressure upon the target state in question to comply with its international and domestic obligations and with international standards. It is for this reason that the authors refer to the 'boomerang effect'. TANs have represented a key player in the 'international rights regime' (Sieder and Witchell 2001: 204).

According to Keck and Sikkink, major actors in TANs include: 1) international and domestic governmental research and advocacy organizations; 2) local social movement organizations; 3) foundations; 4) the media; 5) churches, trade unions, consumer organizations and intellectuals; 6) parts of regional and intergovernmental organizations; and 7) parts of the executive and/or parliamentary branches of governments (1998: 1).

In the context of Latin America, TANs focusing on two particular issues, human rights and indigenous rights, played a fundamental role in the transition from authoritarian rule and in the process of democratization. Initially, in the context of authoritarian rule and, subsequently, of transition, the international human rights regime was the principal constituent actor of TANs. Brysk (2000) has observed that the international Indian rights movement became a key actor in the region after 1992, strengthening the impact of indigenous actors and generating conditions that were conducive to a series of key transformations in the region, including the process of constitutional reform that led to the consolidation of indigenous rights within the constitutions of diverse states within Latin America.

In the case of Guatemala, TANs (notably incorporating Human Rights Watch, Amnesty International, United Nations agencies and foreign governments) pressured the Guatemalan state to adhere to international standards with regard to its formal human rights obligations and to assume broader obligations, particularly in relation to indigenous peoples and women. In this regard, particularly in the early stages of the peace process, TANs were also crucial actors in the transmission of the Liberal Peace, strengthening the impact of heavyweight international actors, including the UN and bilateral donor countries, as they pushed a human rights agenda. Initially, those issues that TANs supporting domestic social movements in Guatemala engaged with and sponsored effectively were restricted to and shaped by those rights that undergirded the Liberal Peace agenda, in particular fundamental human rights, most prominently civil and political rights. Consequently, progressive local activist organizations, including the Ethnic Council Runujel Junam (CERJ), the Mutual Support Group (GAM) and the National Coordination of Guatemalan Widows (CONAVIGUA), initially worked collaboratively with international actors, together wielding the advocacy boomerang to great effect. GAM, CONAVIGUA and CERJ benefited profoundly from their work with TANs, as their visibility and voice were strengthened and their platforms were legitimized at the local level by the pressure imposed by international actors. 'Good advocacy' then worked effectively in favour of human rights at the beginning of the peace process.

As the peace process developed, progressive social movements supported by TANs that advocated indigenous rights and followed a more identity-based agenda, such as Defensoria Maya, also took advantage of their collaboration with TANs. The platforms of these organizations were similarly legitimized and their impact strengthened with regard to specific demands around a restricted indigenous rights agenda, such as the right to language, the indigenous justice system and indigenous dress. However, in the post-Cold War context, local activist movements such as the National Coordination of Indigenous and Peasant Organizations (CONIC) advocating broader issues, such as land reform, collective title to land and peasant rights, did not benefit in the same way from the wave of international activism. While no TANs opposed these issues directly, peasant rights TANs were largely absent on the international stage, ultimately limiting the impact of an already weak national peasant movement. TANs selected strategic issues, such as fundamental human rights and certain indigenous rights, that coincided with the national and international POS.

It is germane to indicate that, despite the role of TANs, the transnational actors active in Guatemala differ significantly in identity, scope and impact from those in the other cases presented in this volume. Several factors may account for this difference. First, the strong tradition of human rights activism in Latin America may have meant that advocates were more intellectually and organizationally self-reliant, depending less upon the conventional US lobby. At the same time, the key episodes examined in this chapter took place (or were at least initiated) before the new forms of US policy lobby advocacy and technology took root, excluding said actors from playing a decisive role.

The Liberal Peace Guatemala's peace negotiations and post-conflict reconstruction processes were framed within the Liberal Peace paradigm. Liberal Peace politics ultimately defined the nature and objectives of international assistance and activism during this time and conditioned the parameters of state-building that were to follow, while entering into tension with indigenous visions of peace-building, as we shall see.

Critics argue that the peace that is configured through international assistance and the activism that is wielded within the framework of the Liberal Peace tends to be 'conceptually and operationally conflated with free-market liberal democracy and those instruments, rights, institutions and concepts that define it' (Brett 2013: 227; Richmond 2005). Consequently, interventions emphasize a specific rights framework that prioritizes those rights that undergird political democracy and economic liberalization, in particular individual and universal civil and political rights and individual property rights.

The composite elements of the Liberal Peace – democratization through elections and democratic governance, rule of law and universal human rights, free market economies and neoliberal development – remain elite-led, exclusionary top-down processes. The Liberal Peace frame situates state and international actors from supporting governments and IGOs as the key decision-makers and executors of economic resources and peace-building policy. Consequently, non-state, non-elite actors, including civil society and indigenous organizations, tend to be *subject to* the peace-building interventions that affect them, rather than being integral in their design, formulation and implementation, leading to lack of ownership of peace-building practices (Mac Ginty 2008; Odendaal 2010: 3). The degree to which non-elite actors may ultimately determine the shape and outcome of peace-building may be restricted within those processes framed through Liberal Peace politics, as we shall see in the case of the indigenous movement in Guatemala.

Critical scholars have tended to overemphasize, however, the dynamic that attests to the crude North–South imposition of the defining political and economic logic of the Liberal Peace – in short, that policies and initiatives are imposed upon unwilling and power-less Southern counterparts. In reality, particularly in the case of Latin America, international assistance and activism waged through the Liberal Peace paradigm have been able to assert a decisive degree of acceptance and legitimacy as a result of buy-in from national elites and, in certain cases, from local civil society (Brett 2013). Buy-in, of course, will likely depend upon the issue at stake. Civil society organizations in Central America and Colombia, for example, have welcomed policies and interventions seeking to establish fundamen-tal human rights norms and practices in contexts of gross violations of human rights, while elites have tended to support initiatives aimed at strengthening institutions that may consolidate their interests and those that incorporate national markets into the global economy. This process does not represent the co-option of Southern elites, but rather their ratification of Northern-led interventions and capitula-tion to aid conditionality in defence of their own interests (Kappler and Richmond 2011: 272).

National elites in Latin America have been adept at recognizing the relevance and strategic importance of Liberal Peace initiatives in those cases where said initiatives would likely consolidate his-torical elite interests and status quo power politics. In this respect, national actors have successfully identified practices and acceded to interventions that guarantee to reinforce the mutual self-interest of international and national elites. Moreover, acceptance of the Liberal Peace agenda is likely to be facilitated in transitional states where economies have been weakened as a result of protracted internal armed conflicts, precipitating increasing dependence upon external assistance. It is here that IGOs and IFIs may step in unchallenged: 'in Guatemala, elites emphatically came to understand that effective competition in the global market place was contingent upon economic modernization, permitting the acceptance of the neo-liberal agenda' (Brett 2013: 226). This dynamic played a key role in shaping the conditions in which civil society emerged during Guatemala's peace process, forging important political space while at the same time generating acute challenges for indigenous activism.

Guatemala case study

Guatemala's internal armed conflict Guatemala's genocidal internal armed conflict (1960–96) was an integral part of Latin America's 'long cold war' (Grandin and Joseph 2010), and represents the region's most bloody and egregious conflict. While the ideological, political and economic logic of superpower politics imposed the contextual framework in which the conflict erupted, Guatemalan actors themselves were decisive in shaping the brutality of the violence and in perpetrating the genocide (Black et al. 1984; Dunkerley 1987; Falla 1988; ODHA 1998; Schirmer 1998; CEH 1999; Sandford 2003). With the support of successive North American governments, the country successfully confronted the communist guerrilla insurgency, the Guatemalan National Revolutionary Unity (URNG), and directly waged war against its indigenous support base to protect the historical interests of Guatemala's racist oligarchy (Casaús Arzú 2009; Brett 2013).

The initial Marxist-Leninist guerrilla uprising of the 1960s did not engage with, nor seek to incorporate or represent, indigenous communities and their politics. It was not until 1972 that the Guerrilla Army of the Poor (EGP) formed, and it subsequently constructed its social base principally from within indigenous communities in the western highlands. The EGP sought to incorporate indigenous peoples within its ranks, citing indigenous exclusion and racism as key motors of armed struggle.

The operative modality of the Guatemalan genocide was characterized by the simultaneous perpetration of instrumentalist and essentialist forms of violence, which served mutually reinforcing purposes. Under the military government of General Lucas García (1978–82), a violent counter-insurgency *'scorched earth policy'* was executed against both the guerrillas, particularly in the capital city and other urban areas, and their principally indigenous civilian social base, mainly in the rural areas of the country. Under the subsequent dictatorship of General Ríos Montt (1982–83), while military operations in urban areas were scaled down, egregious human rights violations escalated in rural Guatemala, as the military sought to wipe out the insurgents' social base. In this regard, the principal military objective and motive behind the counter-insurgency campaign then was to defeat the guerrilla by *draining the sea to kill the fish*. State institutions and institutional arrangements during this five-year period were controlled and held to ransom by the military. After 1980, no space existed for civil society mobilization or for organized opposition to the successive regimes. The justice system was effectively shut down, and the legal system, such as it was, was neutered and subordinated to the violent and arbitrary procedures of military justice. Consequently, organized civil society did not present a collective front against counter-insurgent operations or the mass atrocities that accompanied them, as it did in the Southern Cone.

State forces identified indigenous peoples in highland communities as the *collective internal enemy*, regardless of the presence of the insurgent fighters. The military campaign eventually precipitated the destruction of 660 villages, the massacre of at least 20,000 indigenous peasants, systematic mass public rape, forced sterilization and the internal displacement of approximately 1.5 million people (then amounting to approximately 12 per cent of the population).

At the same time, the genocidal violence was characterized by essentialist acts of violence. In effect, it is arguable that those military forces that perpetrated the genocide did so by explicitly targeting and subsequently seeking to exterminate Mayan indigenous communities, with the aim of building a consolidated whitened, homogeneous nation-state, a project that had not been successfully completed since independence in 1821. Planned and executed by Guatemala's dictatorial regime, with critical support from the US government, by 1983 the counter-insurgency had successfully vanquished the guerrilla uprising and brought about its strategic defeat by literally burning its support base off the map. This victory precipitated the decision by the military command to return the country to civilian rule in 1986 and to accede to the internationally monitored peace process from 1987 onwards. It was in this context that indigenous activism emerged and was subsequently consolidated within a national indigenous movement.

The emergence of the indigenous movement By 1983, the genocidal counter-insurgency had brought with it the military defeat of the guerrillas. The decision to return the country to civilian rule that was hastened by this defeat was further pressured by the economic crisis in the region and the international perception of Guatemala as a pariah state, impeding the country's capacity to garner broad international support. As the political transition advanced, by 1984 the country began to experience a less restrictive political space, despite the persistence of human rights violations. As the state's propensity for repression diminished within this political space, and the POS changed accordingly, particularly after the drafting of a new constitution in 1985 and the return to civilian rule in 1986, Guatemala experienced what O'Donnell has termed the 'resurrection of civil society'.

Civil society began to emerge in the mid-1980s, as human rights activists and victims of state-perpetrated violations poured on to the streets in response to past state-sponsored violence and on-going abuses. Across the region, in fact, social movement activism, in many cases supported by TANs, came to play a critical role in political transition and democratization. With the end of the Cold War, and the respective political and military defeats suffered by the left in Latin America, the politics of civil society became all the more pertinent. However, the post-Cold War context ushered in a rethinking of the left in the region that profoundly shaped activism. Particularist and identity politics and the politics of human rights assumed a more prominent role than did traditional ideological political identities (Dagnino 1998: 47–56), a shift reflected in the platforms of heavyweight TANs and international aid programmes. These factors restricted somewhat the repertoires available for activists, as we shall see.

As the political transition became less determined by the interests of the military, political and economic elites, the process became increasingly open and democratic, subsequently broadening the POS for activists. In the mid-1980s, those initial movements that emerged, Tarrow's 'early risers', articulated platforms framed closely through fundamental individual and universal human rights. Organizations demanded that the state guarantee the right to life and freedom of association, the cessation of human rights violations and political violence and the end to forced recruitment into civilian defence patrols (paramilitaries).

According to the UN-sponsored truth commission, the Historical Clarification Commission (CEH), 83 per cent of the victims of Guatemala's armed conflict were indigenous (CEH 1999). Consequently, the social base of those organizations that emerged in the mid-1980s was predominantly of indigenous origin. These activists mobilized in organizations such as CONAVIGUA, CERJ and GAM, organizations with an indigenous social base led by *ladino* (non-indigenous) leaders. The demands that activists articulated then were framed through those rights consecrated in the international bill of rights and within Guatemala's 1985 constitution. Activists made use of those state entities established within the constitution, such as by filing complaints through the Public Prosecutor's Office and the Human Rights Ombudsman. Significantly, these organizations received key support from those TANs that constituted the international human rights regime, including Americas Watch and Amnesty International. Individual governments, including those of France and the United States, also began to pressure the Guatemalan government to comply with international human rights standards, those standards that were fundamental to the Liberal Peace. Activists welcomed the political opportunities precipitated by these initial Liberal Peace interventions.

With the return to civilian rule in 1986, the political transition gave way to Guatemala's protracted process of democratization. The incremental impact wielded by democratization was itself strengthened by the evolving search for peace at the regional level, instigated in 1987 through Esquipulas II, the regional negotiation initiative that aimed to bring peace to Central America. In this context, activist organizations demanded increasing visibility and leverage, gradually imposing their platforms on the national agenda for peace and orchestrating a series of key achievements. Democratization brought a degree of openness within the institutionalized political system and gradually restricted the state's capacity or propensity to carry out overt repression. At the same time, as international pressure heightened the likelihood of a peace process, so the POS became more conducive for progressive civil society to exert leverage. Said changes, in particular the visibility of indigenous actors and the decrease in human rights violations, both permitted and obliged activists to expand their movement objectives and strategies and transform their identity. To remain relevant, organizations were compelled to change their initial demands for limited human rights guarantees, once these rights were, at least partially, secured. At the same time, the post-Cold War context – characterized by the emergence of particularist identity politics and the developing normative framework for indigenous rights – and the increasing tendency of the international community to emphasize indigenous issues, provided an important set of resources for indigenous activists.

Building on the framework established by historic indigenous mobilizations of the eighteenth and nineteenth centuries and activism by indigenous intellectuals during the second half of the twentieth century, indigenous victims of the armed conflict developed strategies and alliances to take advantage of the shifting POS. A series of factors strengthened this process, which ultimately led to the construction of a broad indigenous movement in Guatemala, a movement that would subsequently shape the peace process.

At the regional level, the Second Continental Meeting of the Five Hundred Years of Resistance Campaign in the hemisphere was held in Quetzaltenango, Guatemala, in 1991. The meeting, attended by indigenous and popular organizations from throughout the Americas, and by European dignitaries, was held in protest against Spain's celebrations of the so-called discovery of the Americas, five hundred years earlier. The meeting placed a spotlight on indigenous peoples in the region, and it strengthened visibility of indigenous struggles at the international level, in a context in which developments relating to indigenous rights within the international system had already taken place. In 1992, Rigoberta Menchú, an indigenous Guatemalan woman, won the Nobel Peace Prize, a key acknowledgement that further legitimized the indigenous struggle at the global level. These achievements were consolidated with the changes within the UN system and the strengthening of the normative framework relative to indigenous rights after 1993.

In the case of Guatemala, indigenous identity became a hegemonic form of political identity during the peace process and democratization. Movement leaders, or social movement entrepreneurs, framed their activism within the language, discourse and symbolic politics that were meaningful to the movement's social base and that resonated, at least in part, within the international policy-making sphere determined by Liberal Peace politics. For example, after 1993, an increasingly wide range of organizations, including Defensoria Maya, CONIC, CONAVIGUA and GAM, began to include Mayan symbols, ceremonies and texts, including from the sacred Popul Vuh, in their publications, demonstrations and national assemblies. After 1995, CONIC began to use the term *Ixim Ulew* (the Mayan term for *Guatemala*) and to carry out training courses in Mayan culture with its activists. This strategic shift in identity and activist discourse and repertoires resonated profoundly with organizations' social bases (principally indigenous victims). Simultaneously, a wide range of donors, including the Swedish and Norwegian governments, supported this strategy as they pushed for an indigenous rights agenda both in the peace accords and within the spheres of the state and political and civil society. However, the agenda stopped short of advocating certain rights, such as the collective title to land, as described previously.

Leaders had initially been non-indigenous, a consequence of the extreme marginalization that indigenous communities had historically experienced. However, increasingly, indigenous men and women, such as Juan Leon de Alvarado and Rosalina Tuyuc, stepped up to lead organizations of indigenous victims. These individuals brought important experience in international indigenous advocacy and impelled further the cultural logic sweeping local-level organizations. This new framework proved difficult for the Guatemalan government and state to oppose, at least on paper, particularly in the wake of the genocide and with international pressure focusing on issues of indigenous rights. Indigenous identity, rights and culture became key terrains of contestation, ultimately defining movement politics; indigenous politics found 'echo in broader regional developments, and most significantly in the guiding principles and conceptual tenets of the internationalized Guatemalan peace process. Demands were made, therefore, on the grounds of indigenous rights to entitlement' (Brett 2008: 23).

However, as we have indicated previously, the complex factors shaping the relationship between Liberal Peace politics and the politics of the indigenous movement ultimately wielded a contradictory impact.

The peace process and the indigenous movement The internationally monitored peace process began in 1994, when the parties signed a series of key accords, including the Framework Agreement, the accord to stipulate the negotiation timetable, and the Comprehensive Agreement on Human Rights. As a result of these accords, the United Nations Verification Mission in Guatemala (MINUGUA) was established. The UN's role in Guatemala was immediately distinguishable from its prior Cold War interventions. In the aftermath of the UN Agenda for Peace, and with lessons learned during the peace process in El Salvador, the UN assumed a broad mandate in Guatemala. The presence of MINUGUA, and particularly its human rights focus, consolidated the human rights tenet of the Liberal Peace. MINUGUA's presence initially legitimized and vindicated the demands and platforms of victims, human rights and indigenous organizations, while in turn strengthening their capacity for leverage with the government and state.

The peace negotiations, in which seventeen accords were signed, represented the process through which parties to the conflict sought to bring definitive closure to the armed conflict by addressing its causes and consequences. However, there was almost no formal acknowledgement of the genocide against the indigenous Maya nor adequate engagement with the conflict's embedded causes (access to and control of land or horizontal inequalities).

An unprecedented aspect of the negotiations was the formal mandate afforded to civil society to participate as secondary actors in the peace process with the establishment in 1994 of the Civil Society Assembly (ASC), a recommendation from civil society that Liberal Peace actors had supported and pressured for. The ASC, an entity bringing together some eighty-two civil society organizations, enjoyed the formal mandate through which to present non-binding proposals for the peace accords to the negotiating parties. A broad range of progressive civil society organizations participated in the ASC, including women's, peasant, human rights and indigenous organizations. Indigenous activists were represented in the assembly through the omnipresent Coordination of Organizations of the Mayan People of Guatemala (COPMAGUA).

COPMAGUA assumed a prominent presence in the ASC, immediately strengthening the visibility and legitimate presence of indigenous peoples within the peace process. The ASC's proposals relative to indigenous peoples, born predominantly of the discussions within COPMAGUA itself and legitimized by international pressure, pushed the developing agenda for peace towards including indigenous rights as a central theme of the accords (Bastos and Camus 1993, 1995, 2003). Indigenous activists lobbied to great effect, not least because COPMAGUA permitted the concentration of indigenous organizations within a single entity, which permitted the 'gradual uniformisation of demands' (Brett 2008: 177). As Caumartin (2005) and Stewart (2005) have correctly argued, a series of unprecedented measures to address historical discrimination and the social, political, economic and cultural exclusion of indigenous peoples were incorporated into the peace settlement, specifically into the Accord Concerning the Rights and Identity of Indigenous Peoples (AIDPI), signed in 1995. Significantly, the AIDPI defined the post-conflict state as *multicultural*, *multi-ethnic* and *pluri-lingual*. Such measures were born of a series of factors, including the pressure exerted by the indigenous movement that had emerged in the aftermath of genocide, strengthened by international aid conditionality signalling the obligation to address indigenous issues as central to the peace settlement and post-conflict reconstruction.

Negotiations for the AIDPI commenced in 1993. That same year, indigenous organizations began to lobby the Guatemalan state to ratify ILO169. As the developing peace process and democratization precipitated changes in the POS, indigenous actors began to broaden the limited rights framework they had originally utilized to articulate their demands. With the signing of AIDPI and the ratification of ILO169 in 1995, indigenous organizations were afforded new political and legal instruments which became the central tenets of the normative framework relative to indigenous rights. Said instruments also formalized and legitimized activists' claims to entitlements based upon indigenous identity and their demands for collective rights, such as the right to autonomy.

From the mid-1990s, then, the normative framework permitted indigenous activists to compound their original claims made on the right to equality with claims made for the right to difference, derived as they were from their focus on collective cultural rights. This development – which immediately entered into tension with the parameters of the Liberal Peace – was consolidated by the presence of the indigenous TAN in Latin America and elsewhere. It was precisely in this context that strategic cultural essentialism became one of the predominant modalities of indigenous movement politics.

In this regard, both AIDPI and ILO169 obliged the state to formulate measures to guarantee indigenous autonomy and to promote rights essential for the recognition of indigenous identity and the elimination of discrimination and exclusion. These instruments also consecrated broader economic, cultural and social rights that went beyond the limited rights that undergirded the Liberal Peace. It would be here that the initial convergence between the demands and platforms articulated by indigenous activists and those that were core to international cooperation (individual human rights) would fracture; the negotiation of broader rights frames that engaged with structurally embedded causes of conflict, as we shall see below, was not permissible.

The Liberal Peace process In the wake of the armed conflict, the implementation of the peace accords was severely restricted. While limited accord implementation was a key impediment to post-conflict reconstruction (Caumartin 2005), it was the design of Guatemala's peace process which represented the principal factor that thwarted possibilities for enduring peace. The initial components of Liberal Peace politics – in particular the imposition of international human rights standards, rule of law and democratization – had been resisted by a reticent elite that only gradually came to capitulate to international conditionality once it perceived said changes to be in its interest. In short, the dependence of Liberal Peace parameters upon a limited human rights framework – which eschewed the inclusion of collective rights to land and the right to territorial and political autonomy – was ultimately welcomed by the political and economic elite and converged with their own programme of supporting those limited reforms necessary to attract international investment.

Similarly, the lack of engagement with the structural causes of the conflict within the peace negotiations, an option insisted upon by the national elite, was logically acceptable to a range of international Liberal Peace actors. The negotiation of indigenous collective rights (guaranteed in the international normative framework) that would assure access to and control of land, facilitate a de facto land reform, and indigenous demands for political and territorial autonomy was not permissible during the negotiations. Clearly, this concession prohibiting the negotiation of indigenous collective rights was demanded by the military, political and economic elite, representing their own historical interests, within the framework of negotiations in which the guerrilla wielded little leverage given its prior strategic defeat in 1983. Moreover, capitulation by international actors to this demand from the national elite likely prevented long-term spoiler actions and kept the peace talks on track. This minimal agenda coincided with Liberal Peace parameters. Provisions aimed allegedly at addressing the causes of the armed conflict were limited to increasing revenue from Guatemala's regressive tax regime, increasing social expenditure for public services, the introduction of a land registry and the establishment of a land bank for peasants. The Agreement on Socio-Economic Aspects and the Agrarian Situation (ASEAAS) and, to a lesser extent, the AIDPI ultimately represented, then, a neoliberal policy response to embedded, historical causes of conflict.

Critics of the Liberal Peace such as Richmond and Mac Ginty have argued that Liberal Peace politics prioritizes fundamental human rights, including civil and political rights, over broader configurations and frameworks of rights, in particular economic, social and collective cultural rights. Collective rights were incorporated into Guatemala's peace settlement only when they did not directly address structural conditions or challenge historical conditions of inequality, such as in the case of the rights to ethno-education, indigenous spirituality, traditional dress, indigenous languages and access to certain sacred sites. While broader rights formed the mainstay of the demands of indigenous activists, they contradicted the undergirding framework of Liberal Peace politics and thus were rejected as part and parcel of the peace settlement. It was here, then, that the demands and visions of indigenous activists diverged from those of international actors that had hitherto supported them so closely and decisively. The sheer financial and political weight of international actors, bolstered by their close links with and capitulation to sovereign government and state actors, assured that indigenous visions were secondary to those of the Liberal Peace. By not addressing the causes of armed conflict, the design of the peace process itself impeded the possibility of generating minimal conditions for preventing future conflict, while sowing the seeds for renewed violence during Guatemala's post-conflict. Moreover, the return to democratic rule itself minimized the impact of indigenous activism, precipitating its demobilization, as we shall see below.

Concluding remarks: indigenous activism in post-conflict Guatemala – a postscript?

The current chapter has demonstrated how, in the context of the peace process and in its immediate aftermath, indigenous activists took advantage of a conducive POS and of the pressure asserted by Liberal Peace actors, ultimately sustaining a series of key achievements that decisively determined the peace agenda. In the wake of genocide, a broad-based indigenous movement was consolidated that, in collaboration with other civil society movements, imposed a framework of rights that shaped the content of a series of peace accords and compelled the negotiating parties to take into account the demands and agendas of victims, indigenous and otherwise.

However, the indigenous movement's ability to maintain its own core agenda and wield leverage over policy formulation after peace was signed was increasingly subject to and limited by the formal democratic framework that the return to civilian rule had imposed, a framework supported financially and politically by Liberal Peace actors and by many activists themselves.

The peace accords had been clearly framed within the parameters of simultaneous liberalization in the economic and political spheres, as the Liberal Peace instructs. Political democratization was a key aspect of this process. In this regard, the formal signing of the peace accords in 1996 brought broad consensus on the rules of the political game, a crucial achievement in itself. Political party and congressional politics formally became the 'only game in town' (Karl 2005; Diamond et al. 2008), strengthened by internationally financed processes of institutional consolidation and decentralization. With power once again vested in formal political channels, the political space afforded to activists during the peace process, particularly through the ASC, logically closed. The restoration of democracy demonstrated that the prior concessions made to and the accepted legitimacy of civil society participation during the peace process had been a state of exception.

With the signing of peace, the state and political parties imposed themselves, once more, as the principal political actors, as the Westphalian international system dictates. The end of armed conflict brought with it the restoration of an albeit nominal democratic political system as the dominant sphere for resolution of political conflict and the formulation of the national political agenda. However, political parties remained weak and personalist vehicles, representing private or sectoral interests. Most political parties and congressional deputies lacked political experience and had little direct relationship to a social base. Guatemala's political democracy remained 'hybrid', as Karl (2005) would define it, characterized by 'brown zones' (O'Donnell 1993), the coexistence of democratic and anti-democratic/authoritarian values and norms. Political parties did not assume their role as interlocutors between civil society and the state. While social movements were relegated to the position of being minor players, no representative, legitimate or effective political actor took their place. In this respect, the demands for popular sovereignty were not channelled through the formal political system. Moreover, political parties continued to be characterized by their historical exclusion of indigenous peoples, at leadership and non-leadership levels, as well as by the systematic absence of a political agenda relating to and democratically representative of indigenous activists as *peoples*. In the wake of the armed conflict and as a result of the democratic transition and Liberal Peace frame, the logical assumption of the political system as the main arena for the resolution of political conflict contributed to the weakening of the indigenous movement.

After 1997, the relative closure of the institutionalized political system to indigenous activists was exacerbated by the growing weakness of their former international allies. Once the peace was signed, the international community's relative capacity for leverage declined. During the peace process, the international community – including the Group of Friends, the United Nations system, the Organization of American States and other donor countries – had maintained an unprecedented capacity to exert pressure upon the Guatemalan state, albeit within the contradictory parameters of the Liberal Peace. This leverage in turn considerably strengthened that of indigenous activists. Sovereignty during the peace process, then, had, to a degree, been mutable.

The political pressure and leverage exerted by the international community during the peace process diminished after 1997. In the post-conflict period, political leverage was replaced by an international role in capacity-building and technical assistance, in particular through the United Nations, the World Bank and donors including USAID, Swedish and Norwegian cooperation. While capacity-building remains a constituent and ideological component of the Liberal Peace, the reassertion of sovereignty and the corresponding increasing weakness of the international community to assert meaningful political leverage immediately restricted the capacity of indigenous activists to take advantage of once powerful alliances.

While international leverage had diminished, donors continued to channel finance to the state and to civil society organizations. Indigenous activists faced a key challenge concerning how to adapt their strategies, discourse and platforms to the nominal democratic context in which the main causes of conflict – poverty, unequal land distribution, exclusion, horizontal inequalities – had not been resolved, conditions in which they remained politically and economically dependent upon international funding.

International assistance was systematically directed towards raising the visibility of indigenous activists and their demands, strengthening technical capacities and consolidating their legitimacy. International donors sought out those partner organizations that resembled Western social movements, as Pouligny has convincingly argued (2005), or otherwise made funding conditional on organizations so doing. Civil society, then, began to assume a homogeneous undifferentiated identity, signifying that those organizations that did not take on Western values and norms ultimately remained voiceless and invisible. As Mac Ginty (2012a) has indicated in other cases, technical assistance may impact severely upon local actors. In this case, it led to the 'NGO-ization' of activist movements. Organizations were obliged both to establish agendas and priorities favoured by donors and to assume impact evaluation frameworks, the *logical framework*, based upon those of North American accountancy firms (ibid.). The platforms of indigenous organizations became depoliticized, as they partially withdrew mass mobilization from the streets and focused upon political lobbying and capacity-building at the grass roots. Significantly, the NGO-ization of the indigenous movement also obliged organizations to compete for financial resources from donors. This process in itself, linked directly as it was to Liberal Peace politics, contributed to the fragmentation of the movement and the neutering of movement politics, demonstrating a key point of tension between indigenous and liberal peace frames.

Finally, indigenous activists also began to compete at national and local levels for positions in state and governmental institutions and positioning within political parties. Knowing full well that the challenge of maintaining their own movement agendas within formal political institutions would be severe, activists faced the dilemma of whether participation would precipitate meaningful impact or lead to co-optation. Moreover, successive governments in the post-conflict scenario demonstrated their ability to co-opt specific leaders and thus to neutralize activists. As Foweraker has cogently argued, movements emerging in transitional contexts will tend to face this challenge as they weigh up the advantages and disadvantages of 'inevitable institutionalization'. In short, as democratization advances, movements must answer the question of whether participation in formal state and political party structures is ultimately the right price to pay for the creation of *agile and effective political actors* (Foweraker 1998: 179). In this case, as indigenous activists began to participate in state and political party structures, they were unable to wield effective leverage and consolidate impact, thus failing to institutionalize the degree of representation that they had previously attained during the mass mobilization and protest that characterized the peace process (ibid.: 280–2).

The research presented in this chapter has documented the emergence of indigenous activists during Guatemala's peace process and in its aftermath, tracing tensions, convergences and fractures between the platforms, demands and strategies of indigenous peoples and those of the actors of Liberal Peace politics. Research has demonstrated how international assistance assumed a Janus-faced role that, while contributing to the construction of a series of unprecedented political opportunities, ultimately impeded the capacity of indigenous activists to assert a politics of emancipation. Simply put, international assistance provided by IGOs and international governments framed within the Liberal Peace paradigm facilitated an important initial space for the demands of progressive local leaders and actors – imposing the logic of a human rights regime – while subsequently promoting national-level political and neoliberal economic policies that would harm the incipient indigenous rights agenda and co-opt the emergent indigenous leadership. Transnational advocacy networks and local-level actors collaborated effectively around certain rights issues (those coinciding with the Liberal Peace paradigm). However, progressive local actors were afforded little leverage by indifferent or, in the worst case, absent TANs around platforms that pushed more emancipatory agendas, in particular those relating to collective rights and structural transformation. In the last instance, then, the Guatemalan experience evidences how international and local advocacy are Janus-faced. The capacity of indigenous actors to reclaim activism, to assert a meaningful leverage around demands for collective cultural rights and those directed towards redressing the causes of armed conflict, was ultimately restricted by the sheer power of Liberal Peace politics. To reclaim activism in this case, mobilizations should move beyond the Liberal Peace to assert Richmond's post-liberal peace-building, a peace-building undergirded by the self-identified needs and priorities and framed through the cultural repertoire of indigenous Guatemalans.

References

Azpuru, D. (1999) 'Peace and democratisation in Guatemala: two parallel processes', in C. J. Arnson (ed.), *Comparative Peace Processes in Latin America*, Stanford, CA/Washington, DC: Stanford University Press/Woodrow Wilson Center Press.

Bastos, S. and M. Camus (1993) *Quebrando el silencio: organizaciones del pueblo maya y sus demandas 1986–1992*, Guatemala: FLACSO.

— (1995) *Abriendo caminos: las organizaciones mayas desde el Nobel hasta el Acuerdo de Derechos Indígenas*, Guatemala: FLACSO.

— (2003) *Entre el mecapal y el cielo. Desarrollo del movimiento maya en Guatemala*, Guatemala: Cholsamaj/FLACSO.

Black, G. with M. Jamail and N. Stoltz

Chinchilla (1984) *Garrison Guatemala*, New York: Monthly Review Press.

Brett, R. (2008) *Indigenous Politics and the Guatemalan Process of Democratisation, 1985–1996*, Boston, MA: Brill-CEDLA Latin American Studies Series.

— (2013) 'Peace stillborn? Guatemala's liberal peace and the indigenous movement', *Peacebuilding*, 1(2): 222–38.

Brett, R. and A. Santamaria (eds) (2010) *Janoy las caras opuestas de los derechos humanos de los pueblos indígenas*, Bogotá, Universidad del Rosario: Colombia.

Brysk A. (2000) *From Tribal Village to Global Village: Indian Rights and International Relations in Latin America*. Stanford, CA: Stanford University Press.

Casaús Arzú, M. (2009) *El Genocidio: la máxima expresión del racismo en Guatemala*, Guatemala: Novo Mundo.

Caumartin, C. (2005) 'Racism, violence, and inequality: an overview of the Guatemalan case', Oxford: CRISE Working Papers Series.

CEH (Comisión de Esclarecimiento Histórico) (1999) *Guatemala: Memoria del Silencio*, Guatemala: United Nations.

Dagnino, E. (1998) 'Culture, citizenship and democracy: changing discourses and practices of the Latin American left', in S. E. Alvarez, E. Dagnino and A. Escobar (eds), *Cultures of Politics/Politics of Cultures: Revisioning Latin American Social Movements Revisited*, Boulder, CO: Westview Press.

D'Anieri, P., C. Ernst and E. Kier (1990) 'New social movements in historical perspective', *Comparative Politics*, 22(4): 445–58.

Diamond, L., M. Plattner and D. Abente (2008) *Latin America's Struggle for Democracy*, Baltimore, MD: Johns Hopkins University Press.

Dunkerley, J. (1987) *Power in the Isthmus: A Political History of Modern Central America*, London: Verso.

Escobar, A. and S. E. Alvarez (eds) (1992) *The Making of Social Movements in Latin America: Identity, Strategy and Democracy*, Boulder, CO: Westview Press.

Falla, R. (1988) 'Struggle for survival in the mountains: hunger and other privations inflicted on the internal refugees from the Central Highlands', in R. M. Carmack (ed.), *Harvest of Violence: The Mayan Indians the Guatemalan Crisis*, University of Oklahoma Press.

Foweraker, J. (1998) 'Social movements and citizenship rights in Latin America', in M. Vellinga (ed.), *The Changing Role of the State in Latin America*, Boulder, CO: Westview Press.

Grandin, G. and G. Joseph (eds) (2010) *A Century of Revolution: Insurgent and Counterinsurgent Violence during Latin America's Long Cold War*, Durham, NC: Duke University Press.

Kappler, S. and O. P. Richmond (2011) 'Peacebuilding in Bosnia and Herzegovina: resistance or emancipation?', *Security Dialogue*, 42(3).

Karl, T. (2005) 'From democracy to democratization and back: before transitions from authoritarian rule', CDDRL Working Papers, Stanford, CA.

Keck, M. and K. Sikkink (1998) *Activists beyond Borders: Advocacy networks in international politics*, Ithaca, NY: Cornell University Press.

Mac Ginty, R. (2008) 'Indigenous peacemaking versus the liberal peace', *Cooperation and Conflict*, 43(2): 139–63.

— (2010) 'Hybrid peace: the interaction between top-down and bottom-up peace', *Security Dialogue*, 41(4): 391–412.

— (2011a) *International Peacebuilding and Local Resistance: Hybrid Forms of Peace*, London: Palgrave Macmillan.

— (2011b) '"Hybrid peace" and "hybridity and hybridisation": beyond top-down meets bottom-up', Paper prepared for HCRI Manchester/Bradford Seminar, 22/23 June.

— (2012a) 'Routine peace: technocracy and peacebuilding', *Cooperation and Conflict*, 47(3): 287–308.

— (2012b) 'Against stabilisation', *Stability: International Journal of Security and Development*, 1(1).

McAdam, D. (1996) 'Conceptual origins, current problems, future directions', in D. McAdam, J. D. McCarthy and M. N. Zald (eds), *Comparative Perspectives on Social Movements: Political Opportunities, Mobilising Structures and Cultural Framings*, Cambridge: Cambridge University Press.

McAdam, D., J. D. McCarthy and M. N. Zald (eds) (1996) *Comparative Perspec-*

tives on Social Movements: Political Opportunities, Mobilising Structures and Cultural Framings, Cambridge: Cambridge University Press.

McCarthy, J. D. and M. N. Zald (1973) The Dynamics of Social Movements: Resource Mobilisation, Social Control and Tactics, Cambridge, MA: Winthrop.

McClurg Mueller, C. M. (1992) 'Building social movement theory', in A. D. Morris and C. M. McClurg Mueller (eds), Frontiers in Social Movement Theory, New Haven, CT: Yale University Press.

Melucci, A. (1985) 'The symbolic challenge of contemporary movements', Social Research, 52(4): 789–817.

— (1988) 'Getting involved: identity and mobilization in social movements', in B. Klandermans, H. Kriesi and S. Tarrow (eds), From Structure to Action: Comparing Movements across Cultures, International Social Movements Research vol. 1, Greenwich, CT: JAI Press.

Odendaal, A. (2010) Local Peace Communities, Some Reflections and Lessons Learnt, New York: UNDP.

ODHA (Oficina de Derechos Humanos del Arzobispado de Guatemala) (1998) 'Informe proyecto interdiocesano de Recuperación de la Memoria Histórica (REMHI)', in Guatemala: Nunca Más, Guatemala City: ODHA.

O'Donnell, G. (1993) 'On the state, democratisation and some conceptual problems: a Latin American view with glances at some postcommunist countries', World Development, 21(8): 1355–69.

Offe, C. (1985) 'New social movements: challenging the boundaries of institutional politics', Social Research, 52(4): 817–68.

Paris, R. (2004) At War's End: Building Peace after Civil Conflict, Cambridge: Cambridge University Press.

Pouligny, B. (2005) 'Civil society and post-conflict peacebuilding: ambiguities of international programmes aimed at building "new" societies', Security Dialogue, 36(4): 495–510.

Richmond, O. (2005) The Transformation of Peace, London: Palgrave Macmillan.

— (2011) From Peacebuilding as Resistance to Peacebuilding as Liberation, University of St Andrews, www. st-andrews.ac.uk/intrel/media/ Peacebuilding%20as%20Liberation. pdf, accessed 26 June 2014.

Richmond, O. and J. Franks (2011) Liberal Peace Transitions: Between Statebuilding and Peacebuilding, Edinburgh: Edinburgh University Press.

Roberts, A. and B. Kingsbury (eds) (1996) United Nations, Divided World: The UN's Roles in International Relations, 2nd edn, Oxford: Oxford University Press.

Sandford, V. (2003) El Genocidio en Guatemala, Guatemala: F&G Editores.

Schirmer, J. (1998) The Guatemalan Military Project: A Violence Called Democracy, Pittsburg: University of Pennsylvania Press.

Sieder, R. and J. Witchell (2001) 'Advancing indigenous claims through the law: reflections on the Guatemalan peace process', in C. Cowan, M. Dembour and R. Wilson (eds), Culture and Rights, Cambridge: Cambridge University Press.

Snow, D. A. and R. D. Benford (1992) 'Master frames and cycles of protest', in A. D. Morris and C. M. McClurg Mueller (eds), Frontiers in Social Movement Theory, New Haven, CT: Yale University Press.

Stewart, F. (2005) 'Policies towards horizontal inequalities in post-conflict reconstruction', CRISE Working Paper no. 7, Oxford.

Tarrow, S. (1994) Power in Movement: Social Movements, Collective Action and Politics, Cambridge: Cambridge University Press.

5 | ADVOCACY DELEGITIMIZED: THE CONVOLUTED CASE OF GAZA

Anat Biletzki

The agenda of the authors of this volume is dedicated to unearthing complexities, nuances and tensions within and between different contexts in which activism occurs. More specifically, we are examining the conditions which pertain to advocacy efforts carried out in or by the West on behalf of victim populations somewhere else, in conflict-affected areas. The 'somewhere else' of our discussion includes the four countries in Central Africa affected by the Lord's Resistance Army, Burma/Myanmar, the Democratic Republic of Congo, Southern Sudan, Latin America (focusing on Guatemala) and Gaza. Each of these localities[1] is, of course, singular and exclusive in its own way; I submit that there is an essential singularity to Gaza, in some way different from that of the others.

This difference arises, first, in the way we understand the additional coinage 'conflict-affected areas'. The generality, almost indeterminacy, of that description might not be unintended, meant to envelop a multi-phenomenal manifestation. Still, certain questions cannot be ignored. Do we mean conflict of groups within one country? Are we suggesting a conflict between two or more countries, or states, or nations, or peoples that affects both (or more)? Can we imply a conflict between certain individuals and the powers that be of said conflicted area? Might we be gesturing towards a conflict between civil society and the official authorities of a state? Or between different factions of civil society?

When we talk, then, of Western advocacy for someone, somewhere else, in conflict-affected areas, we must pose the preliminary question of who the protagonists of the conflict might be. Immediately, in the case of Gaza, complications abound, given the three parties involved in the conflict situation: the Palestinians, who are, themselves, bifurcated between those who are identified with the

Palestinian Authority and those who go under the auspices of Hamas, not to mention other more partisan identities; Israel; and Egypt. Yet these are not the type of complications which make the Gazan story unique; other places similarly exhibit this kind of multiplicity and variability of warring parties. But, in this case, we also require the identification, recognition and placement of the victimizer and the victim, and my discussion, in fact, will presuppose a victim – the Gazans – and a victimizer – Israel, against whom the advocacy for Gaza is addressed.[2] That part of the identification is (almost) a given; but here lies the crux. The uniqueness of the Gazan case, of Western advocacy for someone somewhere else, consists of the fact that Israel itself is perceived – and definitely self-perceived – as a part of the West. In that sense, the advocacy organizations and projects of which I will enquire are asking the West to identify with, show solidarity for and intervene on behalf of a party which is being wronged by Israel, itself of the West. In other words, the West is being asked to speak up and act against one of its own. In that sense the activism of which we speak is somewhat dissimilar to that of the conflict areas above and may be seen as a variant of anti-colonial and anti-apartheid activism;[3] that is the sense we have to make of and give to pro-Gazan, anti-Israeli activism.

Irony – advocacy for Israel in the West

Not unrelated to the problematics of identifying the victimizer, and ingeniously distinguishing Israel as itself being a part of the West, is Israel's own advocacy for itself on Western podia in any context that concerns the Israel–Palestine conflict. Israel's foreign office, its diplomats and its well-oiled public relations and propaganda (*hasbara*) machine carry out, in full force, rhetorical campaigns advocating for both awareness of and support for its positions; these positions are, of necessity and automatically, anti-Palestinian, in general, and more forcefully anti-Gazan, in particular.[4] Pro-Israel advocacy is constructed out of historical and political topic-points that run the gamut from semantics (i.e. the use of certain words and terms), to fact (i.e. the conscription of descriptive data), to interpretation (i.e. a specific construal of the facts), to legal proficiency (i.e. the formulation of all the above in terms of law). Let me spell out some of the policies and devices of pro-Israel advocacy by Israel itself.

Israel as a state, perceived as representative of a nation, a people, a community, a *group* (the Jews), and Israelis as individual Jews claim the status of ultimate victims. The history of centuries of anti-Semitism, culminating in the horror of the Holocaust, is used (and abused?) constantly, in relevant or irrelevant circumstances, as clear and present evidence of a victim position. Advocacy for the historical victim, then, is accepted as appropriate and necessary.[5]

Israel's political system is variously described and acknowledged (and sometimes contested) as a democracy. This is not the place to conduct that conversation; suffice to say that, beyond the theoretical conundrum that goes into definitions of democracy and the associated application of such definitions to specific countries, the label of 'democracy' in the Israeli case can be controversial. Still, public and conventional discourse has accepted Israel's self-proclamation as a 'democratic Jewish state' almost universally, and the refrain that Israel is 'the only democracy in the Middle East' has been ingrained in all Western political and cultural contexts. Related to this positioning is the subsequent alignment of Israel as an American ally – indeed, as 'America's most stalwart ally'. Advocacy for Israel, in the public relations domain, is a natural, albeit simplistic, outcome.

Advocacy for Israel in the West, given the conflict situation, must consist of advocacy against its enemies, the Palestinians. In the case of Gaza, in particular, the descriptive-semantic task of the advocate is temptingly facile. Gaza equals Hamas, Hamas equals terrorism, so Gaza is inevitably identified as a terrorist entity, scarcely needing to be styled in more nuanced terminology. The narrative about Gaza is appropriately replete: Hamas consists of fundamentalist Muslims, Hamas violently 'took over' Gaza, Hamas is intent on targeting Israeli civilians. Subsequently, this storied combination cannot be viewed as anything other than terrorism. Advocacy for the victim of terrorism is an inescapable conclusion.

A case in point is the historical event of summer 2005, also known as the 'disengagement' of Israel from Gaza, which has been leveraged consistently and forcefully in the service of Israeli advocacy in the West. A unilateral Israeli decision and action, the removal of Jewish settlers from settlements in the Gaza Strip is depicted as a grand turn in Israeli policy, born of both military realism (the unreasonable price of defending 8,000 settlers in hostile surroundings) and political compromise. This ostensive, historically significant course of action is then followed, according to the Israeli narrative, by the resulting Gazan comeback in the form of missiles showered on Israeli civilians in the south. Almost no message is more prevalent today in Israeli advocacy than the refrain 'We left Gaza and were rewarded with thousands of Gazan missiles'.

Israel boasts the world's 'most moral army',[6] the Israeli Defense Forces (IDF). This type of aggrandizement is straightforwardly available for advocacy in the form of both anecdotal evidence and educational or cultural frameworks that support conscientious self-reflection about military action. However, in contemporary discourse, it is more in the hands of international law to adjudicate the morality (if it be called that) of military exploits and, indeed, the terminology of both human rights and humanitarian law has come to the foreground of the debate on the wrongness or rightness of what Israel does in Gaza. Accordingly, Israel has a well-developed legal department in government (naturally) and in the military. It is the latter which is charged with scrutinizing the military's work both pre- and post facto, and its deliberation and counsel are used wisely to prevent – or respond to – accusations of wrongdoing by soldiers, commanders and even the political authorities in charge of military policy. In the Gazan case, in particular, intense legal work was done during the last three 'operations' implemented by the IDF: Operation Cast Lead (December 2008–January 2009), Operation Pillar of Cloud (November 2012) and Operation Strong Cliff (July–August 2014).[7] In the first, the legal experts were called upon to defend Israel from Judge Goldstone's report (*The United Nations Fact Finding Mission on the Gaza Conflict*), commissioned by the UN Human Rights Council, wherein Israel's actions in Cast Lead led to an appraisal that Israel may have committed war crimes.[8] The far more careful military conduct of the second operation, Pillar of Cloud, in terms of violations of humanitarian law, is attributed precisely to the lessons learnt in the first and to Israel's concern, in the second, to be seen as morally, and especially legally, unsoiled. The looming possibility of international opprobrium, even to the point of measures on the part of the International Criminal Court, has made Israel's legal advocacy in defence of its operations more careful, wise or, as some would note, cynical.[9]

This partial, but very representative, litany of Israeli advocacy measures highlights the rhetorical wherewithal of a professional, official and institutionally established state operation. Often accused of factual obfuscation, Israel has developed the mechanisms – cultural, political, legal – which can serve the state's agenda of presenting Israel as simultaneously a part of the more powerful West and still needing the West's protection, or, at the very least, support, against the victimizers, that is to say the (Gazan) Palestinians (and the wider forces of which they are said to be the vanguard and which are perceived and presented as resolved to destroy Israel). One must also take note of the huge advocacy arsenal that accompanies the official efforts of the state of Israel, in the form of the Jewish and sometimes non-Jewish networks that work abroad, i.e. in the West. This external-to-Israel but internal-to-the-West advocacy cohort consists of lobbying organizations (such as the right-wing American Israel Public Affairs Committee – AIPAC – and the moderate J-Street); the Jewish community organized into religious congregations, student groups and community associations; and the non-Jewish religious right organizations that have become a powerful, political actor in support of Israel and American foreign policy geared to its defence.[10] Its success in its advocacy efforts underscores two significant points. First, it is based on the same elements of persuasion that service the state of Israel's official advocacy: the Jewish history of victimhood, the current threat of terrorism, Israel's democratic uniqueness in the Middle East, and Israeli military morality and legality. Secondly, its economic and political strength demonstrate the sometimes insurmountable challenges faced by pro-Gaza Western advocacy – that is, Western advocacy against Western actors who have such a strong network of support. It is to that advocacy which we now turn.

Straightforwardness – advocacy for Gaza in the West

Is the ironic phenomenon of advocacy for the powers that be rather than for the side suffering or being oppressed one that is exclusive to Israel and Gaza? Clearly in every conflict situation in which there are two or more warring sides, each side is advocated for by its defenders; the concepts of 'suffering', 'oppression', 'victim', 'aggressor', among many others, are made to do work for all sides. The semantics of conflict are always slack, given to mobilization and manipulation by all. Still, the factual and legal condition of occupation by one country's state and military powers of another's, that is to say, of Israel's occupation of the Palestinians,[11] speaks to the natural assumption adumbrated above: that advocacy for the Palestinian side is the more likely object of our analysis and that therefore advocacy for Israel, by Israel, can be viewed caustically. This is even more pronounced when we move from advocacy – of different types – to overt activism. It is evidently activism in the service of Gaza, against Israel, its occupation of Palestinian lands, and its siege of Gaza, which is the more straightforward version that deserves attention in our investigation.

Gaza and its population, when recognized as the victims of the current Israeli political and military regime, are represented by all forms and styles of contemporary public engagement. A short survey of the operational media and methods of pro-Gaza and, in other words, anti-Israel advocacy serves here to impart both the numbers and variability of these paths of activism. Importantly – and this will be interrogated later – the protagonists of this type of advocacy are usually either Palestinian or Western.

Not surprisingly, the internet has become the most popular and populated stage upon which Gaza activism is practised. Though easily regarded as qualifying for the less respectable level of virtual activism, the contents and force of internet advocacy for Gaza are astounding: blogs, websites, digital journals and even e-books dedicated, either exclusively or inclusive of other issues, to Gaza's predicament. There are personal blogs supplying running reportage of daily life in Gaza, such as Laila El-Haddad's 'Gaza mom' blog (www.gazamom.com), which describes itself as being 'about the trials of raising my children between spaces and identities; displacement and occupation; and everything that entails from potty training to border crossings'. Similar in scope and content are 'In Gaza' (ingaza. wordpress.com/), 'Irish in Gaza' (irishingaza.wordpress.com/), 'Gaza: In the eyes of the beholder' (gazatimes.blogspot.com/), 'A voice from Gaza camps' (gazaphoenix.blogspot.com/) – and hundreds of other individual attempts to present the story of Gaza, usually from the 'inside', so to speak, in order to raise awareness and consciousness among the general internet-using public about the local situation. Somewhat more sophisticated, and usually guided by journalistic conventions, are the blogs created by and on the sites of established, even prestigious, media outlets that are dedicated to implicit advocacy for Gaza, in the context of allegedly objective journalism. And indeed, it is on the sites of the internet newspapers that aspire to – and usually reach – the professional heights of digital journalism that one meets the most articulate, fact-based and coherent examples of well-ordered Gazan reports whose advocacy consists, first, in informing the public of the factual material that is either ne'er to be found in Western media or explicitly contradictory to the well-rehearsed Israeli advocacy. First and foremost is the Electronic Intifada (electronicintifada.net/), where advocacy means exposure of truth and fact. No less effective than Electronic Intifada is Witness Gaza (witnessgaza.com/about/), described as an electronic

> public meeting place where people around the world can access and SHARE information about Israeli violence against the Palestinian people ... All the latest news, videos, notices, announcements, press releases, Twitter, Facebook, and Flickr postings, as well as photos, requests or offers for help, discussions, chats, resourcing, are instantly accessible in one public place at WitnessGaza.com. And interested parties, organizations and individuals can post, share, contribute and update content, plus post information regarding their activities, plans, and progress. These activities can then be accessed by everyone everywhere, and disseminated world-wide.

Interestingly, it is the status of 'witness' and the activity of electronic witnessing, taken as a metaphoric semantic, which provide the literal activism and the effective advocacy, always with the goal of raising awareness.

'Back to the rough ground',[12] however. The traditional venues of activism – demonstrations, marches, sit-ins, teach-ins, conferences and other sundry old-style forms of activism – have not been vacated in the wake of digital or virtual settings. Civil society, student and professional groups, human rights and humanitarian NGOs and political organizations have continued, over the past several decades but most notably since the Israeli blockade of Gaza, creating spaces and activities of protest to rouse civilian publics and, in turn, to move policy – and decision-makers – in a pro-Gazan direction. Although the roster of these exploits is both long and relatively conventional, there have been some significant incidents that deserve special mention for their concrete implementation and, more so perhaps, for their political, or – at the least – promotional, effect.

Of these, the Gaza Freedom March (GFM) of 2009 was one such outstanding event. Organized by a coalition of organizations and individuals, including some celebrities (such as Alice Walker), the GFM was planned as an international group which would march with tens of thousands of Gazans from one point in the Gaza Strip (Izbed Abed Rabbo) to another (Erez crossing), connect with Israelis and Palestinian citizens of Israel at the crossing, and call for an end to the blockade that Israel had imposed on Gaza. Sponsors and endorsers comprised hundreds of NGOs from all over the world – some 'general' humanitarian and human rights organizations (such as CodePink), some with specific missions unrelated to Gaza (such as Focus on the Global South from India), and some with Palestinian or Gazan agendas (such as Forum Palestine from Italy). Individuals signed letters of support in their own names, though hundreds, again, were presented as representatives of the organizations to which they belonged or which they even led and chaired (such as Michael Ratner, president of Center for Constitutional Rights). Palestinian and Israeli civil society organizations were explicit campaigners and supporters of the 'internationals' who went to Cairo. Over 1,300 people from 43 countries (800 from the USA) converged in Egypt, planning to enter Gaza and to march non-violently with the Gazans, with the express purpose of 'lifting the siege on Gaza'. The Egyptian authorities prevented the marchers from proceeding with their agenda, but the march received worldwide attention and publicity, achieving one of the perpetual goals of all activism – awareness of a struggle and support for the victims.

A second noteworthy mode of activism, which purported to hold the same objective of breaking the Israeli blockade on Gaza but adopted a different practical, literally physical, approach, was – and still is – the Free Gaza Movement, organizing boats that would bring humanitarian aid to Gaza. In its most extravagant feat of May 2010 (after eight earlier attempts to reach Gaza by boat), the movement arranged eight boats, the largest of which, the Turkish-registered *Mavi Marmara*, carried hundreds of passengers. Intercepted at sea by the IDF, which claimed that some of those aboard were armed, the flotilla was aborted – after nine passengers were killed by Israeli forces. The 'results' of the freedom flotilla's endeavour included an almost complete breach of diplomatic relations between Israel and Turkey (still being weathered today). More relevant to the very goals of the activist agenda was the attainment of two aims that are the purpose of all advocacy and activism pertaining to Gaza: Israel was generally condemned in the international arena (but it is questionable whether the condemnation was of its pointed actions, or of its siege policy) and the blockade of Gaza was somewhat eased. One can point here to straightforward activism – carried out by international groups (though not all Western) – in the service of Gazan advocacy.

Let me conclude this section, which has outlined and explained the most obvious and intuitively natural modus of advocacy for Gaza by activists in the West, by problematizing, for just a moment, the goals of such activism. And let me note, for just a moment, the sceptical attitude: the kind of activism described here, activism predicated on physical engagement of a few people – and even 1,300 are few, in comparison to the inordinately powerful – is a somewhat unfocused, politically futile, personal feel-good type of doing which cannot and does not, in the end, effect real change in the real policies and actions of the powers that be. This is the oft-heard diatribe against on-the-ground activism, which views politics as necessarily and institutionally professional or as a matter of international policy-making, rather than as motivated or propelled by grassroots movements. The important and, to my mind, authentic answer to this type of practical admonishment turns to the concept of solidarity. It is solidarity which is the goal of such activism; it is symbolic consciousness-raising which is at the root of advocacy, not tangible help (as in blockade-running) or even specific, identifiable, political changes. The most illustrative example of such activism-turned-advocacy can perhaps be seen in the Russell Tribunal on Palestine – a public court made up of eminent personages established to examine the issues of international law that have prevented the Palestinian people (not only in Gaza) 'from exercising its rights to a sovereign State'. Consciously aware of its lack of grounded political power, the Russell Tribunal – which includes, among the members of its jury, luminaries such as Alice Walker, John Dugard, Mairead Maguire, Ronald Kasrils, Jose Pallin and Cynthia McKinney – aims to mobilize civil society, to act as a 'court of the people', and, in the spirit of the original Russell Tribunal of 1966, 'to prevent the crime of silence'. At the least, then, advocacy means the negation of the usual silence of non-advocacy.

Complexity – advocacy for Gaza in Israel

Advocacy for Gaza in Israel is advocacy within a sovereign state (Israel) for the people (Palestinians) living outside the state but in an area that is still under the state's control. This situation is remarkable owing to several factors. There is, first, the dire need for information about Gaza in Israel and the dearth of material precisely in the place where one would think it would be easily available. Sadly and paradoxically, however, Israelis are forbidden to enter Gaza. Whether as functioning journalists, as intentional humanitarian workers, or as visitors of Gazan residents, Israelis, by virtue of their Israeli citizenship, have been legally prohibited, since the 'disengagement' of 2005, from going through the Gazan entry points, which are exclusively manned by the Israeli military. The consequence of this regulation is the lack of first-hand information, whether from journalists or from civilian witnesses. Information is acquired – by those who care enough to enquire – via foreign sources or telephone, e-mail, social media, etc. But nowhere is there an unmediated civilian Israeli encounter with Gaza. Secondly, then, the awareness of the Gazan reality is at a strange level of inadvertent or even wilful indifference; the absence of information and the deficiency of any real knowledge are predictable causes for a lack of the expected human awareness of the suffering next door. So, thirdly, advocacy for Gaza within Israel is primarily conceived as an enterprise of changing attitudes if one is to effect any change. Not surprisingly, the Israeli parties engaged in this enterprise are involved in ethical and legal battles.[13] Their work for Gazan causes is carried out in a fascinating montage of the media and the courts. This is realized by individuals, by certain groups in civil society, and by human rights organizations. Elaboration on some exceptional advocacy work within Israel is in order (in order to later problematize it); I embark on this elaboration in Wittgensteinian fashion, pointing to particulars for the understanding that comes with 'perspicuous representation' rather than attempting to articulate a general hypothesis on such work.[14]

First, individual peace workers and human rights champions, of differing professions and variable effectiveness, are constantly at work in the Israeli arena, using their expert positioning to make the Gazan case. Notable representative names (with respective behaviours and events) come to mind – though there are many others. Parliament member Haneen Zoabi, a Palestinian of Israeli citizenship, was on the *Mavi Marmara*, the ship mentioned above (as a case of outside advocacy for Gaza) that was attacked by Israeli forces in May 2010. She had joined the foreigners on the freedom flotilla to make the obvious point that the Gaza blockade must be broken, but she had done so as an Israeli, advocating for Gaza to other Israelis.[15] Amira Hass is an Israeli journalist who lived in Gaza for several years (before the legal prohibition took effect), reporting to Israelis directly from within the occupied territory about its day-to-day life. Although now based in Ramallah – also in Palestinian occupied territory, though no longer in Gaza itself – Hass has stayed in Gaza several times in order to report directly from an unattainable place but also, by such flagrant reporting, to position herself in the seat of advocacy.[16] In 2004, Ariella Azoulay, an Israeli academic who creates, analyses and critiques art from a political vantage point, produced and directed a short video installation called *The Food Chain* – with a monotonous refrain, 'There is no hunger in Palestine' – driving home to Israelis the point that the population next door was being intentionally and efficiently subjected to malnutrition.[17] Miki Kretzman, a leading Israeli photographer (now director of the Photography Department in Israel's prestigious art school, Bezalel), has routinely photographed the atrocities suffered by the 'ordinary' Palestinian on-site – publishing his photographs in Israeli newspapers, showing them in art exhibits, and volunteering them to those who might use them in additional venues of activism and advocacy.[18] Others too many to name are all a part of a dynamic advocacy project that persists in attempting to make the plight of Palestinians in general and Gazans in particular an active element of Israeli consciousness.

Second, Gisha (Access) – the Legal Center for Freedom of Movement – is an NGO that provides legal assistance and public advocacy to protect the rights, especially to freedom of movement, of Palestinians, especially Gaza residents. Gisha is a legal centre focused on legal work, including much effort in the courts, based on Israeli law, international human rights law and humanitarian law. Paradigmatically, the organization represents students in Gaza who have not been allowed, since 2000, to study in the West Bank (with only three students being exceptions to the rule during that span of time). Indeed, in May 2012, the High Court ordered the state to 'consider allowing students to study in the West Bank',[19] but unsurprisingly, in September 2012, it finally rejected the petition, ruling that the state was not obligated to set up an 'exceptions committee' for anybody. Other issues that Gisha has taken to the authorities or to the courts include innumerable applications under the 'Freedom of Information Act', to acquire information that is usually sequestered under 'security considerations'. Such were, for instance, the criteria used in granting merchants permits to exit the Gaza Strip (finally received from the Coordinator of Government Activities in the Territories [COGAT]), or those for approving construction projects and allowing construction materials into the Strip. As its name attests, applications for travel, such as, for instance, appeals to allow people to travel to Israel for medical treatment, are Gisha's daily bread. This type of advocacy, termed by Gisha itself legal advocacy, is intended to achieve concrete goals; it is subsequently more often than not unsuccessful. But it is a constant irritant, at the least, and a strong moral rebuke of the military and judicial establishments that perpetuate the occupation – i.e. control – of Gaza (more on that in a minute).

Third, B'Tselem – the Israeli Information Center for Human Rights in the Occupied Territories – coined the phrase 'One Big Prison' in its March 2005 report, warning of what might happen after the disengagement.[20] In its report of May 2007 on Gaza, B'Tselem insisted on continuing to use the same title, though certain more polemically oriented workers in the organization suggested '*Still* One Big Prison'. The justification for that name, for that situation, was based on the fact that Israel controlled – and still controls – the Gaza Strip, in the sense of 'effective control' as formulated in international law. It has complete control of the airspace (overhead aircraft, a lack of any airport in Gaza, radio, television and telephone transmissions); the sea (a lack of any seaport, limitations on fishing, both within Gazan jurisdiction and outside it, in international waters); movement of people in and out of Gaza; movement of products and materials – i.e. imports and exports – into and out of Gaza; the population registry of Gaza; and tax collection from Gazans.

The self-identity of B'Tselem involves being an 'information centre' – that is to say, a provider of information. Originally and traditionally this purveyor of information about Gaza supplied reports – long-winded, legally grounded, almost academic reports that earned the accolades of the human rights community all over the world for comprehensiveness and trustworthiness. These reports serve as the basis and the background for public media advocacy, both in Israel and abroad.[21] Interestingly, the mode of advocacy has evolved from periodical statistical and general reports to more personal, varied media, including sponsored blogs, video reports and recorded testimonies. In Israel such advocacy has three explicit goals: documenting human rights violations in the Occupied Territories, educating the Israeli public to human rights, and, perhaps most important, changing Israeli policy in the Occupied Territories. In the USA B'Tselem targets two groups: policy-makers in the capital and the American Jewish community. This is facilely explained by the perceived American one-sided support for Israel, which is purportedly conditioned by Jewish public opinion.

Fourth, beyond the specificity of organizations like Gisha and B'Tselem and their unique, precisely well-defined methodology of human rights engagement and advocacy, there is a motley variety of activism continuously carried out in Israel by several groups and organizations of Israeli civil society. Emblematic of these are appeals to the Israeli government such as 'Open Gaza's borders to prevent a humanitarian crisis', published in June 2007, and signed by the Association for Civil Rights in Israel (ACRI), B'Tselem, Gisha, the Public Committee against Torture, Hamoked (Center for the Defence of the Individual), Physicians for Human Rights (PHR), Rabbis for Human Rights (RHR) and Yesh Din (Volunteers for Human Rights). Similarly, in January 2009, at the height of Operation Cast Lead, the above organizations, augmented by Amnesty International, put up a joint blog, 'Clear and present danger to the lives and well-being of tens of thousands of civilians in Gaza', to provide reports on the circumstances and consequences of the Israeli assault on Gaza. Somewhat differently conceived, but still representative of the kind of work being done by activists and advocacy groups in Israel on Gaza, was the exposure of the outrageous regulations and limitations formulated by Israeli authorities regarding the food being allowed into

Gaza. In 2010 the organizations obtained from military sources the exact list of products permitted into the Strip. (Aniseed, cinnamon, black pepper – permitted; coriander, ginger, nutmeg – prohibited.) More significantly, in November 2012, Gisha petitioned the High Court and succeeded in getting the exact calculations made by the Israeli military for how low the caloric amount could go, during the embargo, if malnutrition was to be avoided (2,279 calories).[22] Presenting the public with such perverse, blatant truths is also a form of advocacy.

There is an aspect of activism in Gaza's defence and advocacy for its travails in Israel by Israelis that garners, to my mind, the label of convolution. In contrast to the straightforward type of advocacy that is encountered in the West on Gaza's behalf, and the ironic promotion of Israel's interests vis-à-vis Gaza in that same West, the presentation of the Gazan case to Israelis by Israelis in Israel harbours a painful, nuanced complexity. On the cusp of a theoretical understanding of humanitarianism and the practical recommendations on how to go forward, there is an intricate viewpoint within the political left admonishing well-meaning Israelis to desist from advocacy that calls for humanitarian help for Gaza. The point here is not that aid is injurious to the Palestinians – it might not be – but rather that organized advocacy for Gaza, by recognized Israeli bodies (NGOs, peace groups, etc.), gives succour to the lie: it presents Israel as a democratic, pluralistic political agora, where various players in a complicated conflict, including Gaza, can have their say and advocate for their positions. In fact, Israeli advocacy for Gaza in Israel, offered up by the Israeli establishment and authorities as a legitimate, even if wrong, political standpoint, functions as a fig leaf for the undemocratic treatment of Palestinians by Israel. Such activism, then, serves to let Israel off the hook and, indeed, becomes one more insidious, even if unintentional, collaboration with the Occupation.[23]

Delegitimization – advocacy for Gaza in Israel, summer 2014

Israelis advocating for Gazans, and for Palestinians in general, have sometimes obliquely, often explicitly, been said to be disloyal, even traitorous. Given a simplistic, popular view of the conflict as a zero-sum us versus them, it is no wonder that support for 'the enemy' arouses such reactions in the general populace and that the arena of political activism in Israel has become so fraught with tensions of political identities. Still, Operation Strong Cliff (aka Protective Edge), launched by Israel against Gaza in the summer of 2014, has given rise to a level of opposition to activism of the several kinds described above that threatens the very core of a supposedly vibrant culture of advocacy. As before, a number of exemplars will suffice to tell the story of the general trajectory that has reached, in the summer of 2014, a bewildering intensity of delegitimization.

On 12 July 2014, on the first Saturday of the first week of Operation Strong Cliff – which came on the heels of the abduction of three Israeli youths in the West Bank, a consequent Israeli military operation called Brother's Keeper assaulting the population of the West Bank and arresting almost all Hamas members there (with the purported aim of saving the youths), and a resulting Gazan launch of rockets into Israel – a group of Israeli activists staged a non-violent anti-war demonstration in the centre of Tel Aviv. A counter-demonstration of self-proclaimed right-wing, 'patriotic', 'Zionist' protagonists materialized in the same centrally located square. Such counter-protests had not been unheard of before; what was novel, however, was the mass and vehemence of this group action and the more ominous abstention of the police in restraining them when they accosted the anti-war demonstrators with physical violence. Thus began a summer of demonstrations and counter-demonstrations during which Israel witnessed a steady consolidation of public vilification of left-wing, anti-war, pro-peace activism. The previous, deviant language of 'Death to the Arabs', itself already becoming portentously popular, rose in volume and morphed into 'Death to the leftists', expressed not only verbally but by threatening, violent attacks on protesters. It is still a matter of interpretive debate among Israelis whether the authorities – usually the police force but sometimes also other security services – were unequivocally instructed and committed to protect civil activists (of the 'left') or whether they could easily take the side of 'patriots'. A telling sign of discriminatory action on the part of the authorities was the number of arrests made exclusively against Palestinian citizens of Israel in protests against the Israeli operation (and thereby perceived automatically as 'pro-Gaza'): 1,500 protesters were arrested during these demonstrations, with 600 indicted. Clearly one could no longer be a pro-Gaza activist without incurring both public and official condemnation.

In a different yet corresponding context, the programmes and activities of human rights organizations (as opposed to individual activists or less formal peace groups) encountered, during the summer of 2014, a pushback previously unseen in the Israeli agora.[24] Almost iconographic was the case of a commercial created by B'Tselem, in which the names of Gazan children killed during the Israeli operation were read aloud.[25] The organization presented the spot as an instance of its legitimate agenda: providing information about the Palestinian Occupied Territories to the public in general and raising awareness of the suspicion of war crimes that may arise in the current circumstances. The Israeli Broadcast Association refused to air the commercial, claiming that it was 'political'. B'Tselem appealed the IBA's refusal, going through government bodies all the way up to the High Court. The court upheld the IBA's decision.

Analysis of such phenomena in the summer of 2014 is called for if one is to understand the political, ethical, social and even cultural significance of a particular occurrence; for us it points to a groundswell of attitudes and behaviours in Israel that has made activism and advocacy for Gaza illegitimate, sometimes even illegal. In the public realm one can identify a change in societal norms that is led by central, mainstream, establishment leaders – politicians (of course), but also the media, the military, academia and cultural icons. When, for example, a very few – no more than four – actors and singers spoke out about the deaths of Gazan children, they were immediately pilloried by the public and the media. In the more official, formal frameworks of government and courts, steps were taken to obviate any signs of pro-Gazan activism and possible avenues of advocacy. The explanation for these manifestations and particularly their climactic eruption during Operation Strong Cliff must turn to deeper currents under and within the Jewish Israeli experience. At the least, these centre on the (previously noted) self-perceptions of victimhood and the convolution of identities that problematize the pro-Gazan position within Israel. Both led, in the summer of 2014, from erstwhile, usually implicit reproach to an explicit (even alarmingly racist) delegitimization of advocacy for the Gazan other.

Conclusion

Gazans, on behalf of whom advocacy in the West is done, are an elusively defined constituency. As Ophir and Azoulay state, 'The [Gaza] Strip is excepted from Israeli law and out of range of the Israeli sovereign responsibility, but completely within its rule and control, effectively preventing the emergence of any other power that could assume the responsibility of a sovereign government. The Palestinians in Gaza are the abandoned people of the Israeli regime.'[26] They are also abandoned by the regime of international law. This absence of sovereignty in a physical space that is and is not a part of some other sovereignty has made the activism born of advocacy for the people of that space a tortuous enterprise. In such a long-lasting clash, where sides to the conflict have internalized their identities as enemies and where advocating for Gazans means advocating against Israel, the well-intentioned Israeli activist is in the condition of a potentially bifurcated identity. This is not merely a critique of one's government or pressure on its policies; it is conceived, by almost all, as an essential taking of sides – on the side of the enemy.

Such graphic representation of the Israel–Palestine conflict may be in keeping with the conventional discourse of conflict resolution; just as common is the appraisal of the story of the conflict as a multiplicity of narratives, all of which must be entertained as legitimate. However, there is a presupposition of symmetry leading to this acceptance of various, even contradictory, positions which is, in the Israel–Gaza case, a false presupposition. In fact, my own premise articulated above insists on a clear victim and a clear victimizer in this story. Although both sides *claim* the status of victim, it is crucial that we understand the differing versions of their victimhood. This is not a symmetrical victimhood. The Israeli side, as we have explained, inhabits a history of victimhood that has become, for Israelis, an all-encompassing identity. The Palestinians in Gaza (but not only in Gaza) claim a victimhood of a specific time and place due to a particular offender.[27] Indeed, the asymmetry is not quantitative, in the matter of numbers of killings, rockets, bombings, attacks and the like, or even in assessment of the stronger or weaker party to the conflict. Israeli victimhood is a fact of the past promulgated into (self-)perception of the present and fear of the future. The fear expressed by ordinary people in Israel is real, but that does not make it any less a manipulated fear – manipulated by the state in its self-advocacy. Palestinian victimhood and its accompanying, justified fear are facts of the present (and the not-very-distant past). It is precisely the false symmetry coming out of a recognition of differing narratives which must be abandoned in our understanding of pro-Gaza advocacy.

But perhaps our emphasis here on victimhood and our insistence on its centrality is also imbalanced. There is well-known discomfort in the community of activists with using terms of incapacitation such as 'victim', which seem to deny the agency and ability of actors in these struggles. I venture that the use of that concept has become immeasurably essential in the Israeli–Palestinian case owing precisely to the predominance of victimhood in Jewish history. Yet even this icon can be interrogated. Not for naught has a relatively new vocabulary made its way into pro-Palestinian and anti-Israeli advocacy, the lexicon of colonialism and apartheid. Viewed as political victims of colonialism and apartheid, Gazans, if they so wish, can be practitioners in a different, perhaps somewhat more political and legal, type of advocacy; Israeli activists, for their part, must not only accept Gazan mentorship in the matter, they must clearly articulate their positions in order to escape the convolution above, born of a group victim identity.

So finally, this seeming tangle posits a recommendation for those 'social movements, political parties, media and NGOs [that] are arguably the most important stakeholder' in the case for Gaza. The protagonist of 'the other side', the Israeli side, must be recognized as an advocate as well, an advocate who has succeeded, to a certain degree, in positioning and advocating for himself as the victim; consequently, his advocacy, sophisticated and powerful, must be deconstructed. Achievement of advocacy for Gaza both in Israel and in the West by Israeli and Gazan actors means the creation of unequivocal pro-Gazan sentiment. Can this be done effectively? Straightforward advocacy is not enough, complex advocacy is trying, and delegitimized advocacy is daunting; together they have been trumped, until recently, by ironic Israeli advocacy in the West. It is critical not just to instil awareness of the real victims but to dismantle the other side's current claim to victimhood. That should be the activist agenda; that is the real challenge.[28]

Notes

1 The categorization here is interesting: two internationally recognized 'countries', one region-become-independent-country, two transnational regions, and one occupied territory.

2 I will return to the question of such presuppositions in the conclusion.

3 See Chapter 2 in this volume.

4 It should be mentioned that a recent, more sophisticated pro-Israel PR agenda, with nary a mention of Palestine, distances itself from 'the conflict' in order to headline the 'positive' elements in Israel. Most well known is the 'Brand Israel' campaign, rebranding Israel, launched in 2006 by the Israeli government and Foreign Ministry. Other, unofficial parties have joined the trend, financed by private funds (such as Sheldon Adelson's ReThink Israel, rethinkisrael.org/).

5 See the conclusion for the implications of historical victimhood.

6 The genesis of this well-known mantra is, like that of most mantras, elusive, but it has been a staple of the conversation about the IDF for decades. A typical example is defence minister Ehud Barak's speech in Jerusalem, following Operation Cast Lead (December 2008–January 2009): 'I have no doubt in my heart that the IDF is the most moral army in the world' (www.ynetnews.com/articles/0,7340,L-3692383,00.html).

7 I use the literal translation of the Hebrew names of these operations. The English counterparts used by Israel's Foreign Office – Pillar of Defense (for Pillar of Cloud) and Protective Edge (for Strong Cliff) – are themselves exercises in the rhetoric of advocacy, inserting the elements of defence and protection into the names of military assaults to enhance their presentation of Israel as victim.

8 It should also be noted, however, that Goldstone retracted some of his findings in a later statement ('Reconsidering the Goldstone Report on Israel and war crimes', *Washington Post*, 1 April 2011, www.washingtonpost.com/opinions/reconsidering-the-goldstone-report-on-israel-and-war-crimes/2011/04/01/AFg111JC_story.html); speculation is rife about the circumstances that brought him to this second assessment.

9 The cynicism I allude to here has been noted and, indeed, turned on its head by anti-Israel advocacy, especially in the hands of astute journalists and politicians. See, for example, Gideon Levy, 'The blood it's acceptable to shed: the further trials and tribulations of the most moral army in the world', *Ha'aretz*, 30 March 2014, www.haaretz.com/opinion/1.582693. I will return to the third, most recent operation, Strong Cliff, and the painful advocacies it gave rise to, shortly.

10 The workings of this formal and informal lobbying effort were (in)famously exposed and analysed in John Mearsheimer and Stephen Walt's *The Israel Lobby and U.S. Foreign Policy* (New York: Farrar, Straus and Giroux, 2007).

11 There have been, over the past several decades, a few legal opinions proffered for the position that Israel's legal status in the West Bank and Gaza is not one of occupation (according to international law). More ominous, but almost consensually derided by international legal experts, was the report of the Israeli government-appointed committee, led by retired Supreme Court justice Edmund Levy, that said that Israel's presence in the West Bank is not occupation. Be that as it may, world opinion – both legalistic and lay – is overwhelmingly consistent in holding that Israel occupies Palestinian lands.

12 Ludwig Wittgenstein, *Philosophical Investigations*, §107 (Cambridge: Cambridge University Press, 1953).

13 The closing off of Gaza might also

explain why this advocacy is distant from on-the-ground activism.

14 Ludwig Wittgenstein: 'A perspicuous representation produces just that understanding which consists in "seeing connexions"' (*Philosophical Investigations*, §122, 1953).

15 It cannot be forgotten that she is Palestinian herself (sometimes misnamed 'Israeli Arab'); her failed advocacy is, of course, then easily explained. After the *Marmara* events some Israeli politicians requested that her parliamentary immunity be revoked but Israel's Attorney General closed the case against her. She was, nevertheless, stripped of some of her parliamentary privileges by a full parliament vote.

16 It should be noted that Hass was twice detained by Israeli military/police for breaking the law in entering Gaza, but legal authorities did not pursue the charges.

17 Ariella Azoulay, *The Food Chain*, 2010, www.youtube.com/watch?v=iGpfq 6COz38.

18 Kretzman's work has appeared in innumerable media and platforms. 'The photographer Miki Kretzman will not let you forget', *Ha'aretz*, 26 August 2011, www.haaretz.co.il/gallery/1.1373123 (in Hebrew).

19 See www.haaretz.com/news/ diplomacy-defense/israeli-court-orders-state-to-consider-allowing-gaza-students-to-study-in-west-bank. premium-1.432210.

20 B'Tselem, *One Big Prison: Freedom of Movement to and from the Gaza Strip on the Eve of the Disengagement Plan*, Joint Report with Hamoked – Center for the Defence of the Individual– March 2005, btselem.org/sites/default/files2/200503_gaza_prison_english.pdf.

21 See, e.g., B'Tselem investigator Yael Stein's 'Killing under the cover of clouds', originally published in *Ha'aretz*, 3 December 2012 (in Hebrew), www.

btselem.org/gaza_strip/20121204_yael_stein_oped, or B'Tselem director Jessica Montell's op-ed in the *New York Times*, 'Let Gaza breathe', 21 November 2012, www.nytimes.com/roomfordebate/2012/11/20/how-to-defuse-the-israel-gaza-conflict/israel-must-lift-the-closure-on-the-gaza-strip.

22 Famously, Ehud Olmert's adviser Dov Weisglass said, 'The idea is to put the Palestinians on a diet, but not make them die of hunger.'

23 Adi Ophir, 'Documentation as resistance', 1991, reprinted in *Present Labor*, Tel Aviv, HaKibutz HaMe'uchad, 2001 (in Hebrew).

24 It is important to note that the assault on such organizations has been apparent for several years now. Most conspicuous were a number of laws, either passed or suggested in parliament beginning in 2012, that have legally narrowed the field of legitimate NGO actions.

25 Of the 2,131 Gazans killed during Operation Strong Cliff, over five hundred were children (UN Office for the Coordination of Humanitarian Affairs).

26 Ariella Azoulay and Adi Ophir, 'Abandoning Gaza', in Marcelo Svirsky and Simone Bignall (eds), *Agamben and Colonialism*, Edinburgh: Edinburgh University Press, 2011.

27 It is not uncommon to hear the Palestinian vernacular: 'Why should we suffer for what the Germans did to the Jews?'

28 This chapter is being written while we are still *in medias res*. I therefore refrain from assessing the American and European scenes of advocacy – for Israel or for Gaza. The ironic (pro-Israeli) and straightforward (pro-Gazan) types of advocacy adumbrated above have achieved new levels of complication at the height and in the wake of Strong Cliff that may become more similar to the complexities seen, up to now, only in Israel.

6 | CONFLICT MINERALS IN CONGO: THE CONSEQUENCES OF OVERSIMPLIFICATION[1]

Laura Seay

An obscure provision of the Dodd-Frank Wall Street Reform and Consumer Protection Act of 2010, section 1502, requires companies listed with the US Securities and Exchange Commission (SEC) to file periodic reports on their efforts to conduct due diligence to determine whether the products they sell contain certain minerals from the eastern Democratic Republic of Congo, the mining of, sale of or other profit from which armed actors in Congo or any of its neighbouring states benefited. This provision, the result of years of advocacy by members of a coalition, was intended to build a norm of responsible supply-chain sourcing by electronics corporations by forcing companies to disclose whether they could demonstrate they were not using Congolese conflict minerals in their products.

As the 2 June 2014 deadline for the first filing under the law's provisions approached, advocates from Global Witness began a push to shame companies that, while they might have met the technical requirements of the law, had not met the standard of due diligence Global Witness and its advocacy partners hoped to see as a result of Dodd-Frank 1502's passage. In one press release, a Global Witness staff member outlined why the organization was not satisfied with most of the submissions:

> Some firms have made strong submissions containing detailed information about the steps they have taken to source minerals responsibly – and demonstrating that oversight of supply chains is possible ... Sadly, these companies are in the minority. The lack of information in most of the submissions we have seen suggests companies have not taken the necessary steps to find out what is really going on along their supply chains – so we can't tell if they are sourcing responsibly or not. (Global Witness 2014)

These comments encompass much of the complexity of the problem of conflict minerals in the eastern Congo. Moreover, the claims made – that supply-chain oversight is possible in a fragile state environment, or that it is even possible for every company, especially those with limited resources, to conduct full due diligence on hundreds of thousands of products – are widely disputed by scholars, regional activists and other long-time observers of Central Africa, as are claims underlying the conflict minerals advocacy campaign that suggest that reducing revenue from conflict minerals will contribute to peace in the eastern Congo.

What explains this discrepancy, and who is right? Are the problems underlying twenty years of conflict easily explained by the presence and sale of four minerals? How did advocates develop the idea that consumer pressure and corporate activity could affect peace-building processes in the Democratic Republic of Congo? In this chapter, I will argue that the international campaign against conflict minerals in the Congo constitutes a case of 'policy-based evidence making' (Boden and Epstein 2006) in which a predetermined narrative overrode evidence contrary to the narrative's claims. Driven by the desire to get attention for an overlooked crisis and to build a norm centred around responsible supply-chain sourcing, advocates pursued a strategy of finding evidence to support the narrative rather than allowing the narrative to be built by evidence. As a result, their efforts led to the creation of a law that has done nothing to lower rates of violence in the eastern DR Congo, but which has caused real harm to the regional economy and citizens who lost employment as a result of Dodd-Frank 1502.

Background

Mired in crisis since the aftermath of the 1994 Rwandan genocide, the Kivu provinces in the eastern Democratic Republic of Congo (hereafter, 'Congo' or 'DRC') garnered some international media attention during the Congo Wars (1997–2002). However, the DRC was never the media's top priority, and any attention on its crisis was long gone by the time the 9/11 attacks and subsequent wars in Afghanistan and Iraq took centre stage in the media and the attention of American policy-makers. Congo, where the 'post-conflict' situation of 2003 on was anything but lacking in violence, was relegated to occasional pieces requiring readers to turn to the later pages of print newspapers or scroll well past the headlines on news organizations' websites.

The lack of attention to the Congo crisis (or, more appropriately, the Congo *crises*, which have involved over fifty armed groups operating with separate agendas in constantly shifting alliances and organizations) largely persisted until the mid-2000s, when a spate of stories regarding the country's rape crisis drew international attention. This attention, however, was fairly sporadic and consisted almost entirely of stories about rape by armed actors, while ignoring the context and the causes of and potential solutions to the DRC's problems.

For years, a number of overseas advocates had been considering the question of how to get more attention for DRC from international media and, it followed, from policy-makers. As Jason Stearns, a researcher at Nairobi's Rift Valley Institute and the International Crisis Group's previous DRC analyst, notes,

> We did complex advocacy until the cows came home. We tried to explain to the public around the world that this conflict is about power and politics and [we tried to explain] the history of the conflict and people basically hit the snooze button. You couldn't mobilize people around complexity like that. It's been amazing to me that ... after the peak of the conflict passed (2000/2001), around 2005 ... all of a sudden media attention started going up around issues of sexual violence and conflict minerals, and it was driven by people like the Enough Project who had had enough ... [and who had said] this has to be a mass issue, we can't be catering to the policy wonks ... [because] the policy wonks serve politicians, and politicians, at the end of the day care about being reelected ... so unless you can actually change the incentives of those politicians and get their constituents calling them on the phone saying, 'We care about the Congo,' at the end of the day you're not going to be able to affect policy. (Chase 2013)

The measured, detailed approach to documenting human rights abuses and explaining the complex causes of Congo's conflicts – among them, disputes over land and mineral concession rights, the citizenship status of Kinyarwanda-speaking Congolese, the lack of state control over the territory, and the absence of functioning national, provincial and local governments – failed to attract the attention needed for policy-makers to commit to anything more than continuing to fund the understaffed, under-equipped and therefore ineffective peacekeeping mission, MONUC (the French acronym for United Nations Organization Mission in the Democratic Republic of Congo, later rechristened MONUSCO, United Nations Organization Stabilization Mission in the Democratic Republic of Congo).

A change of strategy was necessary. John Prendergast, a long-time international advocate who cut his teeth researching the southern Sudan crisis for Human Rights Watch and the International Crisis Group, and who had served in the Clinton administration's Africa team, had been thinking similarly about advocacy regarding Africa in general. Working with another south Sudan advocate who had served in government, Gayle Smith, Prendergast founded the Enough Project in 2007, under the aegis of the liberal think tank the Center for American Progress. Enough's purpose was, and still is, to focus on ending and preventing genocide and other mass atrocities in Africa, with particular attention in its early years on three crises: the conflicts in the DRC, the genocide in Darfur, and the conflict involving the Lord's Resistance Army in Uganda. The idea behind the Enough Project was to create a central organization that could serve as a conduit for mobilizing grassroots advocates, in the USA and abroad, who cared about conflict in Africa and could be counted on to take mass action (e.g. by calling their elected representatives) when asked.

Effectively mobilizing grassroots advocates requires skills in messaging and marketing, as well as the ability to provide clear direction about concrete steps those advocates can take to effect change. With respect to the DRC crisis, it became clear to Prendergast that a narrative encompassing the complexity of the situation would not meet the requirements of an effective grassroots campaign. 'DRC has a series of crises involving multiple state and non-state actors fighting over land rights, ethnicity, governance, and security' does not fit on to a bumper sticker or a T-shirt, and is certainly too complicated to grab the attention of university students, one of Enough's targets for participation in its DRC campaign.

The need to simplify the narrative of a conflict is understandable; it is doubtful any advocacy organization working on any topic could succeed without doing so. However, finding the balance between simplifying and oversimplifying is difficult. How can advocates account for the need to make a message simple enough that anyone can understand, but complex enough to not obfuscate the real challenges that need to be addressed to solve a crisis?

Creating a narrative

Early Enough Project documents on the Congo crisis accounted for the complexity of the crisis and its causes. Minerals were mentioned in most reports, but they were far from central to the analyses and were discussed against the backdrop of the complex nature of governance and authority in eastern DRC. Enough reports from this time addressed a number of issues, including power vacuums filled by non-state armed actors, land tenure disputes, and the contestation of citizenship rights by some Congolese against others (see Prendergast and Thomas-Jensen 2007; Feeley and Thomas-Jensen 2008a, 2008b).

Prendergast led the organization in a major shift to simplify the DRC narrative in 2009 with the launch of Enough's 'Can You Hear Congo Now?' campaign. This campaign, which launched via a report, a YouTube video, blog posts and major media outreach, gave grassroots activists a new, easier-to-understand story. Enough modelled this campaign on the blood diamonds campaign, which some of Prendergast's team, notably consultant Sasha Lezhnev, had worked on with British advocacy organization Global Witness. Both campaigns used a strategy of focusing on Westerners' personal ties to conflict. While the blood diamond campaign drew attention by emphasizing engagement rings and the idea that couples would not want symbols of their love to be associated with violence, the conflict minerals campaign focused on consumer electronics, particularly mobile phones. As almost every young adult in America had a mobile phone by 2009, advocates (correctly) saw this as a way to mobilize interest and make grassroots activists feel they had a personal connection to the DRC crisis.

As expressed by Prendergast and his colleagues, Enough's conflict minerals narrative is thus:

1 Congolese armed groups benefit from trade in four minerals (tin, tungsten, tantalum and gold, known as 'the three Ts and gold').

2 These minerals are valuable because Western demand for consumer electronics is high.

3 The same armed groups are engaged in perpetrating human rights abuses, most notably violent rape.

4 Thus Western consumers' demand for consumer electronics funds violence in the DRC.

Prendergast also proposed a solution, again in simple narrative form:

1 Western consumers can pressure companies to buy only conflict-free minerals from the DRC.

2 Companies will not want to lose consumers' business, so they will respond to their demands.

3 The best way companies can guarantee they are not buying conflict minerals from DRC is to conduct due diligence on their supply chains.

4 When due diligence is conducted on supply chains in DRC and only conflict-free minerals are saleable in international markets, armed groups will stop benefiting from the mineral trade.

5 Without revenue from the mineral trade, armed groups in the DRC will be so weakened that they will stop fighting, and, by extension, stop committing human rights abuses such as rape.

This narrative, while involving at least nine steps, is still relatively simple. It presents a clear theory of change (that consumer demand for conflict-free electronic products will lead to a reduction in violence in the DRC), and Enough provided clear action steps for grassroots advocates to take. These steps included contacting their representatives in Congress and lobbying them to support legislative efforts to require companies to trace their mineral supply chains, pressuring universities to buy only conflict-free computers and other electronic equipment, and petitioning consumer electronics companies to conduct due diligence exercises to verify that they are not using Congolese conflict minerals in their products.[2] Enough branded its overall Congo efforts, including the conflict minerals campaign, under a broader campaign called Raise Hope for Congo.[3]

Enough's efforts received a lot of attention from grassroots activists around the country, particularly university students, people who had been involved in the Save Darfur movement, and others who saw news reports about rape in Congo and wanted to take action. Although Enough was the lead organization, it did not undertake grassroots mobilization actions alone. Rather, as is often the case with US-based advocacy movements, Enough led a coalition of other advocacy groups, including Global Witness, Amnesty International, Campus Progress, Oxfam, the Genocide Intervention Network, Human Rights Watch, Jewish World Watch, STAND (a student-led anti-mass-atrocity organization), and several others.[4] It also formed partnerships with some consumer electronics industry companies, including Hewlett Packard (HP), Intel and Motorola. HP made the conflict minerals campaign a centrepiece of its corporate social responsibility (CSR) portfolio.

The legislative effort

The campaign was a rousing success, at least by the advocacy community's metrics. Enough's campaigns attracted large followings on Facebook and Twitter,[5] and grassroots advocates made enough noise that members of Congress began to pay attention. The latter was helped by the fact that Enough is part of the Center for American Progress, a liberal think tank with which many Democratic members of Congress are closely affiliated.

With a few exceptions, US Representatives and Senators tend to have very limited knowledge of African issues and rely on their staff and on trusted advocacy organizations to provide information and suggestions about the position they should take on issues related to Africa. In the case of conflict minerals, trusting information provided by Enough and its coalition partners was natural for many members of Congress. Several travelled to Goma, where they met rape victims.

For conservative members, the story of rape in the Congo and the presentation of a legislative solution to the crisis that would not cost the US government any money was sufficient to prevent any serious backlash against the campaign before a law was passed. Moreover, no counter-narrative suggesting another path emerged from conservative think tanks or any other actors during the limited debates on conflict minerals. Thus, the advocacy community narrative set the agenda for debate and was the only source of information many members of Congress consulted when making decisions on proposed legislation.

Another motivating factor in the search for a legislative solution to the conflict minerals problem was the view that breaking a black market (in this case, the illicit trade in Congolese conflict minerals) would lead to fewer civilian deaths. This view was expressed by one former congressional staff member who was directly involved in the efforts to combat the issue:

> For markets that are entirely black, when the black market price [for a commodity] goes up, violence levels (the number of people who die per day) go up also. In 2007, according to the State Department, about 1200 people were dying per day in Congo. Our thinking was, 'Can we get it down to 400–500 per day?' in terms of the number of people being killed unnecessarily. When black market prices [drop], death rates drop. Wars burn hotter when black markets exist.[6]

Although Enough and its partners enjoyed a successful advocacy campaign, its efforts to pass legislation soon stalled.

Enough and other advocacy groups working on the DRC pursued a legislative strategy to pass a law that would require companies to be more transparent and accountable in their mineral sourcing practices. Their efforts centred on House Resolution 4128, the Conflict Minerals Trade Act, the purpose of which was to:

> help stop the deadly conflict over minerals in eastern Congo by regulating the importation and trade of tin, tungsten and tantalum – minerals commonly used in cell phones, laptop computers and other popular electronic devices. Under the bill, U.S. Commerce Department-sanctioned auditors would audit mineral mines declaring them conflict free or not. These mines would be mapped to show which ones fund conflict. Furthermore, importers would have to certify whether they were importing conflict minerals – companies that do import conflict minerals will be reported to Congress by the United States Trade Representative.[7]

HR 4128 was submitted by Representative James McDermott, a Democrat from Washington state, and was supported by the Center for American Progress (Enough's parent organization), Human Rights Watch, Hewlett Packard, the International Labour Rights Forum, and the Information Technology Industry Council (ITIC, an industry lobby group). Despite receiving broad support from several sectors and gaining co-sponsorship from other legislators after pressure from grassroots activists, the bill never moved out of the committees to which it was referred.

In July 2010, two provisions focusing on the DRC and conflict minerals were added to the Dodd-Frank Wall Street Reform and Consumer Protection Act. There were no debates or hearings about the inclusion of the two sections prior to the law's passage. Section 1502 requires publicly trading companies to report to the SEC and on their websites whether they source conflict minerals (defined as 'columbite-tantalite [coltan], cassiterite, gold, wolframite, or their derivatives' from DRC or its neighbours).[8] It requires further reporting and auditing from companies that use these minerals, and requires the SEC to create specific rules on how companies will satisfy the legislation's requirements.[9] Section 1504 requires increased transparency from companies registered with the SEC to disclose how much they pay foreign governments for access to minerals, oil and gas.[10]

The definition of conflict minerals in Dodd-Frank section 1502 (hereafter, 1502) is limited to tantalum, tin, tungsten and gold (tantalum is derived from columbite-tantalite, tin from cassiterite, and tungsten from wolframite). This means that the same minerals mined in countries other than DRC and its neighbours are not, by definition, 'conflict minerals' and are not subject to 1502's provisions. It also means that other minerals mined in DRC, even those mined artisanally under horrific and unsafe conditions and those mined by child labourers, are also free from the 'conflict minerals' label. Section 1502 was not intended to stop all human rights abuses associated with the mineral trade in Congo or anywhere else. Rather, it was focused on specific minerals associated with conflict in a specific region of DRC, the Kivu and Maniema provinces and the north-eastern Ituri district,[11] the only part of the country where those minerals are found.

As previously noted, there was no public debate over 1502 prior to its inclusion in the Dodd-Frank Act and its passage into law. As such, most corporations which are now subject to 1502's requirements were unaware of its existence and did not engage in lobbying efforts in favour of or against the legislation prior to its passage.

Rule-making at the SEC

Section 1502's relatively easy passage into law was not echoed in the process of rule-making required under the legislation. Even as the SEC debated potential rules, actors from the business sector raised a number of concerns. The first problem arose in the advocacy coalition's focus on consumer electronics. It turns out that the 3Ts and gold are found in an extraordinarily wide variety of consumer products. This is especially true of tin, which is used in manufacturing everything from food containers to zips. The three T minerals are also present in medical devices including pacemakers, replacement joints and insulin pumps. Similarly, gold is found in products ranging from jewellery to false teeth to home pregnancy testing kits.

TABLE 6.1 Minerals found in selected products[12]

Tin	Tantalum	Tungsten	Gold
Food containers	Cutting tools	Aerospace	Jewellery
Zips	Camera lenses	components	False teeth
Buttons	Jet turbines	Jewellery	Medical
Eyeglasses	Medical devices	Decorative crafts	equipment
Watches	Medical implants	Lawnmowers	Airbag-inflating
Fitness equipment	Vehicle airbags	Power tools	sensors
Metallicized yarn	Mobile phones	X-ray machines	Home pregnancy
Electric toys	Computers	Golf clubs	test kits
Phones		Dental drills	Stained glass
Computers		Darts	Coloured pottery
Audio equipment		Remote-	glazes
GPS devices		controlled toys	Tumour-targeting
Household			technologies
appliances			
Brake pads			

The range of products containing the 3Ts and gold meant that thousands of companies, in addition to the major consumer electronics manufacturers targeted by the advocacy coalition (and graded by Enough in rankings of each company's cooperation with their initiative – Enough Project 2010), would be affected by 1502's requirements. Not surprisingly, corporate industries such as the apparel, food production and medical device industries – which, unlike consumer electronics manufacturers, had virtually no warning that there was a campaign afloat that would affect them – found the new law to be a burden. Corporate compliance officers found themselves facing the task of sorting through the legislation, waiting for the SEC to create detailed rules, and trying to determine whether the raw materials in their end-stage products could possibly contain Congolese conflict minerals. For mega-, multinational corporations like Kraft Foods, 1502 meant that corporate executives would have to ensure compliance by tens of thousands of suppliers. Other problems, regarding how to regulate recycled materials and whether small and medium-size enterprises would be required to participate, also arose in the course of the debate. Industry lobby groups, most notably the US Chamber of Commerce and the National Association of Manufacturers, came out in force against 1502.

Meanwhile, Congress had tasked the SEC to create rules in a topical area well outside its mission 'to protect investors, maintain fair, orderly, and efficient markets, and facilitate capital formation'. Being asked to create rules for what is simultaneously an issue of trade and foreign policy with no precedent in US law or SEC rule-making was a difficult task for which few SEC officials were prepared. As Celia Taylor noted prior to the rules' release in 2012, it is questionable whether the SEC was the appropriate agency to implement the law in the first place given that it 'lacks knowledge of the issues surrounding conflict minerals' and that the law's requirements 'exceed its mandate' (Taylor 2012).

Between the pressures brought by extensive lobbying and the SEC's lack of background in dealing with issues relating to conflict minerals in the DRC, the rule-making process was significantly delayed from the deadline of April 2011 set forth in the legislation. Final rules for the legislation were released in August 2012.[13]

The US Chamber of Commerce and its member companies sued over the legislation because they believe that the SEC has not 'show[n] any benefits to investors, increased efficiencies for the marketplace or capital formation' (Lynch 2011). In other words, the Chamber believes the regulations impose too stiff a burden on commerce without demonstrating market-based reasons for doing so.

As a result of this controversy, the SEC held a roundtable on conflict minerals on 18 October 2011, in which American corporations and advocacy community representatives were invited to participate. Congolese civil society actors, miners and mining executives were not invited. The meeting was somewhat contentious and featured a lively debate over the challenges corporations face in implementing section 1502's potential rules. Most of the corporations present at the roundtable asked the SEC to delay implementation of the rules, owing to the complexity and cost of implementation (United Nations 2011). For example, a Kraft Foods representative noted that, with over 100,000 suppliers, verifying responsible sourcing for every product the company produces will be an enormous challenge (ibid.).

The legal challenges to section 1502 were largely rejected in an April 2014 ruling by the US Court of Appeals for the District of Columbia Circuit. Under the ruling, companies are still required to conduct due diligence on their supply chains and to file public reports on their efforts with the SEC. However, the court struck down two of the law's provisions that required companies to post notices on their websites if a product the company sells is not conflict-mineral-free. This ruling rested on free speech grounds; essentially, the court found, this requirement would have required companies to criticize their own products (Ackerman 2014).

Another problem is the cost of implementation. An independent Tulane University economic impact assessment study commissioned by US Senator Dick Durbin (whose goal was to show that the SEC's estimate was too high) found that the cost of implementing section 1502 will be approximately $7.93 billion dollars – more than one hundred times the SEC's estimated cost of $71.2 million. The authors of the study describe the problem with SEC's estimate:

> Our analysis shows that the published figure of $71.2 million by the SEC underestimates the implementation cost, in part because it does not take into account the range of actors affected by the statutory law. In light of Section 1502, substantial traceability reforms would need to be implemented throughout the supply chain – from the mine to final product manufacturing – in order for disclosure to work. (Bayer and De Buhr 2011)

The SEC's final estimated cost of implementation and ongoing compliance was significantly higher than its initial estimate, but still lower than the Tulane study's figure. The estimated implementation cost for all companies expected to be affected is $3–4 billion, while the ongoing cost (annual costs of compliance after the implementation period) is estimated to be $207–609 million per year (Securities and Exchange Commission 2011).

A series of unintended consequences

Even before 1502 was fully implemented, its consequences had already been far reaching. In September 2010, Congolese president Joseph Kabila instituted a ban on all mining in the Kivu and Maniema provinces. This ban not only largely shut down mining activity in the region, but also led to increased militarization of the mining sector, as the Congolese national army (FARDC, the French acronym for Armed Forces of the Democratic Republic of Congo) took over many mines that had previously been non-militarized.

A de facto embargo of Congolese minerals soon began as well. As the April 2011 deadline for the creation of the rules for section 1502 regulations approached, the Malaysia Smelting Corporation (MSC) began refusing to buy Congolese tin under pressure from the Electronics Industry Citizenship Coalition (EICC), an industry watchdog group. The EICC created a tracing scheme for smelters that requires corporations to show that their ores are conflict-free, and most companies were to work through a tin industry group called ITRI to ensure their minerals were appropriately tagged as conflict-free.[14]

This tracing scheme came into effect on 1 April 2011. However, MSC could not guarantee that all of its minerals would be ITRI-tagged and so stopped purchasing minerals from Congo. MSC had previously purchased up to 80 per cent of eastern Congolese tin, so its exit from the market was devastating to local sellers.[15]

The effect of MSC's decision to exit the Congo's mineral trade means there is now a de facto boycott on almost all Congolese tungsten, tantalum and cassiterite. North Kivu's exports of tin, which is derived from cassiterite, shortly fell by 90 per cent (Kavanagh 2011).

Only three of Goma's twenty-five exporters were operating by late 2011, and they were selling minerals primarily to the Chinese. These purchases may be illegal under a 2010 UN resolution requiring member states to urge their corporations not to purchase minerals that might be financing violence in the region, but this resolution seems to have had little effect (Hogg 2011).

Section 1502's effect on Congolese artisanal miners and their families, however, has been devastating.[16] Congolese artisanal miners normally work under horrific conditions for little pay (Free the Slaves 2011), but in most mining communities it is the only paid employment available. There are virtually no livelihood alternatives in these communities, save subsistence agriculture or joining a militia.

The ban and de facto boycott created mass unemployment in the mines, while unsellable mineral stockpiles sat in mounds in warehouses in Goma and Bukavu. Local mining civil society activists estimated that two million miners were put out of work by the ban; this number is likely far higher than the real figure, but there are no reliable estimates of the impact. Certainly tens, if not hundreds, of thousands of miners were affected by the stoppage. What has happened to these miners is a subject for further research. We know that some migrated to gold mines in far North Kivu and Ituri (where trade did not stop, owing to gold's highly portable and easy-to-smuggle nature), others joined militant groups, and others became destitute, but we do not have specific numbers as to what percentage of miners took each path.

Violence escalated in the period after 1502 began to be implemented, though it would not be accurate to say that this violence was caused by the post-1502 mining ban or de facto boycott. The emergence, triumph and eventual defeat of the M23 armed group (so named because it was founded on 23 March 2012) in 2012/13 was the most notable of the escalations of violence in this period, though the activities of the Raia Mutomboki, the APCLS (Alliance of Patriots for a Free and Sovereign Congo) and the ADF-NALU (Allied Democratic Forces – National Army for the Liberation of Uganda) are particularly notable as well.

Enough, however, claims that section 1502 has improved the situation in the eastern Congo. Their messaging about the effects of 1502 tends to emphasize direct effects on the mineral trade rather than noting that those effects have had little to no effect on violence levels. For example, an August 2014 blog post notes that 'Market regulations instituted by the 2010 Dodd-Frank Act have helped reduce armed groups' involvement in the minerals sector and created a two-tier market for tin, tantalum, and tungsten, helping to incentivize clean-sourcing practices.' No mention is made of the fact that the market for conflict minerals has created a de facto monopoly through which sellers must accept artificially controlled prices.[17]

Other claims are even more dubious. In a March 2014 *Foreign Affairs* opinion piece, Prendergast argued that M23's defeat was in part attributable to the efforts to stop the conflict minerals trade.[18] This claim was made despite there being no evidence that M23 was involved in the conflict mineral trade and that M23 never controlled significant mining areas. Prendergast may have based his argument on Enough's contention that M23 was benefiting from the gold trade, a claim made in an October 2013 report[19] that the United Nations Group of Experts on the DRC could not find evidence to support.[20]

Other advocacy groups have been less sanguine. Global Witness noted its dissatisfaction with the majority of conflict minerals reports filed with the SEC under the first filing deadline in June 2014. Global Witness argues that many companies are only complying with the letter of the law while not taking the steps necessary to actually verify that their supply chains are or are not conflict-free.[21] Unfortunately for these advocates, Dodd-Frank 1502's language arguably leaves the door open for companies to do only minimal due diligence and to satisfy the law's requirements by saying that they cannot verify the conflict-free origins of materials in their products.

The biggest problem for conflict minerals advocates, however, is that the promised reductions in violence in eastern DRC, which were supposed to come about as armed actors lost access to mineral revenue, have not materialized. As of October 2014, there is no evidence that any armed group has laid down its weapons or requested peace talks as a result of having lost revenue from the mineral trade. M23's defeat came at the hands of the new MONUSCO Force Intervention Brigade (FIB), a well-equipped and trained peacekeeping force with a mandate to prioritize the protection of civilians. Working in conjunction with the FARDC, the FIB defeated M23 in late 2013. There is little evidence that M23 benefited from the mineral trade in any significant way (United Nations 2014).

Neither Kabila's ban nor the MSC's decision to stop buying Congolese minerals would have happened had Dodd-Frank not become law. Both the timing of the actual and de facto bans and all rhetoric surrounding them suggests that these were clear responses to the perceived future effects of the legislation. MSC and other international buyers stopped purchasing Congolese minerals owing to uncertainty about the SEC regulations on section 1502 (Hogg and Holliday 2011).

That the consequences were unintentional and unanticipated does not mean they were not direct effects of 1502's passage. While the US-based advocacy community working on Congo has good intentions and wants to improve quality of life for the Congolese, most advocates made several key mistakes in their analysis of the situation. These mistakes were based on misperceptions – notably about the relationship between mineral exploitation and conflict in the Congo, the drivers of Congolese armed group behaviour, and the feasibility of running effective traceability schemes in a failed state. What did the advocates get wrong?

The clash of evidence and narrative

Efforts to pass legislation on conflict minerals in the Congo were based on a mistaken assumption: because the mineral trade is one dynamic in some of the region's conflicts, this means that minerals cause conflict. This underlying belief can be seen in a number of advocacy efforts such as Enough's April 2009 strategy paper 'Can you hear Congo now?' As criticism of this claim mounted, advocates moderated their language to refer to conflict minerals as a 'key driver' of conflict in the eastern DRC.

However, this claim is also misleading. If minerals cause or drive conflict in a failed state, then we would expect most, if not all, of the Congolese mineral trade to be militarized and/or to be the object of competition between armed groups. This is far from true, however. The mines – both artisanal and industrial – of Kasai and most of Katanga are almost entirely free of violence, as were many mines in the heart of the conflict regions in North and South Kivu and Ituri prior to the ban and de facto boycott. One particularly egregious example of misleading claims about the Congolese mineral sector came in a 2009 segment of CBS's *60 Minutes*, in which John Prendergast and CBS correspondent Scott Pelley travelled to Ituri's Chudja gold mine. Ituri gold mines have been at peace since 2006, but the Chudja mine was presented in the segment as a place in which violence against civilians was actively occurring.[22]

Another dynamic is at work in the Kivus and has very little to do with the mineral trade, but is instead about the state's weakness and local disputes over land and citizenship rights. As analyst Jason Stearns told AlertNet, 'There is no doubt that minerals constitute a large part of the conflict economy in the eastern Congo and dealing with the conflict minerals issue is important ... But minerals were not the origin of the conflict in Congo and solving the conflict minerals issue is not going to bring an end to the conflicts' (Fominyen 2011). The militarized mineral trade is much more a symptom of the Congolese state's weakness and inability to govern than it is a cause of the violence.

The logic underlying the advocacy groups' conflict minerals narrative is based on a misperception of what motivates Congolese armed groups and what they do with the money they earn from the mines. First, there is little reason to believe that Congolese armed groups use the bulk of the money they earn from the mineral trade to buy weapons and ammunition. The eastern Congo is saturated with weapons; few soldiers need to buy new ones, and those that are for sale are extremely inexpensive and readily available in local markets.[23]

Instead, most of the money earned by armed groups from the mineral trade is used to pay salaries, buy food, and provide other basic necessities to fighters and their families. This is particularly true in the FARDC, where government salaries are rarely paid, and when soldiers do receive money, it is often only a partial salary. Even if soldiers are paid their salary, the amount (approximately $40–50/ month) is far below what is needed to provide for their families. Thus, they look to earn revenue via the mineral trade.

Secondly, even if armed groups do depend on the mineral trade to finance their activities, most can draw upon other reliable sources of revenue. As Vlassenroot and Adam have shown, Congolese civilians face an enormous burden from informal taxation schemes, many of which are carried out by armed groups. Congolese armed groups have proved remarkably adept at diversifying their revenue streams since the de facto boycott on minerals came into effect. Tactics used to raise funds include controlling border crossings, participating in the timber, charcoal, banana and marijuana trades, and engaging in wildlife poaching and smuggling. In addition, owing to its highly portable nature, the smuggling of gold has significantly increased since 1502's passage (United Nations 2013). As access to mineral wealth has been limited, Congolese armed groups have turned to other forms of revenue extraction with little effect on their violent behaviour.

The argument that breaking the black market for Congolese

conflict minerals will reduce conflict is also based on shaky evidence. It is not clear on what the former congressional staffer quoted above based the claim that civilian deaths decline when black markets are broken. Regardless of the origins of that claim, the use of the figure of 1,200 civilians dead per day suggests a lack of contextual knowledge about the dynamics of violence and mortality in the DRC. The 1,200 deaths per day figure is extrapolated from data from a series of mortality surveys conducted by the NGO the International Rescue Committee (IRC) in Congo in the early and mid-2000s. The last of these surveys was conducted in 2006/07 and estimated that about 5.4 million Congolese had died from all causes as a result of conflict from August 1998 to April 2007 (Coghlan et al. 2007).

The IRC mortality surveys are controversial because of the way they calculate deaths attributable to violence. In the method used in the surveys, all 'excess deaths' above a pre-war baseline are counted towards the total, and the cause of those 'excess deaths' is imputed to be conflict, accounting for the fact that poverty and a poor healthcare system mean that 'normal' mortality rates in DRC are higher than they are in most other parts of the world. The dispute in how deaths are counted arises from the fact that 'excess deaths' in the IRC studies includes deaths that are not the direct result of combat violence. For example, if a family has to flee its home for an internally displaced persons' camp and, owing to contracting cholera in the camp, a child dies, that child's death would be considered an excess death; it would not likely have happened had the family not had to flee their home. Likewise, if the rate of child mortality rises because child vaccination programmes are reduced, those deaths are attributed to the conflict, even though they are not directly caused by violence. In humanitarian emergencies, excess deaths caused by forced displacement, and associated hunger and disease, are usually included in the overall estimate for deaths. The IRC studies introduced a new, broader measurement of conflict-related fatalities by looking at the death rate for the entire population over an extended period of time.

The vast majority of excess deaths estimated in the Congo since 1998 are not violent or combat deaths. Of the 5.4 million excess deaths the IRC projected in 2007, only a tiny minority were from violence, even civilian-directed violence. It is not clear that an observed correlation between lowering rates of violence and lowering death rates would hold in DRC even if this correlation has a causal relationship elsewhere. Thirdly, the mineral trade and access to mines do not motivate most Congolese armed groups to fight. Rather, their violent behaviour stems from anger over inequality and ideology, and it occurs because there are no constraints on such behaviour in the eastern DRC. As Séverine Autesserre notes, despite the international community's overwhelming focus on conflict minerals, only about 8 per cent of Congolese conflicts are actually about the control of natural resources (Autessere 2012: 8). Some groups, including many of the Mai Mai militias, fight simply because they can. Others have specific grievances about their ethnic group's position in society or, in the case of the Democratic Forces for the Liberation of Rwanda (FDLR), about Rwandan political leadership. There is no evidence that any of the armed groups in eastern Congo will simply stop fighting if they lose a key source of revenue. The loss of conflict minerals revenue has not affected their ability to procure weapons and ammunition, nor has it motivated them to negotiate for peace. What has worked in this regard is the recent push by the MONUSCO intervention brigade (FIB) and the most competent units of the Congolese national army, the FARDC, to root out rebel groups through the use of military force.

The idea of ensuring that Congolese conflict-free minerals can make it to market is an attractive one. Unfortunately, it is based on a poor understanding of how trade and governance work in an extremely weak state. The idea for implementing a traceability scheme with respect to the Congo was based on the Kimberley Process for ensuring that diamonds sold on international markets would be conflict-free. However, advocates failed to take into account that the Kimberley Process works well only in relatively strong states with functioning governing institutions.

The situation in the eastern DRC could not be farther from the Western norm. As Carol Jean Gallo notes, even defining what constitutes the 'illicit' mineral trade is problematic in the Congolese context of no rule of law, contract enforcement or fair competition for mineral concession licences or rights (Gallo 2012). What constitutes corruption in a situation when state officials are not paid their salaries makes it even more difficult to enforce provisions like section 1502 (Seay 2012b).

It is not an exaggeration to say that it is possible to bribe almost every border guard, customs official and immigration authority in the region. These officials are not paid regular salaries and thus depend on bribery and the imposition of made-up fees for their livelihoods. This makes smuggling very easy; indeed, it is obvious that a great deal of smuggling is happening even as the de facto boycott continues. Border officials intercepted a load of cassiterite in a MONUSCO vehicle in August 2011, but it is likely that the ton caught there is but a small fraction of what is being smuggled out.[24] In this context, even the most technically perfect efforts to formalize the mineral trade are almost certain to be fraught with difficulty if underlying issues of state control, poverty and broad political challenges remain unresolved. In fact, as Sara Geenen argues, it is more likely to make these problems worse than better (Geenen 2012).

Smuggling has greatly increased since the de facto boycott came into effect (United Nations 2011), and it has continued since the SEC implemented the rules for 1502. It is very difficult to see how any traceability scheme could overcome this situation, for it is not only officials at the borders who will take bribes, but also those at airports and at the mines themselves. An effective traceability scheme would have to involve implementation and monitoring at every step of the process, including transport, by objective outside observers who cannot be bought. But even this may be problematic, as anyone familiar with the Congolese spirit of innovation and entrepreneurial ingenuity expects that smugglers will find a way to fake certification before long. Without effective oversight from functioning government institutions, it is unlikely that even the most carefully planned traceability scheme will effectively prevent Congolese conflict minerals from being sold on international markets.

Many who supported section 1502 made it sound as though it would be the first traceability scheme to address the problems in the Congolese mining sector. This is simply untrue. A number of efforts were under way, many of which were undertaken in consultation with local civil society leaders and Congolese mineral trade experts. In particular, an effort called PROMINES involving the Congolese government, the World Bank and industry actors, had made great strides towards improving transparency and accountability. This effort was intentionally low key, and it had great potential for success.

However, it and other ongoing efforts (most notably the International Conference for the Great Lakes Region's Regional Initiative against the Illegal Exploitation of Natural Resources [RINR] framework[25]) are mired in confusion surrounding section 1502 and a number of other traceability schemes and frameworks in the region. Currently, the ICGLR, the ITRI, the OECD and the European Union are all developing and/or implementing traceability regulations, norms and schemes.

Other schemes include MONUSCO's creation of trading centres, an Extractive Industries Transparency Initiative (EITI) scheme, and the German government's Federal Institute for Geosciences and Natural Resources (German acronym BGR) programme. The problem is compounded in that traceability is possible with some commodities (including diamonds), but extraordinarily difficult with others (namely gold). In short, there is a great deal of confusion surrounding the issue and a desperate need for more collaboration. However, as Dominic Johnson has noted, the negative consequences of 1502 for miners' employment has provoked a high degree of disillusionment among many Congolese in the mineral sector, meaning that they are now less willing to cooperate with or 'buy in' to mineral tracing schemes (Johnson 2013). As Geenen notes, artisanal mining in many communities is a generational economic activity, passed from fathers to sons and forming the backbone of village and regional economies (Geenen 2011, 2013).

Misperceptions and their consequences

Why did advocates fall prey to these misperceptions? Many of those who conceived the strategy for dealing with conflict minerals had worked to put together the Kimberley Process, and some had also worked on the movement to end sweatshop labour practices in clothing production in South-East Asia.

With the exception of Liberia, none of the wars cited by advocates as support for the idea that creating a mineral supply chain traceability scheme will reduce conflict had ended by the time the Kimberley Process came into effect. There is no evidence suggesting that fighters in any of these conflicts were primarily – or at all – motivated to lay down their arms owing to the fear that they might lose sources of revenue from the diamond trade. Rather, each conflict ended with decisive battlefield victories, external pressure and negotiated political solutions.

That the Kimberley Process did not end the wars in Sierra Leone or Angola is not in and of itself a reason not to pursue traceability schemes and responsible sourcing for other mineral resources in conflict areas. If implemented well, such schemes can theoretically build more accountable and transparent economies in countries that need them. To some advocates who supported Dodd-Frank sections 1502 and 1504, the creation of such an international norm is the most important aspect of the legislation, arguably more so than whether the law will lead to greater peace and stability in the eastern Congo. These advocates see the potential failure of the law as disastrous for their goal of building international norms to hold corporations responsible for where and how they source materials for their products.

While there is no question that most DRC stakeholders want to see less violence and more peace and prosperity in the conflict regions, the overarching focus on the creation of a norm with respect to conflict minerals is problematic. Advocates used the horrific nature of the violence in the Congo to draw attention to the crisis, and leveraged emotional language, shocking images and testimony about rape to promote the need for legislation on conflict minerals, while promising that the violence would abate if the legislation were passed. However, many overstated the potential of a traceability and transparency scheme to alleviate some of that violence. Meanwhile, the unintended effects of the passage of section 1502 have put thousands of Congolese artisanal miners out of work, and the violence has not abated despite the fact that few armed groups are making money from the nearly halted mineral trade. Many policy-makers and legislators feel that they were deceived about the consequences – positive and negative – section 1502 would produce, particularly with respect to preventing civilian-directed violence.

These consequences were unanticipated by the advocacy community, but not by the academics, local stakeholders and other observers who have deep contextual knowledge, language skills and access to social networks in the DRC. Many of us who worked on the issue predicted well before the passage of Dodd-Frank that the ideas contained in section 1502 would not work.[26] Had the advocates involved in developing the conflict minerals narrative based their policy prescriptions on the realities of life in a fragile state, their policies might well have had more positive consequences, or, at the very least, done no harm. Instead, most of the political capital available for addressing this issue was spent on a policy driven by an inaccurate narrative. The consequences of getting that narrative wrong are not borne by the advocates who did so, but rather must be endured by ordinary Congolese civilians who are simply trying to survive in one of the most difficult environments on earth.

Reclaiming conflict minerals advocacy

As noted above, the notion that governments and consumers should hold corporations accountable for responsibly sourcing the materials and labour used to build their products should not be controversial. Many consumers have shown that they prefer to pay higher prices for fair trade and ethically produced goods. However, we must decouple the value of creating a norm about supply chain tracing from the notion that doing so will end violence against Congolese civilians. There is no evidence that this occurs, and however Dodd-Frank section 1502 is implemented, it is unlikely it will do so in the DRC. Violence in the Congo is rooted in political disputes and requires a political solution, not an economic one. Stakeholders could have a more productive and honest debate by delinking these issues and focusing on finding appropriate solutions to distinct problems.

Though the damage of Dodd-Frank section 1502 is done, it is not too late to reclaim the narrative around conflict minerals for the purposes of activism and advocacy. Indeed, a number of Congolese community leaders and international advocates are trying to do just that. In September 2014, a group of seventy Congolese and international civil society leaders, journalists and analysts released an open letter on conflict minerals.[27] The letter outlines positive steps that all stakeholders of good will in the conflict minerals debate could take in order to move towards more productive and realistic efforts. These include increasing consultations with a wider sector of civil society actors, creating incentives for better practice on the ground, and 'widening the lens' through which international actors view the crisis. The story of violence in the Congo is not just about minerals, and solutions must take into account land issues, identity disputes and contested politics if they are to lead to sustainable peace.

Notes

1 Portions of this chapter were previously published in Seay (2012a).

2 Conflict-Free Campus, www.raisehopeforcongo.org/content/conflict-free-campus-initiative. Enough Project, www.enoughproject.org/.

3 Raise Hope for Congo: An Enough Campaign, 'Conflict free campus initiative toolkit', www.raisehopeforcongo.org/sites/default/files/Enough%20Conflict-Free%20Campus%20Toolkit.pdf.

4 For a full list, see 'Our partners', Raise Hope for Congo, www.raisehopeforcongo.org/content/about/our-partners, accessed 11 February 2014.

5 As of February 2014, Raise Hope for Congo's Facebook page (facebook.com/raisehopeforcongo) has almost fourteen thousand followers and over six thousand people follow its Twitter account (@RaiseHope4Congo).

6 Public remarks by former congressional staff member, 'Implementing Dodd-Frank 1502/1504: advancing human rights through financial reporting', Event, Dodd Center, University of Connecticut at Storrs, 8 April 2014.

7 OpenCongress Summary, HR 4128: Conflict Minerals Trade Act, submitted to Congress 19 November 2009, www.opencongress.org/bill/111-h4128/show.

8 Resource Consulting Services has an excellent explanation of the full implications of section 1502. US Legislation on Conflict Minerals: RCS Private Services Guidance on the Dodd-Frank Act Section 1502 (April 2011), www.resourceglobal.co.uk/documents/RCS_DF_ACT_GUIDANCE_APRIL_2011_lowres.pdf.

9 'The "conflict minerals" provision in the Dodd-Frank Act imposes new disclosure requirements on manufacturers', McDermott Newsletters, 22 July 2010, www.mwe.com/index.cfm/fuseaction/publications.nldetail/object_id/13114620-b2dd-466a-8392-e53e3da0a162.cfm.

10 Ibid.

11 Under the DRC 2006 constitution's decentralization mandates, Ituri is supposed to be an independent province with its own provincial administration. However, these provisions of the constitution have never been implemented. Ituri still largely functions as a semi-autonomous administrative unit within Orientale Province.

12 Data source: summarized in David Aronson, 'Why companies will avoid the DRC', Congo Resources blog, www.congoresources.org/2013/03/why-companies-will-avoid-drc.html, accessed 11 February 2014.

13 Securities and Exchange Commission, 17 CFR Parts 240 and 249b, Release no. 34-67716; File no. S7-40-10.

14 'GeSI and EICC announce update to conflict-free smelter program', Press release, 22 April 2011, www.gesi.org/Media/GeSINewsFullStory/tabid/85/smid/503/ArticleID/75/reftab/37/t/GeSI%20and%20EICC%20Announce%20Update%20to%20Conflict-Free%20Smelter%20Program/Default.aspx.

15 'Congo in talks with Malaysia Smelting over tin foundry', Reuters, 3 October 2011, af.reuters.com/article/investingNews/idAFJOE7920KM20111003.

16 'GeSI and EICC announce update to conflict-free smelter program', op. cit.

17 Christoph Vogel and Ben Radley, 'In Eastern Congo, economic colonialism in the guise of ethical consumption?', Monkey Cage blog, *Washington Post*, 10 September 2014, www.washingtonpost.com/blogs/monkey-cage/wp/2014/09/10/in-eastern-congo-economic-colonialism-in-the-guise-of-ethical-consumption/, accessed 18 October 2014.

18 John Prendergast, 'The new face of African conflict: in search of a way forward', *Foreign Affairs*, 12 March 2014, www.foreignaffairs.com/articles/141027/

john-prendergast/the-new-face-of-
african-conflict, accessed 18 October
2014.

19 Ruben de Koenig and the Enough
Team, 'Striking gold: how M23 and its
allies are infiltrating Congo's gold trade',
October 2013, www.enoughproject.
org/files/StrikingGold-M23-and-Allies-
Infiltrating-Congo-Gold-Trade.pdf,
accessed 18 October 2014.

20 United Nations, *Final report
of the Group of Experts submitted in
accordance with paragraph 5 of Security
Council resolution 2078 (2012)*, January
2013, www.un.org/sc/committees/1533/
egroup.shtml, accessed 18 October 2014.

21 'Global Witness warns that
majority of inaugural conflict minerals
reports are inadequate', Press release,
2 June 2014, www.globalwitness.org/
library/global-witness-warns-majority-
inaugural-conflict-mineral-reports-are-
inadequate, accessed 18 October 2014.

22 I thank Daniel Fahey for this
observation. See Pelley (2009).

23 Author's observations, 2005–07,
2010. A Small Arms Survey report on the
illicit weapons trade between southern
Sudan and north-eastern Congo made
clear just how many small arms are
in the region. The Small Arms Survey
researcher set out to explore the scale
of illicit arms trading between the two
regions, but found that weapons flows
there are limited because civilians in
north-east Congo do not perceive a
need for arms, the Congolese army
rigorously disarms civilians, and southern Sudan was already saturated with
arms. See Marks (2007).

24 'DR Congo tin "smuggled by UN
man"', BBC, 23 August 2011, www.bbc.
co.uk/news/world-africa-14629354.

25 My own prediction is available here: 'Show me the data', *Texas in
Africa*, Blog post, 10 December 2009,
texasinafrica.blogspot.com/2009/12/
show-me-data.html.

26 I thank Amanda Taub for her
insights with regard to who bears the
consequences of incorrect advocacy
narratives in reference to the advocacy
campaign against the Lord's Resistance
Army, as noted in her remarks at a Congo
in Harlem panel, New York City, 2012.

27 'An open letter', 10 September 2014, ethuin.files.wordpress.
com/2014/09/09092014-open-letter-
final-and-list.pdf, accessed 18 October
2014. The author is among the letter's
signatories.

References

Ackerman, A. (2014) 'U.S. Appellate
Court faults SEC's "conflict minerals"
rule', *Wall Street Journal*, 14 April,
online.wsj.com/news/articles/SB100
014240527023038878045795015908
09000188, accessed 2 June 2014.

Autesserre, S. (2012) 'Dangerous tales:
dominant narratives on the Congo
and their unintended consequences',
African Affairs, 111(443): 202–22.

Bayer, C. and E. de Buhr (2011) *A
Critical Analysis of the SEC and NAM
Economic Impact Models and the
Proposal of a 3rd Model in View of
the Implementation of Section 1502
of the Dodd-Frank Wall Street Reform
and Consumer Protection Act*, Tulane
University Law School Payson Center
for International Development,
October, www.payson.tulane.edu/
sites/default/files/3rd_Economic_
Impact_Model-Conflict_Minerals.pdf,
accessed 16 June 2014.

Boden, R. and D. Epstein (2006) 'Managing the research imagination?
Globalisation and research in higher
education', *Globalisation, Societies
and Education*, 4(2): 223–36.

Chase, S. (2013) 'Western media spin',
Interview with Jason Stearns,
Obama's Law, Film, www.obamaslaw.
com/congo-experts/jason-stearns/,
accessed 10 February 2014.

Coghlan, B. et al. (2007) *Mortality in the Democratic Republic of Congo: An Ongoing Crisis*, International Rescue Committee, www.rescue. org/sites/default/files/migrated/ resources/2007/2006-7_congo mortalitysurvey.pdf, accessed 2 June 2014.

De Koning, R. and the Enough Team (2013) 'Striking gold: how M23 and its allies are infiltrating Congo's gold trade', October, www.enoughproject. org/files/StrikingGold-M23-and-Allies-Infiltrating-Congo-Gold-Trade. pdf, accessed 2 June 2014.

Enough Project (2010) 'Getting to conflict free: assessing corporate action on conflict minerals', December, www.enoughproject.org/files/ corporate_action-1.pdf, accessed 11 February 2014.

Feeley, R. and C. Thomas-Jensen (2008a) 'Beyond crisis management in eastern Congo', Enough Project Strategy Paper, December, www.enoughproject.org/files/easterncongo_1208. pdf, accessed 10 February 2014.

— (2008b) 'Getting serious about ending conflict and sexual violence in Congo', Enough Project Strategy Paper 15, www.enoughproject.org/ publications/getting-serious-about-ending-conflict-and-sexual-violence-congo, accessed 10 February 2014.

Fominyen, G. (2011) 'Mineral certification? The path to end Congo's violence?', AlertNet, 6 May, m.trust.org/ alertnet/news/mineral-certification-the-path-to-end-congos-violence/.

Free the Slaves (2011) 'The Congo report: slavery in conflict minerals', June, www.freetheslaves.net/Document. Doc?id=243.

Gallo, C. J. (2012) 'The informal economy and resource exploitation in the Democratic Republic of Congo', *St Antony's International Review*, 7(2), January, pp. 8–31.

Geenen, S. (2011) 'Relations and regulations in local gold trade networks in South Kivu, Democratic Republic of Congo', *Journal of East African Studies*, 5(3): 427–46.

— (2012) 'A dangerous bet: the challenges of formalizing artisanal mining in the Democratic Republic of Congo', *Resources Policy*, 37(3): 322–30.

— (2013) '"Who seeks, finds": how artisanal miners and traders benefit from gold in the eastern Democratic Republic of Congo', *European Journal of Development Research*, 25(2): 197–212.

Global Witness (2014) 'Global Witness warns that majority of inaugural conflict mineral reports are inadequate', Press release, 2 June, www.globalwitness.org/library/ global-witness-warns-majority-inaugural-conflict-mineral-reports-are-inadequate.

Hogg, J. (2011) 'U.S. buyers shun conflict minerals in Congo's east', Reuters, 4 October, af.reuters. com/article/drcNews/ idAFL5E7L31S720111005?sp=true.

Hogg, J. and G. Holliday (2011) 'Conflict minerals crackdown backfiring in Congo', Reuters, 30 December, af.reuters.com/article/drcNews/ idAFL6E7NU25720111230?sp=true.

Johnson, D. (2013) *No Kivu, No Conflict? The misguided struggle against 'conflict minerals' in the DRC*, Goma: Pole Institute, April.

Kavanagh, M. (2011) 'Congo tin sales tumble 90% as companies avoid "conflict minerals"', Bloomberg News, 23 May, www.bloomberg.com/ news/2011-05-23/congo-tin-sales-tumble-90-percent-as-companies-avoid-conflict-minerals-.html.

Lynch, S. (2011) 'U.S. SEC to hold round-table on conflict minerals', Reuters, 29 September, af.reuters.com/article/ idAFS1E78S0R920110929?sp=true.

Marks, J. (2007) 'Border in name only: arms trafficking and armed groups at the DRC–Sudan border', Geneva: Small Arms Survey, www.smallarmssurveysudan.org/pdfs/HSBA-SWP-4-DRC-Sudan.pdf.

Pelley, S. (2009) 'Congo's gold', *60 Minutes*, 29 November, www.cbsnews.com/video/watch/?id=5825990n, accessed 3 June 2014.

Prendergast, J. and C. Thomas-Jensen (2007) 'Averting the nightmare scenario in eastern Congo', Enough Project Strategy Paper 7, September, www.enoughproject.org/files/congonightmare_0.pdf, accessed 10 February 2014.

Seay, L. (2012a) 'What's wrong with Dodd-Frank 1502? Conflict minerals, civilian livelihoods, and the unintended consequences of Western advocacy', Working Paper 284, Center for Global Development, January.

— (2012b) 'What is "illicit"? A response to Carol Jean Gallo, "The informal economy and resource exploitation in the Democratic Republic of Congo"', *St Antony's International Review*, 8(1): 167–73.

Securities and Exchange Commission (2011) *Conflict Minerals Final Rule*, RIN 3235-AK84, www.sec.gov/rules/final/2012/34-67716.pdf, accessed 2 June 2014.

Taylor, C. (2012) 'Conflict minerals and SEC disclosure regulation', *Harvard Business Law Review*, January, www.hblr.org/wp-content/uploads/2012/01/Taylor-Conflict-Minerals.pdf, accessed 11 February 2014.

United Nations (2011) *Final Report of the UN Group of Experts on the Democratic Republic of Congo*, www.un.org/ga/search/view_doc.asp?symbol=S/2011/738.

— (2013) *Group of Experts on the Democratic Republic of Congo, Final Report of the Group of Experts*, United Nations S/2012/843, www.un.org/ga/search/view_doc.asp?symbol=S/2012/843, accessed 2 June 2014.

— (2014) *Group of Experts on the Democratic Republic of Congo, Final Report of the Group of Experts*, United Nations S/2014/42, www.un.org/ga/search/view_doc.asp?symbol=S/2014/42, accessed 2 June 2014.

7 | 'MAKE HIM FAMOUS': THE SINGLE CONFLICT NARRATIVE OF KONY AND *KONY2012*

Mareike Schomerus[1]

Introduction

> Something called ... what? Invisible Children of the where? ... Theirs was just a video. It started in America. I'm not familiar with it.[2]

Gabriel Ayoor Reckuei, an officer in the special task force of the Sudan People's Liberation Army (SPLA), could see little connection between his military task of pursuing the Ugandan Lord's Resistance Army (LRA) and an American advocacy phenomenon he had vaguely heard about. Ten months after the widely viewed video *Kony2012*, produced by California-based NGO Invisible Children (IC), had brought the Ugandan conflict to the attention of millions of people around the world, people in South Sudan who were directly affected by the events it recounted had very little idea of what this phenomenon meant. Named after the LRA's elusive leader Joseph Kony, *Kony2012* aimed to bring him to 'justice' before the end of that year.

Invisible Children's strategy was to 'make Kony famous'. This idea was reminiscent of a joke by George Clooney, in which he said of Sudanese president Omar al-Bashir that, as 'a war criminal ... I think it should be fair enough that he should enjoy the same amount of celebrity that I do'.[3] Invisible Children applied this logic to Kony: the implication was that, if millions of young Americans knew about Kony's heinous crimes, then the US administration would be compelled to act. Kony would be captured, and this would bring to an end a violent conflict that began in Uganda in the late 1980s and twenty-five years later was affecting people in South Sudan, the Democratic Republic of Congo (DRC) and the Central African Republic (CAR).

This is a simple assumed chain of events at best. Yet in addition to the shortcomings of the advocacy logic, *Kony2012* highlighted a pressing need for international activism in general to reinvent itself in a way that allows the complexity of a conflict situation to become just as compelling an advocacy tool as feigning simplicity has been. Activism's next generation will need to challenge those in power in a better way by reclaiming the art of second-guessing causes, solutions and the centrality of their own role.

Because it was not the affected people who were the focus of *Kony2012*: it was American youth. At a public event in Washington, DC to support the message of *Kony2012*, some of the Ugandan actors visible in the video briefly walked on stage to roaring applause, they barely spoke a word. Both makers and viewers of *Kony2012* were overwhelmingly Western,[4] and the video's success proves how well it served Western viewing preferences. While at a public showing in Uganda people threw stones at the screen (Flock 2012), the *Guardian*'s film critic, Peter Bradshaw, called *Kony2012*:

> quite simply brilliant ... a piece of digital polemic and digital activism ... a slick, high-gloss piece of work ... already achieving one of its stated objectives: to make Kony famous, to publicise this psychopathic warlord's grotesque crimes: kidnapping thousands of children and turning them into mercenaries, butchers and rapists. (Bradshaw 2012)

The portrayal of Ugandans in the video is of lesser concern to my argument in this chapter than the fact that, for the people who lived in the Central African regions where the LRA was active, the idea of 'making Kony famous' made little sense. Not only did they know as much as they wished or needed to about the man and his armed band, but a campaign that aimed to generate Western clamour for yet more military action in their countries was not serving their needs as they saw them.

My central argument is that the Ugandan belligerents jointly constructed a narrative about the conflict that shares a number of elements, including a focus on individual responsibility of leaders, the strength of the LRA rebellion lying in the spiritual sphere, and the capacity of violence to solve Uganda's problems. Early on, the US government bought into the Ugandan official narrative, and activists have faithfully followed that line, with IC as the most conspicuous example. The internationalization of the conflict, through humanitarian NGOs, the International Criminal Court (ICC), foreign

; and more recently popular culture and social media, has nhanced that shared narrative. Given that the LRA exerts ts power through its fearsome reputation for violence and spiritual sanction, the attention given to it by its adversaries has perversely enhanced that power. What greater testament could there be to Kony's standing as a supernatural warrior than the fact that the world's temporal superpower is relentlessly searching for him?

In this chapter, I also draw upon the LRA's own version of events, based on my own first-hand research and the documents produced by the LRA and its obscure political wing, the Lord's Resistance Movement (LRM). This narrative has been wrongly silenced. We should take the LRA's account of itself seriously, as it provides a window into why the conflict has endured for so long, and why Kony has earned the respect, even political support, of a not insignificant number of people in northern Uganda. Suppressing this account only nurtures grievances.

From the late 1980s onwards, northern Uganda was the locus of many grievous violations of human rights worthy of an international advocacy campaign. The most well known of those abuses are those perpetrated by the LRA, many of which are conspicuous atrocities designed to send messages to the population and aggrandize the LRA's reputation. But the abuses by the Ugandan army and government, including very large-scale forced relocation, have been deeply resented by the population of northern Uganda, and have arguably caused as much human suffering (or more) as the LRA's violations themselves. Invisible Children, following the lead of earlier American advocacy efforts, has focused exclusively on the well-established horrors of the LRA. Its narrative converges with that of the Ugandan government and the US administration. This is important: IC does not campaign for policy change but rather advocates for existing policies to be sustained or intensified. It is an echo chamber for a certain set of values and policy priorities already established.

Invisible Children contributes to a single conflict narrative, namely an account of the war to which all the belligerents subscribe, and which marginalizes or eliminates certain important issues and options. This narrative obscures not only failures of Ugandan governmental and international policy – for example, the massive population displacement of the 1990s and early 2000s and the militarization of a large swathe of Central Africa – but also successes, such as the de facto ending of the war in Uganda when the LRA withdrew its forces at the time of the Juba peace talks in 2006. The *Kony2012* video and its attempt to 'make Kony famous' was a tribute to IC's faith in the liberating power of information. The argument, usually implicit, is that if enough people know, enough people will care, and enough will be done. In this chapter I will argue that this confidence in the uncomplicated role of information is unfounded. Flaws will be found both in the idea that telling a lot of young Americans about Kony will make it impossible for him to prevail, and also that telling South Sudanese about LRA activities will enable them to protect themselves better.

The principle of 'making someone famous' at first comes across as a laudable way of raising awareness. Yet the makers of *Kony2012* packaged awareness in such a way as to promote a simple solution (military force) rather than responses to the much wider issues affecting people in northern Uganda and the areas affected by the LRA. The campaign promoted a linear process of cause and effect, making strict divisions between good and bad, perpetrators and victims, problem and solution. The value of the awareness it raised is difficult to measure. Having information is valuable in itself, but the belief that one-dimensional Western awareness of a complicated African problem can lead to a solution, is questionable. As Nonviolent Peace Force commented, 'a revolutionary medium reduces itself to a reactionary solution'.[5]

The chapter concludes with an example of how the IC strategy has worked in practice in South Sudan. The practice under examination is broadcasting of information using FM radio about supposed LRA threats alongside messages to encourage LRA members to desert. In South Sudan, such radio campaigns have contributed to an atmosphere of fear among communities, leading to the establishment of a substantial local militia whose size and arms are out of proportion to the real threat of the LRA, which is a potentially damaging trickle-down effect from *Kony2012*.

War and peace in northern Uganda

Uganda's first president, Milton Obote, hailed from the north. He was deposed by Idi Amin, and reinstated following the Tanzanian-led invasion of 1979, only to wage an exceptionally brutal war against several insurgent groups, and ultimately to be overthrown again. His nemesis was not, however, his own generals who took power from him, but the leader of the National Resistance Army (NRA) guerrillas, Yoweri Museveni, who finally triumphed in 1986 over Tito Okello, who had himself overthrown Obote, who had claimed victory in Uganda's 1980 post-Amin elections. Museveni's military victory was acclaimed by many in the centre and south of Uganda, but by few in the north and east. The new Ugandan leader was also welcomed internationally and given considerable latitude to develop his political and economic policies.

From the outset, northern Ugandans were excluded, and increasingly felt repressed and abused. Obote wrote that 'the walls of protection which the international media and Human Rights Organizations have erected to protect the regime are such that Museveni, like the mythical James Bond, is thereby licensed to kill and to do whatever he likes with the lives of the citizens of Uganda' (Obote 1990). The LRA emerged from the Holy Spirit Movement led by Alice Lakwena, which mounted an early and surprisingly effective military challenge to the Museveni government by convincing its soldiers of their invincibility – which ultimately failed them at their defeat at the hands of government forces.

Lakwena's relative, Joseph Kony, picked up the baton of armed rebellion. While the victims of his brutalities were almost entirely the civilian population of the Acholi region – the people on whose behalf he claimed to be fighting – his message of invincibility appealed to some members of that population who felt humiliated and degraded by the way the new government was treating them. A succession of military offensives by the NRA (renamed the Uganda People's Defence Force, UPDF) further antagonized the northern population. A belief spread that Museveni intended to destroy the Acholi (Doom and Vlassenroot 1999; Jackson 2009). Particularly unpopular was the government policy of forcing people into so-called 'protected villages' (Omach 2002; Branch 2011; Lamwaka 2011). These were squalid camps of forcibly displaced people who were to live and die there (WHO 2005).

Much has been made of Kony's appeal to supernatural powers in his management of the LRA and its fearsome reputation. This has a natural appeal to foreign journalists who wish to sell copy as well as to Ugandan government leaders who want to discredit their enemies. Yet the stories of wizardry and spiritual sanctions should not obscure the more mundane political messaging of the LRA. The LRA's conventional political statements are rare but significant. Kony's four-hour-long speech at the 1994 peace talks is generally considered to be the first major effort of Kony to articulate his case in a cogent manner. The substance was repeated in a 1996 communiqué: 'We are fighting for our land and our lives. The Acoliland is threatened and it can be safe only if Museveni is toppled. The whole of Uganda will be safe only if Museveni is removed. Museveni is one man in this world that Ugandans must not trust' (LRA 1996).

Kony tried to justify his violent actions – including atrocities against civilians[6] – as necessary to challenge the authority of Museveni.[7] This propaganda of the deed established the LRA's reputation as a fearsome and fearless rebel group, fully committed to its spiritual rules. But the atrocities were also the government's best tool for discrediting the LRA's political messages.

The Ugandan government personalized and demonized the politics of rebellion, using the same approach as the LRA but to better effect. It also enlisted international endorsement of its definition of the problem and proposed solutions. Former Ugandan government minister and peace negotiator Betty Bigombe and US activist John Prendergast asked in a joint article: 'How do you end a 19-year insurgency led by a messianic guerrilla leader with an army of abducted, tortured, and brainwashed children?' (Bigombe and Prendergast 2006). President Museveni and the then-Prosecutor of the ICC, Luis Moreno Ocampo, stood side by side to make a joint announcement of the ICC's opening of an investigation into LRA crimes in northern Uganda.[8] In the same vein, the UN High Commissioner for Human Rights, Louise Arbour, called the LRA a 'well-armed criminal enterprise' that does not have 'any kind of political agenda' and ought not to be 'romanticized' (Inner City Press 2007). Most mainstream information on the LRA is heavy on atmospheric description, helping to perpetuate the myths about the sources of the LRA's mysterious power.[9] However, in their eagerness to demonize Kony, his international adversaries may well have aggrandized him, with their condemnations serving as an echo chamber for the very reputation that Kony so ably built. For President Museveni, Kony has been a convenient enemy. The LRA's conspicuous atrocities over-shadow those of the UPDF, and help to justify the UPDF's size, large budget and deployment up to and beyond the country's borders.

The single (international) conflict narrative

Both belligerents and activists use simplified narrative tools to create jointly what can best be described as 'narrative conflicts'. These consist of single narratives, which are simplified versions of events, usually focused on one aspect from which all other conclusions are drawn. Conflicts are driven in part by narratives, anecdotes and rumours, all of which are strengthened when they cohere around a single simplified script.[10] The activity of war thus becomes a reflec-tion of the narrative of war. The armed actors and those involved in propaganda and activism can collude in constructing such a conflict narrative, and as a result advocacy messages may legitimize the behaviour of *all* conflict actors, including those against whom the advocacy is directed.

The voiceover in *Kony2012* tells us the intention of the video is to educate the '99 per cent of the planet' who do not know who Kony is: 'If they did, he would have been stopped years ago.' To achieve this, the video's makers used techniques that, as McIntosh argues,

> [fit] squarely into the propaganda/persuasion traditions developed in the work of Frank Capra, Leni Riefenstahl, and Pare Lorentz. But KONY 2012 pushes the boundaries of these traditions. It attempts to go for the heart strings and not just tickle them but instead rip them out and stomp on them. (PBS 2012)

Presented as the personal quest of IC's Jason Russell to stop the LRA, the video's main narrative device is him explaining to his young son that there is a bad guy out there and how Russell learned about this when he met Jacob Acaye in Uganda in 2003. Acaye had been attacked by the LRA and seen his brother killed. Russell promised Jacob, on camera, that he would do whatever it took to stop Kony. He is grandiloquent: 'If we succeed, we change the course of human history.' The juxtaposition of the humanity of the film-makers and their followers on the one side, and the dehumanized Kony on the other, quickly establishes a dichotomy of good and evil. Russell's and

IC's impressive campaigning over years on behalf of the Ugandans – who at times contribute a voice to the campaign, but primarily appear as powerless victims or to confirm the need for the international campaign – also confirms that true power in the matter rests in the United States.

The way IC has long portrayed the LRA has been to focus on Kony as the undisputed centre of the conflict, whose movements and decisions determine its continuation or end. He is seen as a spirit-possessed leader of charisma and brutality who has fought the war fuelled by a mixture of spiritual force, religious extremism and military support from Sudan (another fully paid-up member of the advocates' axis of evil). Part of Kony's appeal and ability to evoke utter terror lay in his invisibility as a rebel leader who is known only from the stories of those who have escaped.

The power of invoking 'the invisible' should not be lost on an organization calling itself Invisible Children. In April 2008, the former LRA spokesperson Obonyo Olweny explained that the mysticism that surrounded Kony gave him such power. Therefore, he reflected, making Kony a public figure during the Juba peace talks of 2006–08 was a mistake: 'He was stronger when he was not exposed to the world.'[11] In person, Kony appeared banal. When he was an elusive legend, stories of Kony's mysterious strength and unspeakable brutality made the descriptions of this ghost-like figure even more poignant. This generated fear in a manner that became a strategic 'force multiplier' for the LRA (Vinci 2005). The LRA was feeding off the image of the unknown spirit-driven superhuman commander. The outside world and its most visible activists did exactly the same, an example of what Agamben in another context has called the commodification of evil and the messianic (Agamben 1993). The result was that the LRA received regular confirmation from advocacy campaigns that the image of the spirit-driven madman remained one of its strongest assets.

Having established that the spiritual realm is a battlefield, both the LRA and the anti-LRA advocates have fought for spiritual hegemony, using narrative devices.

One striking example of the activists' moral logic was revealed in a 2009 episode of the popular crime series *Law & Order: Special Victims Unit*. In this, an American prime-time television audience watched as a young African asylum seeker in New York City struggles to come to terms with having killed as a child soldier with a Ugandan rebel group. The episode, entitled 'Hell' to alert even the most obtuse viewer, brought the notion of the African madman as the driver of conflict on to American television screens. Another refugee, Miriam – who is mute and thus literally a voiceless victim – spots her Ugandan tormenter, who is now living in Harlem. The police identify him as the warlord Joseph Serumaga, nicknamed 'The Devil', who is wanted by the ICC for war crimes – and rather casually and in a surprisingly uncomplicated way, extradite him for trial in The Hague. Redemption of the former child soldier, however, comes through prayer and faith, although he does not survive a confrontation with the police.

A piece of gripping television, this episode was also an advocacy-driven depiction of the single narrative of modern conflict resolution – with a romanticized image of how international justice procedures provide the solution. The evil of the single perpetrator is coupled with the idea that higher powers – in this case the ICC – will wipe out evil.

The TV programme implies that claims to righteousness come from a higher being. In *Law & Order*, only God can exonerate and prayer alone will create the best of all awareness campaigns. The LRA found itself on familiar terrain. When its political spokesmen objected to the flawed factual basis of *Kony2012*, they wrote:

> African people are profound believers in Christian, Islamic and
> Indigenous African faiths. They take most seriously and highly
> value for instance, the admonition of Jesus – the Christ (Prophet
> Issa in Islam) – whose teaching to all believers was: 'Seek ye
> the truth and the truth shall set thee free.' This prophetic and
> spiritual admonition is relevant to all in the world, particularly
> those who exercise vast earthly powers for which one day they will
> be made to account. The US African Command and the US special
> forces-led military adventure and intervention in Central Africa
> are best evaluated with the benefit of the Prophetic and Messianic
> admonition of Jesus – the Christ – on truth.[12]

The Association of Concerned Africa Scholars in its statement criticizing *Kony2012* emphasized the problem of 'the religious messianism that implies we can save Africans from their leaders and that Americans can "change history," "change the world" in Africa with a few simple actions' (Association of Concerned Africa Scholars 2012).

Single-narrative advocacy is concerned with shaping collective memories of events – what Halbwachs termed '*mémoire collective*' (Halbwachs 1992 [1925]) – with the aim of strengthening internal group structures. Brockmeier calls it 'a shared horizon of experience, understanding and orientation – a common experiential ground for a sense of coherence and belonging' (Brockmeier 2002). Both the LRA and IC created such a sense of belonging in those they sought to influence: the LRA by maintaining that their voice was not heard and everyone was against them; IC by instilling a sense of community drawn from its campaign against Kony.

The two endeavours feed off each other in interesting ways. In a conversation with me, Kony's deputy at the time, Vincent Otti, spoke about how the LRA's goals had been misunderstood. Matter-of-factly, he mentioned the injustice of being labelled 'terrorists', 'killers' and 'animals'. The label terrorist was the greatest insult of the three. He did not seem particularly fazed by the label 'killers'. In previous conversations he had alluded to the fact that the LRA took a lot of pride in being such an efficient military force. Being called a good killer by your enemies is a badge of honour, rather than an insult.

Faith in force

The LRA and Invisible Children share the belief that solutions are brought by force. Both support military intervention to end political conflict. Invisible Children's members were seduced by the power of heavy weaponry, a fact that became particularly evident when the group's leaders posed for a photograph with SPLA guns.

Both the LRA and the Ugandan government have promoted the idea that the conflict will be resolved by military victory. Both have also tried to tap into Western cultural histories of war, albeit not always in the same way. Most Western advocacy has worked hard to portray the LRA war as the ultimate manifestation of the 'African hell of colonial imagination' (Finnstroem 2008a), which warrants an international civilizing mission. The LRA has tried to co-opt this same militaristic tradition. On my first visit to the LRA camp, I saw soldiers carry what to me was unexpected reading material: Clausewitz's seminal treatise *On War*, a book by Tom Clancy entitled *Special Forces* and *The Idiot's Guide to Special Forces*. Possibly the LRA commanders were really reading these books. Perhaps these were put on display to portray a particular image of the LRA to a foreign visitor. If it was strategic placement, this only strengthens the point that the LRA was shaping the narrative of the conflict not just internally but also externally.

In 2010, the US Congress passed the LRA Disarmament and Northern Uganda Recovery Act (2010), providing domestic legislation to back a US military operation to pursue rebel forces in a foreign country which presented no obvious danger to US interests. Invisible Children had lobbied for the bill; the photograph of the signing ceremony in the White House is remarkable primarily because of the overwhelming dominance of white, male faces. In a familiar tactic for campaigning organizations, IC also tried to claim credit for the bill, at least when communicating with its supporters. The numbers of US military personnel assigned to the LRA case are small, and most of them are stationed in the Ugandan capital, far away from the action. But the Act, the deployment of US troops on a mission that has no obvious connection to American national security, and the endorsement of Uganda's military activities all contribute to the militarization of US policy in central Africa (Schomerus et al. 2011).

At the time when the *Kony2012* video was released, the Obama administration had already extended the US military mission in Uganda and the neighbouring countries. While there was a hypothetical possibility that the policy might change and the troops withdraw, this was not happening or even being discussed. However, only the most careful viewer of the video, and attentive-to-detail follower of the story, would understand that IC's efforts at influencing policy amounted only to opposing a hypothetical policy change. The implication of the advocacy was that America needed to ramp up its military effort to catch Kony, and only with massive popular support would the president take the necessary action to do so.

Consequently, IC's advocacy supports US government positions, in detail and in spirit. Insofar as Jason Russell and his staff criticize the administration, it is for hypothetically contemplating scaling back its military effort. The US government, the Ugandan government and non-governmental advocates converge on endorsing a military solution.

The notion of teenage activists fighting international evil with the support of the US government and army feeds into a prominent American foreign policy narrative: that of the evil and single enemy as a threat to the values and safety of America itself. When trying to disentangle how this rather implausible chain of reasoning became such a driving force, it is helpful to draw on Bruner's encouragement to look beyond logical thought to a way of thinking 'that is quite different in form from reasoning: the form of thought that goes into the construction not of logical or inductive arguments but of stories or narratives' (Bruner 2004). The religiously coloured, hyper-moralistic narrative developed by IC – and exemplified in the *Law & Order* television programme – shows how this argument can be constructed.

The militaristic narrative has not gone without challenge. The Association of Concerned Africa Scholars called *Kony2012* 'misleading', stressing its deep concern 'that the recent campaign in the United States to pursue and arrest Joseph Kony, leader of the Lord's Resistance Army (LRA), could have dangerous unintended consequences' (Association of Concerned Africa Scholars 2012). The group spelt out what these consequences were: militarization of the region, with civilians left vulnerable to attacks not only from the LRA but also from the state forces pursuing them, with an emphasis on the fact that the 'Ugandan and other armies ... have killed more Africans than Kony's LRA'.[13]

Silenced narrative

In 1996, the LRA published a document containing its 'Policy definitions and explanations'. Written in simple language, the document covered social rights, social obligations, economic policy and foreign policy. It argued that human life is sacrosanct and in need of protection and stressed the right to a good life with education, healthcare, religious freedom and creative output as aspirations. The paper also made a particular point of saying that peace also meant rejecting 'stereotypes, clichés and derogative remarks' (LRA 1996).

A number of scholars have tried to penetrate the obfuscation around the LRA, and the infamy that arises from its atrocities (Tindifa

2006; Allen 2006; Dunn 2004; Bøås and Dunn 2007; Finnstroem 2008b; Accorsi et al. 2005; Branch 2011), to challenge the simplistic depictions of good and evil (Bailey et al. 2003; Ahadi and Stoltz 2004). The scholarship is excellent but mainstream media and government communication remain largely unchanged, still dominated by 'stereotypes, clichés and derogative remarks', focusing on Kony as a mad Satan-like figure.

Making use of its often-absent political wing, the LRM, which regularly publishes commentary and open letters on the conflict, Kony's lieutenants and supporters have made some effort to criticize their adversaries' narrative, and – more importantly – to articulate the grievances of people in northern Uganda.

The LRM described *Kony2012* as an attempt 'to prepare world opinion to accept as "inevitable and necessary" the military campaign to "kill and then capture" Joseph Kony and the Lord's Resistance Army Field Command'. They called it 'a cheap and banal panic act of mass trickery to make the unsuspecting peoples of the world complicit in the U.S. rogue and murderous activities in Central Africa' (LMP Team 2012). The LRM does not enjoy much credibility, but nonetheless its view that such advocacy was deeply intertwined with American politics was not far fetched.

Having been appointed spokesperson for the LRA/M during the Juba peace talks, Obonyo Olweny was elated at what he saw as a potential sea change in the communication strategy because the 'LRA never had a proper spokesperson'. He saw this as an opportunity to build a new LRA narrative, which was to focus on political issues and legitimate grievances. The LRA/M delegation at the Juba talks argued that they had been unsuccessful in reaching out to the media and that 'failure of the LRM/A to have access to the mass media to express its political agenda loudly in intellectual form does not mean the lack of it' (Olweny 2006). LRA commanders were adamant that their political message was well known in Uganda, stressing that the mass media were not their most important communication channel. Otti argued that it was difficult in a 'bush war' to distribute strong messages, especially because 'rebel supporters' faced persecution. Yet Otti was also aware of the need to shape positive perceptions, something in which the LRA had fallen far behind. He mentioned several times that he wanted to write a book just as Museveni had done with his autobiography, *Sowing the Mustard Seed*, about the establishment of modern Uganda (Museveni 1997). Within the LRA, Otti was seen as the best person to create the LRA narrative – in fact no one else was considered capable of doing so. This also made the LRA's advocacy very difficult. As an LRA member explained, 'We did not have a manifesto because we did not have anybody who could do such a thing. Otti could not be waiter, cashier and cook at the same time.'[14]

The International Crisis Group made a similar point, stating that 'until the legitimate grievances and feeling of marginalisation of northern Uganda's communities are genuinely addressed, LRA fighters remain a possible vehicle for the expression of northerners' frustrations' (ICG 2008).

Giving a voice to the silenced, complex narratives of the people of northern Uganda is not an advocacy priority for any of the high-profile actors – belligerents and Western activists – engaged in the LRA issue.

The fear factor

Invisible Children followed up *Kony2012* with a few activities; support for broadcasting information relating to the LRA on the radio was part of what they called their 'Protection Plan' (Invisible Children 2013b). This included sponsorship of broadcasts in LRA-affected regions in the DRC, the CAR and South Sudan. One was so-called 'come-home' messaging, targeting LRA fighters and encouraging them to defect. According to Invisible Children's annual report in 2012 (Invisible Children 2013a), two FM radio stations broadcast such messages in South Sudan's Western Equatoria state, along with information about LRA movements and its suspected attacks. Invisible Children claim that these broadcasts on radio stations are part of a strategy that saves lives (Invisible Children 2011). Yet it is possible to look at their effect as mirroring the *Kony2012* campaign. Both *Kony2012* and the radio stations in South Sudan create awareness with a notion of empowering people. Implicit in this is the view that information is in itself valuable – or that information is a base for social power (French and Raven 1950). Yet the effects of sending a radio message are more complicated. In two counties in South Sudan – Ezo and Tambura – the radio messages did not increase safety for the populations, but contributed to a complex social change in which new groups and people were able to increase their power, while others became potentially more vulnerable.

This involved several steps, none of them linear or clear cut. In 2005, the LRA moved into Western Equatoria state, having had bases in Eastern Equatoria state since the early 1990s (Prunier 2004; Schomerus 2007). Although rebel activity in the state subsided during the Juba peace talks, residents of Western Equatoria state remained suspicious of the rebel presence, and dubious about the government's willingness to provide protection (Gordon et al. 2007). In December 2008, the Juba peace talks ended with an ill-fated military offensive against the LRA camp in Garamba National Park in DRC.

The 2008 military intervention triggered a series of LRA attacks, to which Southern Sudanese government forces barely reacted (Schomerus and De Vries 2014). As a result the communities mobilized their own protection. Ad hoc groups of armed civilians patrolled the roads and bush and continued to mobilize, particularly when information about security threats was received. In 2010, the Southern Sudan Legislative Assembly allocated the equivalent of nearly $2 million to supply these 'community militias' with more sophisticated weaponry such as 'guns, communication systems and training' (Martell 2010) to defend themselves against LRA attacks. This response, although the weapons were desperately needed for protection, also caused great concern with regard to its long-term implications.

The LRA remains present in DRC, CAR and South Sudan, but its activities have decreased considerably since the terrible events of 2008 (Human Rights Watch 2009). Invisible Children's LRA Crisis Tracker reports an increase in LRA activity from 112 LRA 'events' in 2008 to 718 in 2010, but with a comparable decrease thereafter.[15] On the southern Sudanese side of the border, LRA activities decreased in 2009 and stopped almost completely in 2010. Survey responses confirm this picture. Reported victimization by the LRA peaked in 2009, and reports from later years have been sporadic. Even at the height of LRA activity, however, levels of LRA-related violence were much lower in southern Sudan than in the DRC and the CAR. There was, explained an international security worker, only one 'genuine LRA attack in Ezo', which happened in 2009.[16] What is crucial to this argument is that LRA attacks on the population in Western Equatoria have been rare, so that people are statistically at low risk of being the victim of an attack. Yet the perceived risk among the population is very high, and to a noticeable extent this is because they hear about the LRA on the radio.

Having researched the effects of radio messages on the population,[17] Anouk Rigterink's and my first finding was that the radio coverage that IC claims in its annual report is not correct, as one of the radio stations has long been defunct. The other one, Yambio FM, has reliable reception in only the two villages closest to Yambio town. In fact, the unreliability prompted the commissioner of Ezo County to file a complaint with the state minister for information and to ask for a booster.[18] Even those who can hear radio information do not necessarily trust what they hear. This is because they do not see how the radio security warnings match up with the lack of follow-up action by such official actors as the army, the SPLA or the UN. Some respondents had heard about US soldiers being in the area, but had never seen them and thus did not believe they existed. Respondents were also scared of army movement and acutely aware that the radio would not warn them when either the South Sudanese or the Ugandan armies were on the move. Being able to receive information over the radio without witnessing any action that corresponds to what they hear means that people have a general sense of feeling unsafe.

With both national and international forces largely discredited in their eyes, our respondents turned to a local militia that was formed to protect the villages: the so-called Arrow Boys. The long-term effects of this shift in protective authority are unclear. We could see from our research that in areas with better radio reception, people are more frightened of the LRA and their trust in the Arrow Boys is stronger than in areas with poorer radio reception (Rigterink and Schomerus forthcoming; Schomerus and Rigterink forthcoming). From what we found it is clear that simply getting information about a threat does not make people feel safer, but triggers a whole range of other reactions. Instead of there being a linear cause-and-effect relation between greater information and an increased feeling of security, the information is just part of a messy chain of cause and effect that fuels fear and lack of trust among some actors, while increasing the authority of others.

evoking radio information as part of a 'protection' effort suggests clear path from problem to solution. But this case study warns of the unintended consequences that may arise. What sounds like a useful development – civilians taking up arms to protect themselves after hearing about threats on the radio – may result in the increased militarization that the Concerned Scholars feared. What we see in Western Equatoria is that the Arrow Boys are becoming a permanent fixture of society, regardless of whether or not there is a threat from the LRA. One respondent, an important local leader, said:

> If the situation is now [improving] – there is no LRA – I'm trying to have an institution to train them, transform them to normal citizens. We can train them in carpentry. Because if you leave them like this they can even turn against the community. What will happen? Who will they be? Will they be good citizens?[19]

Conclusion

Kony2012 highlighted a disconnect between the world of contemporary lobbying and those who are caught in the complex situation that is the ostensible focus of that lobbying. In this disconnect lies the explanation for the video's simplistic narrative and its success in generating public attention and acclaim. Thus, contemporary activism, despite being able to draw upon better communication networks and technologies, and more information, largely relies on repackaging a simple story of good and evil. Invisible Children demonstrated that contemporary activism, like propaganda down the ages, relies on setting narratives and manipulating perceptions.

Kony2012 demonstrates the importance of critically assessing the power of single narratives to shape conflicts and structurally entrench a conflict. The increased militarization that purported military solutions bring is just one example of the broken link between local needs and international activism. Substantial unintended consequences are disregarded, and genuine narratives of grievance remain silenced. The lesson to be drawn seems simple: activism that depicts a conflict as driven by a single actor, and which offers a simple strategy towards a solution, must be discarded, particularly if the power between activists and victims is as unequally distributed as was the case with *Kony2012*. Yet the stand-off between advocacy and its critics rather deepens the divide and triggers further advocacy of the same kind. Evera describes such a situation as the 'kill the messenger' syndrome, in which those expressing doubt inadvertently contribute to a reputation-saving continuation along the same path (Evera 2002). Modern activists and their critics both need to overcome this 'kill the messenger' syndrome if they are to find a better way forward.

Yet there is more to be learned from understanding the power of narrative conflicts and single narratives: what is lacking is a compelling narrative of complexity in both cause and solution. Woody writes about the need for 'integrated' narratives, which draw together single narratives into a more complex one, developing 'centred' narratives 'in which all the strands fit together – though not without some tension, various confusions, and much second guessing' (Woody 2003). Similarly, integrating the focus on damaging narratives with a more holistic principle of 'do no harm' is necessary. That might bring an end to justifying means and advocacy could turn a corner. However, a considered and nuanced form of advocacy requires notions of success and failure to be redefined. If a complex, nuanced advocacy campaign lobbies unsuccessfully against single-minded government policies, it has not failed. The existence of nuanced advocacy needs to be seen as a success, even if its impact seems diminished. With such a redefinition, conflict actors who drive single narratives might one day find that their nuanced opponents in advocacy have become a much greater challenge to the structures of conflict.

That simplification does not have a positive effect in the long run was shown in a surprising twist of events in late 2014. Only two years after an advocacy stunt that stunned the world (and resulted in a huge fundraising success), Invisible Children announced that it would dissolve. One of the reasons for this, it was argued, was the backlash against how the organization had depicted both the conflict and the way it might end when they released *Kony2012* (Titeca and Sebastian 2014). Maybe unexpected lessons will be learned from one of the most successful advocacy campaigns of the last years.

Notes

1 Thanks to Anouk Rigterink, Danielle Stein and Craig Valters for their research, which helped inform this chapter.

2 Gabriel Ayoor Reckuei, CDC, Regional Task Force AU, 15 December 2012.

3 George Stephanopolous, 'George

Clooney "surprised" by success of Kony2012 video', *ABC News*, 14 March 2012, abcnews.go.com/blogs/politics/2012/03/george-clooney-surprised-by-success-of-kony-2012-video/.

4 The RightsViews blog of Columbia University tracked Google searches and reached the same conclusion (Rights-Views 2012). Acknowledging several shortcomings in their data collection, Floating Sheep's mapping of Twitter trending nonetheless shows the focus of the debate in the USA and Europe (Floating Sheep 2012).

5 Nonviolent Peace Force, 'Kony 2012: Viral, dangerous?', www.non violentpeaceforce.org/blog/kony-2012-viral-dangerous.

6 Particularly in Uganda, the interaction between civilians and the LRA is complicated, as being a member of the LRA was at times a choice for those wasting away in displacement camps. For a further discussion, see Allen and Schomerus (2006). For a more detailed outline of how Sudanese civilians developed protection mechanisms by working with the LRA, see Schomerus (2007).

7 Richards, Hoffman and Ellis all point out that localized armed groups root themselves firmly in the global narrative of violence, drawing inspiration from other armed groups that were acting with more international attention focused on them, namely al-Qaeda and the Taliban (Richards 1996; Ellis 1999; Hoffman 2005).

8 The ICC later explained that it would be investigating the situation in the whole of northern Uganda, not just the violations committed by the LRA.

9 Good examples of atmospheric, often disturbing, memoirs that are at the same time infused with symbolism are Cook (2007), Dunson (2008), Eichstaedt (2009), McDonnell and Akallo (2007) and Caruso (2006). A comedic approach to asking why Museveni has

not been able to defeat Kony has been offered by Bussmann (2010).

10 A vast and varied literature exists on the importance of personal narratives, of creating agency through voice and of empowerment through speaking. See Fassin (2007: 519); Bruner (2004).

11 Conversation with former member of LRA/M delegation, Nairobi, 2008.

12 LRM Team (2012).

13 See also a range of publications that addressed either directly *Kony2012* or were intended to provide background information about it, such as Taub (2012), Schomerus (2012), Schomerus et al. (2012).

14 Author fieldwork notes, 'With delegation in Juba', Juba, 6 June 2006. Otti was killed in a leadership struggle at the order of Joseph Kony in October 2007.

15 www.lracrisistracker.com.

16 Author interview, Ezo, 4 May 2013.

17 Research conducted in Ezo and Tambura consisted of different types of interviews – about seventy open-ended and unstructured interviews or group meetings and a structured survey with 433 individuals. For a more detailed description of methods, see Rigterink, Kenyi and Schomerus (2014), Schomerus and Rigterink (forthcoming) and Rigterink and Schomerus (forthcoming).

18 Author interview, Ezo, 30 April 2013.

19 Author interview with local leader, Tambura, 13 May 2013.

References

Accorsi, S., M. Fabiani, B. Nattabi, B. Corrado, R. Iriso, E. O. Ayella, B. Pido, P. A. Onek, M. Ogwang and S. Declich (2005) 'The disease profile of poverty: morbidity and mortality in northern Uganda in the context of war, population displacement and HIV/AIDS', *Transactions of the Royal Society of Tropical Medicine and Hygiene*, 99(3): 226–33.

Agamben, G. (1993) *The Coming Community*, Minneapolis: University of Minnesota Press.

Ahadi, A. S. and O. Stoltz (2004) *Lost Children*, Germany/France, 90 mins.

Allen, T. (2006) *Trial Justice: The International Criminal Court and the Lord's Resistance Army*, London: Zed Books.

Allen, T. and M. Schomerus (2006) 'A hard homecoming: lessons learned from the reception centre process on effective interventions for former "abductees" in northern Uganda', Washington, DC and Kampala: USAID/UNICEF.

Association of Concerned Africa Scholars (2012) 'ACAS statement to the U.S. government about the Lord's Resistance Army and Central Africa'.

Bailey, B., L. Poole and J. Russel (2003) *Invisible Children*, USA, 55 mins.

Bigombe, B. and J. Prendergast (2006) 'Stop the crisis in northern Uganda', *Philadelphia Inquirer*.

Bøås, M. and K. C. Dunn (2007) *African Guerrillas: Raging against the machine*, Boulder, CO: Lynne Rienner.

Bradshaw, P. (2012) 'Kony2012 – review', *Guardian*.

Branch, A. (2008) 'Gulu Town in war … and peace? Displacement, humanitarianism and post-war crisis', Crisis States Working Paper.

— (2011) *Displacing Human Rights: War and Intervention in Northern Uganda*, New York: Oxford University Press.

Brockmeier, J. (2002) 'Remembering and forgetting: narrative as cultural memory', *Culture & Psychology*, 8(1): 15–43.

Bruner, J. (2004) 'Life as narrative', *Social Research*, 71(3): 691–710.

Bussmann, J. (2010) *The Worst Date Ever: War Crimes, Hollywood Heart-throbs and Other Abominations or how it took a comedy writer to expose Africa's secret war*, New York: Pan.

Caruso, N. (2006) 'Refuge from the Lord's Resistance Army in Uganda: a report from a Médecins Sans Frontières team leader', *Emerg. Med. Australas.*, 18(3): 295–8.

Cook, K. (2007) *Stolen Angels: The kidnapped girls of Uganda*, Toronto: Penguin Canada.

Doom, R. and K. Vlassenroot (1999) 'Kony's message: a new Koine? The Lord's Resistance Army in Uganda', *African Affairs*, 98(390): 5–36.

Dunn, K. C. (2004) 'Uganda: the Lord's Resistance Army', *Review of African Political Economy*, 31(99): 139–42.

Dunson, D. H. (2008) *Child, Victim, Soldier: The loss of innocence in Uganda*, Maryknoll, NY: Orbis.

Eichstaedt, P. H. (2009) *First Kill Your Family: Child soldiers of Uganda and the Lord's Resistance Army*, Chicago, IL: Lawrence Hill.

Ellis, S. (1999) *The Mask of Anarchy: The Destruction of Liberia and the Religious Dimension of an African Civil War*, New York: NYU Press.

Evera, S. V. (2002) 'Why states believe foolish ideas: non-self evaluation by states and societies', *Security Studies Program*, pp. 1–46.

Fassin, D. (2007) 'Humanitarianism as a politics of life', *Public Culture*, 19(3): 499–520.

Fine, S. and A. Nix Fine (2007) *War/Dance*, USA, 105 mins.

Finnstroem, S. (2008a) 'An African hell of colonial imagination? The Lord's Resistance Army/Movement in Uganda, another story', *Politique Africaine*, 112: 1–21.

— (2008b) *Living with Bad Surroundings: War, history, and everyday moments in northern Uganda*, Durham, NC: Duke University Press.

Floating Sheep (2012) 'Mapping #Kony2012 on Twitter', www.floatingsheep.org/2012/04/mapping-kony2012-on-twitter.html.

Flock, E. (2012) 'Kony 2012 screening

in Uganda met with anger, rocks
thrown at screen', *Washington Post*.

French, J. R. P., Jr, and B. H. Raven
(1950) 'The bases of social power', in
D. Cartwright, *Studies in Social Power*,
Institute for Social Research.

Gordon, S., C. Vandewint and
S. Lehmeier (2007) 'Reluctant hosts:
the impact of the Lord's Resistance
Army on communities in Western
Equatoria state, Southern Sudan',
World Vision.

Halbwachs, M. (1992 [1925]) *On Collective Memory*, Chicago, IL: University
of Chicago Press.

Hargitay, M. and J. Prendergast (2009)
'Law & Order: SVU takes on the issue
of child soldiers and sex slaves in
Africa', *Huffington Post*, 30 March.

Hoffman, D. (2005) 'West-African warscapes: violent events as narrative
blocs: the disarmament at Bo, Sierra
Leone', *Anthropological Quarterly*,
79(2): 328–53.

Human Rights Watch (2009) 'The Christmas massacres: LRA attacks on civilians in northern Congo', New York.

ICG (International Crisis Group) (2008)
'Northern Uganda: the road to peace,
with or without Kony', Africa Report
no. 146, Nairobi/Brussels.

Inner City Press (2007) 'UN's Louise
Arbour calls Lord's Resistance
Army a "criminal enterprise" with
no political agenda', M. R. Lee,
28 February, www.innercitypress.
com/arbour022807.html.

Invisible Children (2011) *Protection Plan:
A look at Invisible Children's Protection Plan, our comprehensive strategy
to protect LRA-affected communities
in central Africa*, Video, uploaded to
YouTube 17 June.

— (2012) *Kony2012*.

— (2013a) 'Annual report 2012', San
Diego.

— (2013b) 'Protection Plan', San Diego.

Invisible Children and Resolve (n.d.) LRA
Crisis Tracker, www.lracrisistracker.
com.

Jackson, P. (2009) '"Negotiating with
ghosts": religion, conflict and peace
in northern Uganda', *The Round Table*,
98(402): 319–31.

Lamwaka, C. (2011) *The Raging Storm:
Civil War and Failed Peace Processes
in Northern Uganda, 1986–2005*,
Kampala: Fountain.

Lee, M. R. (2007) 'UN's Louise Arbour
calls Lord's Resistance Army a
"criminal enterprise" with no
political agenda', InterPress Service,
28 February.

LRA (1996) 'LRA policy definitions and
explanations', Unpublished LRA
document.

LRM Team (2012) 'Behind the "Kony2012"
facade: the fear of the political
triumph of native and indigenous
African people and other hidden and
real reasons for the United States led
"Rambo" type military campaign in
central Africa', LMP Team.

Martell, P. (2010) 'South Sudan to arm
militias against Uganda rebels', Juba:
AFP.

McDonnell, F. J. H. and G. Akallo (2007)
Girl Soldier: A story of hope for northern Uganda's children, Grand Rapids,
MI: Chosen.

Museveni, Y. K. (1997) *Sowing the Mustard Seed: The struggle for freedom
and democracy in Uganda*, New York:
Macmillan Education.

Obote, A. M. (1990) 'Notes on concealment of genocide in Uganda', Lusaka.

Olweny, O. (2006) 'LRA/M opening
speech at first Juba Peace Talks
opening ceremony', Juba.

Omach, P. (2002) 'Civil war and internal
displacement in northern Uganda:
1986–1998', Network of Ugandan
Researchers and Research Users
(NURRU).

PBS (2012) 'KONY 2012: analyzing
the viral documentary video',

H. McIntosh, www.pbs.org/pov/
blog/2012/03/kony-2012-analyzing-
the-viral-documentary-video/.
Prunier, G. (2004) 'Rebel movements
and proxy warfare: Uganda, Sudan
and the Congo (1986–99)', *African
Affairs*, 103(412): 359–83.
Richards, P. (1996) *Fighting for the Rain
Forest: War, Youth and Resources in
Sierra Leone*, London: James Currey.
RightsViews (2012) 'Opinion and
research from the human rights
community at Columbia University',
Google web search interest by
region and date, search term 'Kony',
3–10 March, CBR Views, blogs.
cuit.columbia.edu/rightsviews/
files/2012/03/google-search-kony.
jpg.
Rigterink, A. S. and M. Schomerus
(forthcoming) 'Information is liberating? The impact of exposure to
radio on fear and political attitudes:
results from a natural experiment'.
Rigterink, A. S., J. Kenyi and M. Schomerus (2014) 'Report of the Justice
and Security Research Programme
survey in Western Equatoria South
Sudan (first round May 2013)',
London: London School of Economics
and Political Science.
Schomerus, M. (2007) 'The Lord's
Resistance Army in Sudan: a history
and overview', Working Paper no. 8,
Geneva: Small Arms Survey.
— (2012) 'How not to change the world:
Kony2012', CNN.com, March.
Schomerus, M. and L. de Vries (2014)
'Improvising border security: a
situation of "security pluralism"
along South Sudan's borders with
the Democratic Republic of Congo',
Security Dialogue, 45(3).
Schomerus, M. and A. Rigterink (forth-
coming) 'The fear factor is a main

thing: how radio influences civilians'
perception of security and political
structures in areas of South Sudan
affected by the Lord's Resistance
Army'.
Schomerus, M., T. Allen and K. Vlassenroot (2011) 'Obama takes on the
LRA: why Washington sent troops
to Central Africa', *Foreign Affairs*,
15 November.
— (2012) 'Kony2012 and the prospects
for change: examining the viral
campaign', *Foreign Affairs*, 12 March.
Taub, A. (ed.) (2012) *Beyond Kony 2012:
Atrocity, Awareness and Activism in
the Internet Age*, E-book, Leanpub.
Tillon, N. (2012) 'GuestBlog: Beyond
Kony2012', E. S. Kangoyangala.
Tindifa, S. B. (2006) 'Listen to the peo-
ple! A call for an inclusive approach
to the peace process in northern
Uganda: a report on the study on
peace and reconciliation in northern
Uganda', Kampala: Human Rights and
Peace Centre, Makerere University.
Titeca, K. and M. Sebastian (2014) 'Why
did Invisible Children dissolve?',
Washington Post Monkey Cage,
30 December.
US Embassy Kampala (2007) 'Northern
Uganda notes: (Aug 11–Aug 24,
2007)', Kampala: Wikileaks, 07KAM-
PALA13.
Vinci, A. (2005) 'The strategic use of fear
by the Lord's Resistance Army', *Small
Wars and Insurgencies*, 16(3): 360–81.
WHO (World Health Organization)
(2005) 'Health and mortality survey
among internally displaced persons
in Gulu, Kitgum and Pader districts,
northern Uganda', Kampala: Ministry
of Health, Republic of Uganda.
Woody, J. M. (2003) 'When narrative
fails', *Philosophy, Psychiatry, & Psychology*, 10(4): 329–45.

8 | GETTING AWAY WITH MASS MURDER: THE SPLA AND ITS AMERICAN LOBBIES

Alex de Waal

Introduction: unscripted atrocities

South Sudan's civil war began on the evening of 15 December 2013. Over the next three days, government soldiers killed hundreds of civilians in Juba, immediately after which rebel soldiers also went on a killing spree as they overran the town of Bor (UNMISS 2014). The atrocities were also described by John Prendergast of the Enough Project (2014b: 2):

> At the outset of the conflict in mid-December 2013, Dinka soldiers of the Presidential Guard conducted targeted killings in Nuer neighborhoods in Juba and Bentiu, going door-to-door in search of Nuer and executing hundreds. We visited the main U.N. compound in Juba, where over 27,000 internally displaced people – mainly Nuers – have sought sanctuary, and listened to harrowing stories of ethnic targeting.

Prendergast concluded (ibid.: 7):

> The opportunity certainly presents itself for President Kiir to rebuild [his] legacy of reconciliation in the way he approaches the peace process, the constitution, and national dialogue. Through grand gestures and inclusive initiatives, President Kiir can reset the post-independence clock and create opportunities to address governance shortcomings and conflict drivers in a transparent, inclusive manner.

One suspects that if Prendergast or other American advocates had compiled first-hand evidence for mass ethnic killing by Sudanese president Omar al-Bashir's elite units, they would have made different recommendations. It is unusual for the Enough Project to be more cautious in speaking out against human rights violations than the chairperson of the African Union Commission, but this is what happened.[1] One month after civil war broke out, Enough's Satellite Sentinel Project, intended to provide real-time information on atrocities (SSP 2011), had yet to provide a single image or issue a single report. This was not due to ignorance. Prendergast's testimony to the Senate on 9 January 2014 showed that he understood the dimensions of the crisis (Prendergast 2014a). But atrocities by the Sudan People's Liberation Movement/Army (SPLM/A) were not in Enough's script, and its public figures struggled to explain them. George Clooney wrote an op-ed that reads as an apologia for the Juba government, trying to explain away the violence as the inevitable growing pains of a young nation (Clooney 2013). Pointing out this instance of double standards would be a trivial exercise were it not for the fact that American advocates had, over the years, extended a remarkable moral indulgence to the leaders of the SPLM/A that is not only distasteful but arguably a contributor to the sense of impunity enjoyed by those who perpetrated the mass atrocities of December 2013 and thereafter. This demands our scrutiny.

The background supposition of this chapter is that a progressive, transformational activism requires two main preconditions, namely (1) a progressive social or political movement in Sudan as the principal actor and (2) an international activist group ready to recognize and support this. This chapter argues that Sudan did indeed possess such a movement, but it was not the SPLM/A. Indeed, the democratic forces in Sudan were overtaken by a regressive resistance army masquerading as a liberation movement. Members of a policy lobby in Washington, DC well knew the nature of the SPLM/A, but decided to set aside their knowledge and concerns in favour of unconditional support.

This policy lobby group had one foot inside government and one foot outside. Over the years, the most important advocacy positions arose within successive administrations – those of Clinton, Bush Junior and Obama – and were then endorsed by advocates outside government. However, the Washington activists were not simple mouthpieces for official policy, in two main respects. First, they reflected the views of only a select group of people inside the administration, and not others. In fact, they were used as an instrument in internal policy struggles within the government. Secondly, the advocates took high-profile and inflexible positions that created difficulties for policy-makers who wanted to adjust US policies to respond to changing conditions, or to criticize the SPLM/A.

The American position had far-reaching impacts on South Sudanese domestic politics. The leaders of the SPLM/A came to believe that the normal rules did not apply to them. This disposition was conducive to corruption, militarism, recklessness and ultimately to perpetrating mass atrocity.

This chapter summarizes the SPLM/A's record on democracy and human rights, seeking to identify the particular role that US lobby and advocacy organizations played at key moments. It does not deal with the record of the Sudanese government and how Western governments and lobbies have dealt with that government. This is because, whatever the misdeeds of that government, the record of the SPLM/A and its fellow travellers is a worthy topic of study in itself. The chapter deals in passing with the Sudanese democratic opposition, noting mainly that a non-violent civic movement achieved goals that the SPLM/A aspired to, but never achieved.

Being on the 'right side'

Since it was founded in 1983, the record of the SPLM/A, during the war and then in the governments it headed, first the autonomous Government of Southern Sudan from 2005 to 2011 and subsequently the sovereign Government of the Republic of South Sudan, has been unremittingly deplorable. The SPLM/A did not tolerate dissent, systematically failed to build institutions, encouraged corruption, tribalism and militarism, and perpetrated grievous human rights violations, often amounting to war crimes and worse. This record, not the purported inevitable fragility of a new African country, was the root of the political and human rights crisis of 2013.

When American activists adopted the SPLM/A as their partners in the late 1990s, it required them to forget what they knew. For the previous decade, American policy-makers and advocates had no illusions about the SPLM/A (Human Rights Watch 1994; Prendergast 1996). The turning point occurred in 1997 when, following an intensive internal review, President Bill Clinton quietly adopted a policy of regime change in Sudan by proxy. He had decided that, because of the Sudanese government's policy of destabilizing its neighbours and hosting terrorists, the USA would discreetly support the efforts of the 'front-line states' – Eritrea, Ethiopia and Uganda – as well as Egypt, to give military support to the armed opposition and in particular the SPLA (De Waal 2004). On 10 December 1997 in Kampala, Secretary of State Madeleine Albright met with the SPLM chairman, Dr John Garang, and other opposition leaders. Her intentions were made clear in a statement attributed to a senior member of the administration: 'This meeting is a demonstration of support for a [future] regime that will not let Khartoum become a viper's nest for terrorist activities.'[2] Three individuals within the administration were identified with the new policy: Susan Rice (Assistant Secretary of State for Africa), Gayle Smith (National Security Council) and John Prendergast (deputizing for both).

Before that date, US advocacy on southern Sudan had been focused on humanitarian issues and was highly critical of both the Khartoum government and the SPLA factions. Afterwards, advocates extended political support to the SPLM/A and went quiet on its record, sub-ordinating judgement on human rights violations to the perceived justice of the wider cause.

American advocates inside and outside the administration did not create the SPLM/A, nor did they turn its leadership into an abusive, militarized, anti-democratic, corrupt and feckless elite. However, for fifteen years they held the SPLM/A and its leaders in high regard but to low standards, creating the impression among southern Sudanese that honesty and integrity did not matter. The advocates' motivations appear to have been as much hatred of Khartoum as friendship with the SPLM/A leadership, a combination that contributed to a Manichaean account in which Khartoum was designated as evil, while the comparably corrupt and militaristic SPLM/A was good. Hamilton (2012) writes of a group of Washington activists who called themselves 'the council':

> The group was united by a respect for Garang. The men acknow-ledge that his SPLM fighters committed horrific crimes during the war, and say they often had highly critical conversations with Garang. But they say they never doubted that they backed the right side. 'You have these well-trained guys in Khartoum who are murderers and never keep an agreement,' said [one]. 'How do you treat them equally?'

The American activists on Sudan were inside and outside government, associated with both Democrats and Republicans, and represented human rights and humanitarian lobbies, the Christian right, Jewish groups and the Black Caucus. It was a remarkably broad and resilient coalition, each member of which had joined for its own reasons. Human rights groups had become interested in Sudan in the late 1980s, and humanitarian agencies had become active in southern Sudan following the launch of Operation Lifeline Sudan, a ground-breaking initiative for delivering relief to civilians on both sides of the civil war, in 1989. For the Jewish groups, southern Sudan became a means not only of opposing an Islamist government with ties to Israel's enemies, but also a way of making political connections with African-Americans and the Christian right. They scored a notable success in 1996. The immediate precursor to this was a visit by Louis Farrakhan of the Nation of Islam to Khartoum, where he denounced criticism of Sudan's human rights record as propaganda, and made the provocative error of saying that reports of slavery were invented. Eager to damage Farrakhan's credentials among African-Americans, for whom the issue of slavery resonated deeply, Christian groups organized for two journalists from the *Baltimore Sudan* to travel to southern Sudan and 'buy back' African slaves for $500 each. African Rights noted, 'Slavery therefore became the locus of a proxy war between political opponents in the U.S.' (1997: 353) This broad-based advocacy coalition meant that when the administration adopted a regime-change policy the following year, it was readily embraced by activists.

Thereafter, although the activists followed official US policies rather than generating them, they had a very important policy impact: once they had adopted a position, they clung tenaciously to it. As a result, it was difficult for the administration to change its policies. For example, when the SPLM/A misbehaved, US government officials had limited scope for rebuking its leaders or threatening to cut assistance, because they would be subject to high-decibel public criticism. By the same token, when the USA imposed sanctions on the Sudanese government in response to a particular violation, it was extraordinarily hard for the administration to lift that sanction, even when Khartoum complied with the US demand.

The position I take in this chapter will, for sure, be vigorously challenged. Lobbyists will make the principal counter-argument that the government in Khartoum is untrustworthy, venal and violent, and that it is the root cause of the ills that afflict South Sudan. The Government of Sudan may indeed be these things, and worse. However, a liberation movement worthy of the name surely ought to hold itself to *higher* standards than its oppressor. Part of the tragedy of South Sudan and of the hopes for democracy in northern Sudan is that the SPLM/A did not hold itself to a higher standard, and was rarely pushed to do so by its friends. The foreign champions of the SPLM/A will argue that they made private representations to the South Sudanese leadership. This may be true, but such quiet diplomacy was never matched by tough action or public words until it was too late.

Formative days: the 1980s

Sudan has a vibrant history of progressive politics (Abu Sharaf 2010). However, progressive secularism suffered three major setbacks in the 1970s and early 1980s. The first was the decimation of the Sudanese Communist Party after a failed coup in 1971. The second was the failure of Sudan's developmental decade of the 1970s, a time when the prospects for multiculturalism and economic development appeared bright. The third was the turn to Islamism and intolerance in the late 1970s and 1980s. Nonetheless, such was the resilience of Sudanese civil society that a broad-based non-violent popular uprising brought down the dictatorship of Jaafar Nimeiri and ushered in a transitional government committed to returning the country to democratic rule (El-Affendi 2012). The popular uprising not only sought to end the war but also to bring the SPLM into government. Sudanese democrats stood on the brink of achieving their goals.

This democratic opening failed, for several reasons. One was that it was dealt a shattering blow by the IMF, which suspended Sudan for failure to service its debt. Another was divided and ineffective leadership. But the third, and possibly the most important, blow to democratic hopes was the summary rejection of the popular uprising and its democratic programme by the SPLA (De Waal 2013). The SPLA commander-in-chief pronounced the transitional government of 1985 a fraud and insisted that the SPLM/A was the only truly democratic movement in Sudan. He did not consult his comrades in making this decision (Nyaba 1996).

Why did John Garang do this? His defenders will argue that he presciently foresaw the descent of the democratic government into a sectarian jihadist agenda. But that overlooks the extent to which the SPLA's rejectionism was self-fulfilling: it placed the new government in an impossible position. It was bankrupt and unable to prosecute the war. To preserve his coalition, the elected prime minister, Sadiq al-Mahdi, turned to the Islamists, and to fight the war he turned to a strategy of arming tribal militia, principally groups known as the Murahaliin, which were responsible for massacre, enslavement and destruction across a large swathe of Bahr al Ghazal (Amnesty International 1990).

A more credible explanation is simple political ambition on the part of Garang. He did not want to share power and had little interest in the well-being of the Sudanese people, save in the broadest historical sense of wanting them to achieve a socialist united Sudan. The SPLA spent much of the mid-1980s fighting other southern Sudanese groups such as Anyanya II and various Equatorian militias such as the Murle and Mandari (Africa Watch 1990; Nyaba 1996). Garang imposed starvation sieges on southern towns and shot down civilian planes, and publicly justified these actions. He disposed ruthlessly of potential rivals. These decisions were Garang's alone. The purported decision-making body of the SPLM/A, the Political-Military High Command, met for the first time only in September 1991, when Garang's leadership had been challenged.

This record of dictatorial ruthlessness and disregard for civil administration, humanitarian needs or political accountability characterized Garang's entire political-military career. Like many such dictators, however, he also possessed charisma and vision. Rebecca Hamilton (2011) describes how he won over a group of Americans, including professional humanitarians such as Roger Winter and Brian D'Silva, John Prendergast, who turned to public advocacy after he left government in 2001, Ted Dagne, a long-time staffer at the Congressional Research Service, and Eric Reeves, a professor of English at Smith College, Massachusetts, who was an indefatigable writer on Sudan and a relentless critic of Khartoum. Susan Rice and Gayle Smith were honorary members. Hamilton writes of Garang's impact: 'Over six feet tall and more than 200 pounds, the rebel leader had a laugh – and a personality – that filled a room. "You meet Dr. John, you get converted," said Winter, who first met Garang in 1986.' The SPLA leader was often more comfortable with foreigners than with his own people, who were not so easy to convert with size and charm.

Towards a rebel–NGO coalition

The fall of the military regime in Ethiopia in 1991 and the end of tight control of the SPLA's political management were heralded by many in the SPLA as an opportunity for opening up. Instead, however, they led to a disastrous split in the SPLA and horrendous massacres perpetrated by contending factions. The very existence of Garang's 'SPLA-Mainstream' at times seemed precarious. Thereafter, Garang's survival depended largely on his value to external patrons – Sudan's neighbouring countries, as well as the USA. By this point, Garang's greatest assets were his reputation for never having compromised with Khartoum (unlike his rivals), and his ability to articulate a political vision for Sudan – which, crucially, included a genuine commitment to a united country rather than southern secession.

Garang strenuously resisted any form of political reform or structuring of the movement. Compromise was forced on him, resulting in a grudging commitment to a platform of self-determination for southern Sudan and a 'National Convention' (Rolandsen 2005). Garang had many critics within the SPLM/A, and their strategy was patience: to stick with the leadership until peace was achieved, and then pursue their divergent agendas, which included (*inter alia*) independence for South Sudan and democratization. Garang endeavoured to implement only the minimum concessions. Throughout the decade, his priority was always to shore up his internal supremacy, striking first at an internal rival in preference to fighting Khartoum.

Garang's embrace of Western humanitarians and advocates was opportunistic. He did not trust international NGOs, especially after a number of them appeared to sympathize with his challenger, Riek Machar, in 1991, and when the churches seemed to be gaining political influence based on mediating internal conflicts within southern Sudan.

During the early 1990s, there were competing models of international engagement with southern Sudan, none of which focused on political solidarity with the SPLM/A – although Garang sought to benefit tactically from each one. The major engagement was the UN-run Operation Lifeline Sudan (OLS), which involved major international NGOs under conditions of neutrality. Established in 1989, the OLS was the first instance of the UN providing humanitarian assistance across battle lines and across borders to civilians under the control of an insurgent group. It was a pioneering instance of impartial humanitarianism that challenged the sovereignty of a state, albeit with government consent. Harsh criticism was directed at OLS for giving the Sudanese government undue control over what relief assistance was allowed into SPLA-held areas, and allowing both sides to manipulate aid to their advantage, possibly prolonging the war (Karim and Duffield 1996; African Rights 1997). Nonetheless, in the 1990s the OLS model appeared set to be the dominant conduit for international humanitarian and human rights engagement with Sudan.

In parallel, led by groups such as Christian Solidarity International, were anti-Muslim campaigners, many of whom focused on slave redemption. This became a useful exercise, especially for local SPLA commanders, who thereby gained access to ready cash. The SPLA high command struggled to centralize this source of revenue. A third strand was efforts by established missionary churches in southern Sudan seeking 'people-to-people' peace. The SPLA at first resisted these, but later saw opportunities for co-opting the efforts in support of mobilizing support against Khartoum. Lastly, there were secular political solidarity efforts, including Norwegian People's Aid (NPA), which sometimes directly supplied the SPLA, and African Rights, which ran an operation to the SPLA-held areas of the Nuba mountains with a reformist-solidarity spirit based on promoting self-reliance and local leadership. The SPLA gladly made use of the NPA logistics and support, but felt threatened by the African Rights programme with its emphasis on building a local judiciary and encouraging democratization, and moved to shut it down as soon as it expanded beyond the Nuba mountains, where it had enjoyed the protection of the local command.

The political context of humanitarian and human rights efforts changed in the mid-1990s. This began when the three front-line states – Eritrea, Ethiopia and Uganda – coordinated political and military support to the Sudanese opposition, in reaction to Khartoum's destabilization of their countries. American policy-makers were thereby drawn into supporting the SPLA and the regional policy of containment and possible regime change. The USA toyed with the idea of direct military support to the SPLA but was dismayed by the extent of corruption and disorganization it found, and so preferred to provide arms to the neighbouring countries instead.

However, USAID initiated direct assistance to SPLM institutions, through an ad hoc programme called Sudan Transitional Assistance and Relief (STAR). Part of the impulse for these efforts was a belief that the SPLM should be governing its own affairs, and to do this it needed to build capacity for its institutions. The implicit model was to establish civilian and humanitarian organizations in southern Sudan, comparable to those which had existed in rebel-held Eritrea and Tigray ten years earlier. Some of those instrumental in the US policy shift were strongly influenced by Ethiopian and Eritrean policy and by the experience of solidarity with the Ethiopian and Eritrean rebels in the 1980s (Duffield and Prendergast 1994). However, this approach required that the SPLM/A shift from its military-first paradigm of liberation warfare to adopting an agenda of socio-economic transformation and institution-building, even while the war continued. The SPLM/A leaders were unwilling or unable to do this: they were building an entirely different political system based on patrimonialism (Pinaud 2014). The UN agencies could not directly fund a rebel organization, and indeed USAID itself was required to develop innovative operating principles in order to work hand-in-glove with the SPLM/A. The STAR programme did not meet its goals, but nonetheless it allowed for the development of camaraderie between American aid workers and their southern Sudanese counterparts.

Advocacy, peace and democracy

The premise of the 1997 US policy shift was that the front-line states would remove President Bashir by force of arms. In 1998, however, Eritrea and Ethiopia went to war with each other, and Uganda and Rwanda also fought in the Democratic Republic of Congo. The Sudanese government was spared, and because the SPLA was too small and poorly led to win, the war entered a stalemate. But the US lobby on Sudan – the liberals in the Clinton administration and the broad coalition including the religious groups – was uninterested in a peace process, still wanting regime change. Peace advocacy was confined to a handful of groups, such as Justice Africa. The principle of Justice Africa's activity was that the peace process should be civilianized and inclusive, building upon the model of the 1985 non-violent civic movement in Khartoum – a movement that had achieved more for democratic regime change than the armed struggle. The proposal for the 'Committee for Human Rights in the Transition in Sudan' stated that 'the armed struggle has run its course', and intended to bring northern opposition (armed and unarmed) into the peace process. Particular emphasis was put on the Beja in eastern Sudan and Darfur – both locations in which rebellion was under way or incipient. The USA offered to support it as part of the STAR programme but then, when Garang objected, withdrew offers of funding and political backing. Nonetheless, Justice Africa's Kampala conferences went ahead, bringing representatives from civil society, civilian parties, from Darfur and the Beja, and gaining traction among non-governmental donors (Abdelsalam and De Waal 2000; De Waal and Ajawin 2002), but not the USA. This is important because the same government policy-makers who rejected the broadening of the peace process to include (among others) the Darfurians and the civilian parties included individuals who reappeared as 'activists' just a few years later.

In early 2001, the American initiative to support peace in Sudan came from the Republican Party, newly in office. It drew upon more conservative officials in the State Department who had opposed Clinton's regime-change policy and upon a report by Francis Deng and Stephen Morrison that articulated a 'one country, two systems' model. One key actor in the administration was Andrew Natsios, who reached across party lines to involve some of the veteran humanitarians, such as Roger Winter and Brian D'Silva. The principal worries of the incoming administration were, first, that peace was improbable, so the burden of taking the initiative forward should be shared with other international partners (such as Britain and Norway), and secondly, the religious right would be opposed to compromises with Khartoum. For that reason, the candidate first tapped as Special Envoy turned it down, and President George W. Bush instead chose a senior Republican and minister, Jack Danforth, whom he hoped would be able to keep the more militant Christians at bay.

Garang was a reluctant peacemaker, but nonetheless finally entered into negotiations with Vice-President Ali Osman Taha, which led to the Comprehensive Peace Agreement (CPA). Even as he entered government, Garang kept his plans secret and most likely had several different options under consideration. The key elements of the agreement, negotiated privately between him and Ali Osman Taha, are still not known. But Garang undoubtedly saw the CPA as a chance to build a national power base in the north. The SPLM as a political party would now be tested: for the first time since the 1980s, would it be able to live up to its promise of being the vanguard of national democratization?

Garang met an untimely end in a helicopter crash in July 2005, leaving the SPLM leaderless. The movement spent much of the next five years unclear about whether it was in government or opposition, and no more interested in the prospects for national democratization than was the National Congress Party (NCP) headed by President Bashir. Meanwhile, the war and atrocities in Darfur emboldened those US activists who nurtured dreams of regime change. Along with the polarization of politics in northern Sudan, the aggressive posturing of Washington advocates encouraged the SPLM/A also to prepare for a military option against Khartoum. Based on the signals they received from those lobbyists, the SPLM/A leaders were confident that the USA would support their plans for an armed takeover. In October 2007, the SPLM withdrew from the Government of National Unity and SPLA generals prepared to relaunch the war. The northern generals – who had done much to provoke the crisis in the first place – were so alarmed by the prospect of an SPLA-led attack on Khartoum that they agreed to a US proposal for de-escalation, but it required an intervention from President Bush for the SPLA to stand down its troops (Natsios 2012: 182–4).

The greatest missed opportunity of the CPA was the chance for democratization. The ruling NCP was at most a reluctant convert to political pluralism, but the SPLM had formally espoused democracy since the early 1990s. However, the SPLM was unable to put together a cogent strategy for the 2010 national elections. In the south, the SPLM leadership understood that participating in the elections was a *sine qua non* for continued cooperation from the NCP, but the 'northern sector' of the SPLM decided, after long prevarication, to support radical elements in the northern opposition and boycott the polls. The result was that the party emerged from the elections weakened and divided: in the south, it won a handsome plurality but the electoral violations were comparable to, or exceeded, those of the NCP in the north, while in the north the SPLM failed to inherit the mantle of organized progressive politics.

The 2010 elections showed again that Washington advocates stood in uncritical solidarity with the SPLM. They were vocal about electoral abuses by the NCP but silent on SPLM violations. They focused on endorsing (and encouraging) the tactical manoeuvres of the SPLM, without attending to the bigger challenges of building a democratic system in Sudan.

Independence

The struggle to separate southern Sudan from Sudan took more than fifty years and was a bloody and bitter affair. But the actual moment of secession was smooth. The SPLM/A leadership and their foreign supporters had long prepared for a showdown with Khartoum. It did not happen. The most remarkable event in the story of the creation of South Sudan did not fit the script, and has been little noticed.

On 4 January 2011, just five days before voting began in the referendum on self-determination, President Bashir travelled to Juba. Setting aside the drafts that his advisers had prepared, Bashir made his own personal speech. He promised to respect the southerners' wishes. Having spent his life fighting for the unity of the country, Bashir said that if secession were the price of peace, he would accept it.[3] It was a remarkably gracious speech, which set the tone for an uncontested vote, carried out in an atmosphere of celebration. That same evening, after returning to Khartoum, Bashir addressed a protest rally, in which residents of the city were complaining about austerity measures that were already coming into effect.

The USA had pressed President Bashir to concur with an exercise in self-determination that clearly had a foregone conclusion. It was not only an enormous, possibly irreparable blow to the legitimacy of Bashir's government, but also a huge economic loss. With the separation of the South, Sudan lost 50 per cent of its government revenues, and 80 per cent of its foreign currency earnings. Because of the financial sanctions imposed at various times during the previous twenty years, and the accumulation of debt dating back to the 1970s, Sudan faced a huge fiscal crisis. A month before the referendum, President Obama sent Senator John Kerry, chairman of the Senate Foreign Relations Committee, to Khartoum to offer a deal: the USA would begin to lift the economic sanctions on Sudan, to alleviate the coming economic crisis, in return for Bashir allowing the peaceful secession of the South.

Bashir kept his side of the bargain, but Kerry was unable to deliver on his. Fired up by the Washington lobbies, Congress was not ready to make even the smallest step to lift the economic pressures on Sudan. By the time that Bashir travelled to Juba on 9 July to fulfil his promise to celebrate the independence of South Sudan, he had received no material credit for his action. At those independence celebrations, he received not a word of thanks from Kiir, nor from the Americans who spoke. This should have been a worrying augury for the future: a mood of reconciliation is a far better start for relations between the halves of a partitioned country than a sense of triumphalism on one side, and grievance on the other.

In the referendum tally, the vote in favour of separation was a remarkable 99.83 per cent. In any other country, such a result would have been scorned, but in this case international observers heralded it as a triumph for democracy. This should have been another warning, about the nature of the SPLM's democratic commitment and the standard to which it was being held.

The border war

Just six months after independence, South Sudan took the extraordinary decision to shut down its oil production. It did this in response to an unresolved dispute over the level of payments to be made to Sudan for use of the pipeline and export infrastructure and over other elements of the post-secession transitional financial arrangements, as well as Khartoum's illegal diversion and lifting of a proportion of South Sudan's oil in December 2011 and January 2012. The African Union had drawn up proposals to address all of these issues. Nonetheless, South Sudan went ahead with a comprehensive shutdown.

Oil revenues accounted for over 70 per cent of South Sudan's GDP and 98 per cent of government revenue at the time, and the shutdown was predicted to bring South Sudan's economy to disaster within a few months (World Bank 2012). In fact, the economic crisis was slower to mature than predicted, but by early 2013 government ministries had ground to a halt, and the government could pay the army only by borrowing billions of dollars at commercial rates against future oil production. Northern Sudan had also undergone considerable hardship, which contributed to urban protests in September and October 2013. But South Sudan's crisis was more immediate.

The principal reason for South Sudan's decision to shut down its oil production was that it expected it would win a war with Sudan and would therefore have a friendly government in power to the north, as members of the SPLM/A leadership candidly explained to this author. It was a monumental miscalculation, possible only because those leaders were confident of the international economic, political and military support they expected to receive. In the event, the support they received was wholly incommensurate with the financial gap that opened up.

The border war began in January 2012, as a spillover from the renewed conflict in southern Kordofan and Blue Nile in northern Sudan, with the SPLA in South Sudan providing logistical support and weaponry to their brethren, and even deploying their own forces in support. Three months later it escalated into a military encounter between the armies of the two nations, with the SPLA briefly capturing the town of Heglig, just north of the border, which is also the single largest oil-producing location in northern Sudan. The SPLA forces were driven out shortly afterwards, mainly by dissident South Sudanese militia. The invasion of Heglig prompted immediate condemnation from the African Union (AU), the UN and the international community, including a communiqué from the AU Peace and Security Council and UN Security Council Resolution 2046 under Chapter VII. The South Sudanese were shocked by their sudden disfavour.

This was the war that many had feared at the time of the South's separation. The Satellite Sentinel Project (SSP), run by Enough and funded by George Clooney, was set up in 2010 with 'the goals of deterring a return to full-scale civil war between northern and southern Sudan and deterring and documenting threats to civilians along both sides of the border' (SSP 2011). However, it appears that it was set up to report only on violations by northern Sudan. In a total of eighteen reports between the first SPLA incursions in January 2012 and the withdrawal of SPLA forces from almost all their positions in June 2013, there are just three passing mentions of the possibility that the SPLA might have crossed the border. When SPLA forces occupied Heglig and were condemned, implicitly for aggression, by the UN Security Council, the SSP mentioned only that there was 'evidence for destruction of key oil pipeline infrastructure ... SSP cannot make a determination based on the evidence currently available as to ... who destroyed [it]' (SSP 2012). For more than twelve months, SPLA forces were positioned some tens of kilometres north of the Bahr al-Arab in eastern Darfur. The SSP was entirely silent about these. In May 2013, it published a report on the presence of troops in the Safe Demilitarized Border Zone (SDBZ), claiming to have identified a Sudan Armed Forces (SAF) garrison positioned just 3 kilometres north of the centre line, therefore 7 kilometres inside the zone, contrary to the agreement (SSP 2013). What the SSP identified, however, was not an SAF garrison but rather a long-standing SPLA position that had not withdrawn, whose presence had been confirmed by a UN patrol in April.[4] Presumably prompted by officials inside the US administration, who had better information sources, the SSP did not repeat the claim in its next report, but still had the audacity to write to the AU and the UN to tell them what they should do, based on its satellite images, without any ground verification.

The fact that American lobby groups were telling a one-sided story had implications. The SAF high command pays no attention to the lobby groups, but it does communicate with British and American security officers. The SAF generals know they are being watched and know that if they transgress, for example by dropping bombs in South Sudan, they will be caught. So they tend to be careful. For example, in July 2012 a convoy of 108 armed pick-up trucks belonging to the rebel Justice and Equality Movement (JEM) were stationed in Aweil in South Sudan, preparing to move north to attack Sudan. Sudanese generals told the USA that they intended to bomb the convoy and were told that if they attacked before the JEM forces crossed the border, it would be a major infringement. The Sudanese air force mounted a series of attacks on the convoy as it crossed into northern Sudan, and six bombs fell just over one kilometre inside

South Sudan, killing one civilian. Susan Rice, who was serving as US ambassador to the UN, immediately issued a statement which 'strongly condemn[ed] Sudan's July 20 bombing ... [which] constitutes a serious violation of resolution 2046' (US Mission to the UN 2012). The Sudanese generals privately admitted their error.

South Sudan, in contrast, is less sophisticated and has an expectation of impunity. In meetings with senior US officials, including President Kiir's meeting with President Obama on the sidelines of the UN General Assembly in September 2011, South Sudan simply denied that it was supporting northern rebels, or intending to cross the border, or had troops inside northern Sudan. Such denials flew in the face of facts known by US intelligence, and made the South Sudanese look amateur and impudent. Their credibility within the administration suffered. But, confident that they could call on friendly members of Congress, the SPLM leaders appeared not to care.

The new crisis in the South

The SPLM/A and the Government of South Sudan were confident that the established rules of international relations did not apply to them. This was also seen in their internal military operations, which routinely involved large-scale killings.

During the CPA period, the SPLA undertook several campaigns of forcible disarmament that involved very high levels of violence (Small Arms Survey 2006/07). The election results of 2010, especially for a number of governorships, were clearly fraudulent, with SPLM candidates being returned despite good evidence that independent candidates were more plausible winners. International outrage over this fraud was muted because of a focus on the upcoming referendum and relief that there was very little violence associated with the election and its immediate aftermath. However, southern Sudanese unity and restraint were transient, lasting just long enough for the referendum to be held, before a number of rebellions erupted in various parts of South Sudan. The most significant of these was led by George Athor in the northern part of Jonglei State. The conduct of the SPLA in combating these rebellions indicated that it had not undergone significant reform since the end of the civil war: counter-insurgency involved large-scale burning, stealing and killing. The largest and best-documented case of mass atrocity during

SPLA counter-insurgency operations occurred in Jonglei in 2012/13, in response to an insurgency led by David Yau Yau, at the head of mostly ethnic Murle forces. Humanitarian NGOs, diplomats and mainstream human rights organizations documented large-scale violations (MSF 2012; Human Rights Watch 2013), and foreign diplomats – including the US ambassador in Juba – made strong démarches (US Embassy Juba 2013).

The most common explanation for the SPLA's disorderly, tribalistic and abusive conduct is that it is a liberation army that has not transitioned to a regular army, and that effort is needed to regularize and professionalize the army. Such an explanation seems to assume that it is acceptable for a guerrilla army to behave in an undisciplined and hateful manner. This is unfounded. The fact that it named one unit the 'Locust Division' and that newly graduating soldiers were taught the slogan 'Food, wife and property wherever you find them are to be acquired through your might' (African Rights 1997: 84) show that this attitude was not a lapse: for years the SPLA had celebrated destruction. Other liberation armies have a fine record of holding themselves to a higher standard than their adversaries. The disciplined conduct of the SPLA in the Nuba mountains showed that this was possible in Sudan's civil war (African Rights 1995). Although in many cases (Uganda's National Resistance Movement, the Eritrean People's Liberation Front) standards slipped after gaining power, the key observation is that the fact of being a guerrilla army is neither a political nor an ethical justification for misconduct or disorder. The SPLA's problem was never that it was an irregular force, but that it was a militarized, factionalized, authoritarian and politically regressive force from the outset, and never reformed during or after the war.

Nonetheless, as the Jonglei counter-insurgency unfolded during 2012, American lobbyists were at best silent, or at worst publicly defended the indefensible. For example, Eric Reeves tried to explain away the shooting down of a clearly marked UN helicopter by SPLA forces (Reeves 2012). The Enough Project described the conflict in words that could have been taken from a government press release, as 'intercommunal violence' combined with '[a] Sudanese government-backed rebellion led by former council official David Yau Yau [which is] currently destabilizing Jonglei state' (Heaton 2012). Rather than the calls for international military and judicial intervention that have been the hallmark of vocal Western advocacy groups, Enough used language more characteristic of quiet diplomacy, noting that the Jonglei massacres posed a test 'of the ability of the South Sudanese government to fulfill its responsibility to protect and govern in a more inclusive and transparent manner' (Heaton and Hsiao 2012: 1).

The Jonglei atrocities occurred against a deepening crisis of corruption and power struggle within the SPLM leadership. An open letter by four American 'friends of South Sudan' in July 2013 was as close as the American advocates came to public criticism of the SPLM/A (Sudan Tribune 2013). This was not early warning of a political crisis and mass atrocity – such warnings had been sounding for years. Neither was it the first such call, as it followed private and public statements by foreign diplomats.

Conclusions

This chapter has endeavoured to show that the SPLM/A was, from the outset, the perpetrator of systematic human rights violations. The fact that the people of southern Sudan had a fundamentally just cause in resisting the Sudanese government obscured the profoundly flawed nature of the political-military instrument that they were obliged to use in pursuit of their goals. During the early part of the SPLM/A struggle, a powerful civic movement in northern Sudan delivered many of the goals for which the SPLM/A was ostensibly struggling, but the SPLM/A leadership spurned this opportunity. For many years subsequently, international advocacy stood with the people of southern Sudan but was justifiably cautious about embracing the SPLM/A and its leadership, focusing instead mostly on humanitarian issues, local conflict resolution and broadly impartial human rights questions. However, a shift in US policy in the late 1990s generated a new alignment between the SPLM/A and a group inside the US government and some associated individuals. That group very effectively repackaged the SPLM/A and its leadership.

For the SPLM/A leadership, its political alliance with lobbyists in Washington, DC was a formidable political asset. Unfortunately, rather than using this political solidarity to develop and deepen a democratic agenda, the southern Sudanese leadership used it to advance narrow political interests and to ignore or postpone reform. Sudanese progressives have a long history of pursuing their own struggle and enacting democratic change. Some, such as Salah Hassan (2010), have felt that Western advocacy groups have tended to demean and distort their roles. But others have recently identified closely with Washington, DC-based lobby groups. For example, Alhaj Warrag, who shares a political background similar to Hassan's but who is a member of the SPLM, writes that he feels that the Enough Project 'represents' him (Warrag 2013). Is this a cry of despair from a frustrated Sudanese radical or does it represent an important dimension of the predicament of oppressed people, for whom international lobbyists are an important resource? Evidently, the links to the Washington lobbies provide political opportunities and livelihoods, but might they also be a route towards political emancipation? The 'boomerang model' of national and international activism suggests that external links can, over time, lead to a domestication of human rights norms and practices – perhaps not the short cut to revolution of which some Sudanese radicals have dreamed, but a credible road nonetheless.

Unfortunately, despite the progressive rhetoric, the case study of the SPLM/A suggests that this has not happened in South Sudan. The close association between the SPLM/A leadership and the lobbyists exempted South Sudanese elites from the kinds of scrutiny that they long warranted.

This chapter has shown a consistent pattern in US policy-making on southern Sudan since 1997, which is that the administration is in the lead, and activists outside government follow. For the most part, they endorse the official policy, paddling along in the wake of the ship of state. A similar pattern was also observed during the American campaign on Darfur, in which the US administration took a lead on most issues and lobby groups such as the Save Darfur Coalition responded to these initiatives (Hamilton 2011). The activists amplified policy positions and made them less flexible, making it difficult for the administration to respond to the excesses of the SPLM/A with credibility, or to respond to positive changes in Sudanese policy. American policy towards Sudan and the SPLM/A has had poor outcomes with tragic results for the Sudanese and South Sudanese people.

Since 15 December 2013, the Washington lobbyists have, like a spurned lover, turned on their erstwhile best friends. But their favoured instrument, while clothed in democratic language, is coercion. In an open letter to leading members of the US administration, Prendergast and David Abramovitz (of Humanity United) began their list of recommendations with the line, perhaps more candid than they intended: 'the U.S. must invest much more deeply in cultivating coercive influence'.[5]

Notes

1 Enough Project, 'Memorandum: ongoing SPLM political crisis and violence in South Sudan', 18 December 2013, www.enoughproject.org/reports/ memorandum-ongoing-splm-political- crisis-and-violence-south-sudan; African Union Commission, 'The African Union stresses the imperative and urgency of an inclusive political dialogue to address the current crisis in South Sudan; the AU calls for an immediate humanitarian truce', Press release, 21 December 2013.

2 'Quote of the day', *Washington Post*, 11 December 1997, p. A30.

3 Bashir's speech is available at: embed.verite.co/timeline/?source=oAk A4FvqGoYhvdEd1ZmZiMWhPdHItQUN seVpQdUp4NEE&font=Bevan-Potano Sans&maptype=toner&lang=en&heig ht=650.

4 The post was still there in April 2014.

5 Enough Project and Humanity United, 'Open letter on enhancing U.S. policy towards Sudan and South Sudan', 29 April 2014, p. 2.

References

Abdelsalam, A. H. and Alex de Waal (2000) *The Phoenix State: Civil Society and the Future of Sudan*, Trenton, NJ: Red Sea Press.

Abu Sharaf, R. (2010) 'Introduction: Writing the dialectic', *South Atlantic Quarterly*, Special Issue, 'What's left of the left? The view from Sudan', 109(1): 1–8.

Africa Watch (1990) *Denying the 'Honor of Living': Sudan, a human rights disaster*, London and New York.

African Rights (1995) *Facing Genocide: The Nuba of Sudan*, London.

— (1997) *Food and Power in Sudan: A Critique of Humanitarianism*, London.

Amnesty International (1990) 'Sudan: human rights violations in the context of civil war', London.

Clooney, G. (2013) 'George Clooney on how to stop an inferno in South Sudan', *Daily Beast*, 20 December, www.thedailybeast.com/articles/ 2013/12/20/preventing-south-sudan- s-inferno.html.

De Waal, A. (2004) 'The politics of destabilization in the Horn', in A. de Waal (ed.), *Islamism and Its Enemies in the Horn*, London: Hurst.

— (2013) 'Sudan's elusive democratization: civic mobilization, provincial rebellion and chameleon dictatorships', *Journal of Contemporary African Studies*, 31(2): 213–34.

De Waal, A. and Y. Ajawin (2002) *When Peace Comes: Civil Society and Development in Sudan*, Trenton, NJ: Red Sea Press.

Duffield, M. and J. Prendergast (1994) *Without Troops and Tanks: The Emergency Relief Desk and Cross-border Relief Operation into Eritrea and Tigray*, Trenton, NJ: Red Sea Press.

El-Affendi, A. (2012) 'Revolutionary anatomy: the lessons of the Sudanese revolutions of October 1964 and April 1985', *Contemporary Arab Affairs*, 5(2): 292–306.

Hamilton, R. (2011) *Fighting for Darfur: Public action and the struggle to stop genocide*, New York: Palgrave Macmillan.

— (2012) 'Special report: the wonks who sold Washington on South Sudan', Reuters, 11 July, www.reuters.com/article/2012/07/11/us-south-sudan-midwives-idUSBRE86A0GC20120711.

Hassan, S. M. (2010) 'Darfur and the crisis of governance in Sudan: a left perspective', *South Atlantic Quarterly*, Special Issue, 'What's left of the left? The view from Sudan', 109(1): 95–116.

Heaton, L. (2012) 'Root causes of violence in Jonglei, South Sudan', Enough Project, www.enoughproject.org/multimedia/root-causes-violence-jonglei-south-sudan, accessed 5 July 2013.

Heaton, L. and A. Hsiao (2012) '"Sometimes we see ourselves as apart": South Sudan's response to violence in Jonglei', Enough Project, www.enoughproject.org/files/Jonglei-Report.pdf.

Human Rights Watch (1994) *Civilian Devastation: Abuses by all parties in the war in Sudan*, New York.

— (2013) *They are Killing Us: Abuses against civilians in South Sudan's Pibor County*, New York.

Karim, A. and M. Duffield (1996) *OLS: Operation Lifeline Sudan: A Review*, University of Birmingham.

MSF (Médecins Sans Frontières) (2012) 'South Sudan's hidden crisis: how violence against civilians is devastating communities and preventing access to life-saving healthcare in Jonglei', November.

Natsios, A. (2012) *Sudan, South Sudan and Darfur: What everyone needs to know*, New York: Oxford University Press.

Nyaba, P. A. (1996) *The Politics of Liberation in South Sudan: An insider's view*, Kampala: Fountain Press.

Pinaud, C. (2014) 'South Sudan: civil war, predation, and the making of a military aristocracy', *African Affairs*, 113(451): 192–211.

Prendergast, J. (1996) *Frontline Diplomacy: Humanitarian aid and conflict in Africa*, Boulder, CO: Lynne Rienner.

— (2014a) 'The situation in South Sudan', Testimony of John Prendergast, co-founder of Enough Project, Senate Foreign Relations Committee, 9 January.

— (2014b) '"Peace must come soon": a field dispatch from South Sudan', Enough Project, 19 February.

Reeves, E. (2012) 'Why the armed forces of South Sudan shot down a UN helicopter', *Sudan Tribune*, 22 December, www.sudantribune.com/spip.php?article44950.

Rolandsen, O. H. (2005) *Guerrilla Government: Political changes in the Southern Sudan during the 1990s*, Uppsala: Nordiska Afrikainstitutet.

Small Arms Survey (2006/07) 'Anatomy of civilian disarmament in Jonglei State: recent experiences and implications', Human Security Baseline Assessment 3.2, November 2006–February 2007.

SSP (Satellite Sentinel Project) (2011) 'Our story', www.satsentinel.org/our-story, accessed 5 January 2014.

— (2012) 'Pipeline: evidence of the destruction of key oil infrastructure', 21 April, www.satsentinel.org/report/pipeline-evidence-destruction-key-oil-infrastructure-heglig.

— (2013) 'Broken agreement: violations in the demilitarized border zone by Sudan and South Sudan', 6 May, www.satsentinel.org/imagery-broken-agreement-violations-demilitarized-border-zone-sudan-and-south-sudan.

Sudan Tribune (2013) '"Friends of South Sudan" go public with call for "significant changes and reform" in Juba',

7 July, www.sudantribune.com/spip.php?article47220.

UNMISS (2014) 'Interim report on human rights: crisis in South Sudan. Report coverage: 15 December 2013–31 January 2014', Juba: UNMISS Human Rights Division, 21 February.

US Embassy, Juba, South Sudan (2013), 'Press Release: Joint Statement on Ending Conflict in Jonglei State', 18 May.

US Mission to the UN (2012) 'Statement by Ambassador Susan E. Rice, U.S. Permanent Representative to the United Nations, on implementation of UN Security Council Resolution 2046, July 27, 2012'.

Warrag, A. (2013) 'In defense of international activists', Reinventing Peace, sites.tufts.edu/reinventingpeace/2013/05/19/in-defense-of-international-activists/.

World Bank (2012) 'Briefing by Marcelo Guigale, World Bank Director of Economic Policy and Poverty Reduction Programmes for Africa', Note-to-file, 1 March.

Young, J. (2012) *The Fate of Sudan: The origins and consequences of a flawed peace process*, London: Zed Books.

9 | FROM WHOSE PERSPECTIVE ANYWAY? THE QUEST FOR AFRICAN DISABILITY RIGHTS ACTIVISM

Tsitsi Chataika,[1] Maria Berghs, Abraham Mateta and Kudzai Shava

Introduction

Disabled people have always been involved in activism and are situated at the vanguard of myriad forms of protest, such as those for a country's independence, political liberty, peace, and civil and human rights. Nonetheless, this global history has largely been ignored owing to the marginal position of disability within human rights discourses and activism in general, as well as disabled activists from the global South in particular. Furthermore, there has been a kind of delegitimization and re-creation of disability in the global South by the global North through associations with contagion, deficiency, disease, suffering, burden and now poverty in development discourses. Disability thus intersects with neocolonialism, racism, sexism and (dis)ablism, so that situations of double or triple discrimination and oppression come into existence (Sherry 2007).

In recent years, there has been a reappropriation of what Negash Gebrekidan (2012) terms 'histories from below' to question the idea of a disabled 'subaltern' that does not speak (Spivak and Guha 1988). Disabled activists from the global South are reclaiming their own and other forgotten histories by, for example, calling attention to the role disabled people played in peaceful protest for social change in Lebanon (Kabbara and Khalil 2014), arguing for self-representation in legislation (Herald Reporter 2013), and pointing to effects of poverty on a forgotten generation in Zimbabwe (Tsama 2014).

Further, nuances have been built into analyses of disability activism to dislocate what we understand by it, where it occurs (i.e. the grass roots) and whether we should define it as a social movement (Shakespeare 1993). Taking seriously the ideas of double or triple disability oppression means interrogating forms of hegemonic power and identity, as well as locating resistance. In this sense, when Skelton and Valentine (2003) examined the 'weapons of the weak' (Scott 1985), they found volunteering was a political site of activism for 'D/deaf' people and sign language was used as a tacit act of resistance.

The sites of disability resistance thus dislocate spaces of activism from global to local, and challenge our perceptions of what it means to have a voice and be heard. This is especially so when it comes to understanding and defining disability in the global South and the exploitation and inequality that create impairment. Additionally, disabled people are not just vulnerable victims, and may not identify themselves as disabled, or even live in poverty. In tune with the heterogeneity of African realities, disabled people are just as likely to be transnational entrepreneurs, teachers, farmers, middle-class or wealthy politicians. Likewise, disabled people can be perpetrators of violence, pimps, prostitutes and criminals, as well as located in the margins and slums, thus outside the reach of legislative instruments. People's identities may not in any way be linked to biomedical ascription of impairment and yet this is where most Northern debates on activism and rights, largely driven by international institutions like the World Health Organization (WHO), begin.

The medical model was called into question owing only to the efforts of disabled people, disabled people's organizations (DPOs) and activists. Thus, while they were seemingly covered by general human rights conventions (Harpur 2012), an awareness of the rights and needs of disabled people came on to the global agenda only in the early 1970s and 1980s with United Nations (UN) declarations (i.e. Rioux and Heath 2014). The late 1990s saw the UN move towards advocating legislative change and implementing social changes to support the inclusion and human rights of disabled people. The culmination of these human rights and social model approaches was the UN's Convention on the Rights of Persons with Disabilities (CRPD), which came into force in May 2008 (United Nations 2006). The CRPD was heavily influenced theoretically by the social model of disability developed, mainly, by academics and activists in the global North.[2] The social model of disability distinguishes between biological impairment and social barriers that disable, such as lack of access to education or employment. Rioux and Heath (2014: 320-1) argue that the CRPD

... entails moving *away from viewing people with disabilities as problems* toward viewing them as rights holders. Importantly, it means locating any problems outside the person and especially in the manner by which various economic and social processes accommodate the difference of disability ... *The debate about disability rights is therefore connected to a larger debate about the place of difference in society.* (Quinn and Degener 2002: 1, emphasis added)

The CRPD also states that disability 'mainstreaming' is an integral part of global policy needed for sustainable development to occur and should be a part of poverty reduction strategies. Disability mainstreaming, akin to gender mainstreaming, means that inclusion of disability should be a feature of all development programming, aid and policy development. Thus, DfID (2000) argues for the implementation of a 'twin track' approach to development, wherein it funds projects for the empowerment of disabled people and requires that all aid projects have a disability component.[3]

Notwithstanding its widespread adoption by international bodies, national governments, charities and NGOs, implementation of the CRPD proves challenging, especially in the global South (Harpur 2012). The same can be said about monitoring the CRPD, and the ability of disabled people, activists and DPOs from the global South to be involved. This is despite efforts to ensure that their needs are part of the agenda of research evidence, activism, policy and practice (Stein and Lord 2010). Considering that disabled people are mainly located in the global South and predominantly in low-income countries, a strange state of affairs is instantiated (WHO and World Bank 2011).

In this chapter, we illustrate how disability rights are framed within charitable and neocolonial approaches, which delimit activism and ignore sites of resistance. We expose the links between the disabling norms and values of neoliberalism, and how disability rights are subsumed in development discourses and debates (i.e. linked to poverty reduction work). We thus note a top-down flow of information, terminology and discourses of rights and empowerment, which pander to a stratification of Africa, and stereotypes of disabled people in particular, as on the lowest levels of global society.

While a lot of hope is invested in the CPRD, we show how genuine partnership and social accountability are rarely achieved. Rather, there is a focus on soft rights, such as the right to vote, and the soft laws or conventions where there are no real legal consequences for lack of implementation.[4] This affects both activism and true empowerment. In response, we challenge the African disability movement and its allies to reclaim notions of rights in their own terminology (i.e. *ubuntu*), and work on 'hard' rights, leading to economic and social change in policy and practice. Using examples from southern and West African contexts, we illustrate seven challenges to true inclusion and respect for rights based on a framework developed by the activist Abraham Mateta. Our quest is thus to push for a legitimate marriage of commitment between the global North and Africa in the rights debate (Chataika 2012; Shava 2008). We believe that it is this form of activism which can foster social justice and empowerment of African disability rights activism, with the hope of realizing the post-2015 sustainable development goals.

Reflecting on disability rights, definitions and development issues in Africa

Contesting neoliberal development and the values and norms it incorporates means rethinking the terminology and definitions we espouse. We adopt the terms global North and global South in order to avoid binary thinking (Stubbs 1999). We could also use majority world with regard to minority world of global North to illustrate inequality (Stone 1999). More common terminology, such as developed/ underdeveloped/developing, high/low income, thriving/failing, First/ Third world and centre/periphery, not only communicates but also evokes a reality of divisions, superiority, inferiority, hierarchy and subordination (Charlton 2010; Grech 2009; Meekosha 2008; Sherry 2007). The struggle here is challenging oppression, voicelessness, stereotyping, neocolonization, post-colonization and 'them and us' ideologies to bridge gaps in the disability and development agenda (Chataika 2012). It requires thinking critically about how to develop new paradigms based on African self-emancipation, partnership and attention to the inclusion of third spaces and overlooked sites of resistance.

Development is a part of neoliberalism tied to economic interests at the heart of globalization (Harrison 2010). Neoliberalism is primarily an economic free market policy implemented by the World Bank and the International Monetary Fund (IMF) to ensure social and economic interests that delimit the role of the state in the provision of services, championing privatization and profit. Within a development context, when an African country needs funds owing to poverty or after a disaster or conflict, it must go to the World Bank and the IMF. Conditions of aid now require Poverty Reduction Strategy Papers (PRSPs) and adherence to international targets, such as Millennium Development Goals (MDGs), international conventions and rights.

Neoliberalism thus has had a profound effect on the creation of civil society, politics and culture in an African context. Harrison (ibid.) argues that neoliberalism has led to global social engineering in terms of the creation of citizens as free market consumers. Forms of sensitization or socialization programmes for 'capacity-building' illustrate this in the African context. In post-conflict Sierra Leone, for example, there were numerous programmes targeting issues from disability terminology to governance usually organized by institutional bodies, e.g. the WHO and NGOs (Berghs 2011a, 2012). Giving an overall understanding of the CRPD and involving disabled people in Sierra Leone's PRSPs was, however, neglected (Berghs 2012). This has also been found in other studies documenting marginalization from PRSPs (Chataika et al. 2011; Mwendwa et al. 2009; Yeo and Moore 2000).

Citizen-consumers need choices, but these are governed through scientific evidence appraisal by the very institutions setting agendas for interventions and programmes. This extends to how 'rights' are understood in terms of individual freedoms and risks, but also how they are invested with economic and political interests linked to charity, relief, governance, peace-building and biomedicine. It is noteworthy that most programme aid is not bilateral, but is channelled through multilateral funding agencies, and thus circumvents national governments to go directly to implementing partners, especially global institutions, international NGOs and local civil society organizations, thereby ensuring a neoliberal hegemony. This is particularly the case where the state is defined as fragile (e.g. post-conflict Sierra Leone) or autocratic (e.g. Zimbabwe), and this trickles down to locally run NGOs, DPOs and institutions.

Furthermore, twin-track systems, such as DfID's, are called into question when the promotion of rights and legislation takes second place to economic and political stability. As long as a government is seen to be aiding market reform (i.e. good economic governance), the political elites are rewarded and even an autocratic status quo will remain, such as in Rwanda and Angola. Hanlon (2004) argues that in such cases donors allow corruption and foster predatory elites under the guise of a delimited democracy and rights (e.g. Mozambique). What happens at the macro level of a state is also mirrored at the micro level in terms of disability governance, or the creation of policy that curtails democracy.

This neoliberal bias lies at the heart of dominance of theories from the global North, and it affects the construction and definition of disability and the importation of disability models, as well as how the disability business and rehabilitation are constructed without local input. For example, in community psychiatry in India, Jain and Jadhav (2008: 561) found that 'a cultural asymmetry between health professionals and wider society, the search [for] legitimisation of psychiatry and WHO policies' all interacted to silence rural community voices. In an African context, Chataika and Mckenzie (2013) illustrate how indigenous knowledge systems can be undermined by, for example, the importation of Western ideas of childhood in disability studies, which lack agency. Thus, the complexities and uniqueness of specific geopolitical environments and culture are misunderstood owing to top-down bureaucratic patterns of administration and control (Chambers 1997). The undemocratic imposition of rights within neoliberal development discourses has consequences for activism.

We argue that most programme aid is now multilateral, thus bypassing national governments, NGOs and DPOs. Historically, bilateral and multilateral aid relied on the idea that the global South should be aided with funding on condition that it be held accountable (Wehbi 2011). This is not currently possible. The exclusion or limited participation of disabled people in decision-making within international organizations and development work in various African countries has been documented (Chataika et al. 2011; Mulumba 2011; Swartz and MacLachlan 2009). Similarly, Wehbi (2012) describes how neocolonialism shapes what happens when foreign funding crosses national boundaries during a conflict. She argues that in Lebanon, aid brought necessary support, but the strategies, approaches and conditions imposed through foreign funding reinforced the exclusion of disabled people and their DPOs from humanitarianism. In post-conflict Sierra Leone, imposition of identities such as 'persons with disabilities' or 'victim' became gateways to ensuring access to resources, but also imposes dependency owing to the charity approach (Berghs and Dos Santos-Zingale 2012).

Furthermore, Wehbi (2011) argues that when disabled activists are poached and moved into institutional settings as professionals, this leads to fragmentation of disability activism with the real grassroots activists relegated to the status of volunteers, weakening their roles. Accordingly, she argues that we must '... critically re-evaluat[e] funding practices in the age of shifting global boundaries in an act of solidarity and resistance of neo-colonial agendas and their impacts on the continued oppression of disabled people' (ibid.: 519).

Disability activism has been endorsed by many Southern DPOs and NGOs, providing an invaluable platform for lobbying, but the flow of ideas has been too one-sided (Grech 2009; Meekosha 2008). Charlton (1998) clarifies that a slogan like 'nothing about us without us' was born out of social movements and the consciousness of disabled activists in the global South in terms of their oppression. Yet if the global North controls the purse strings and people, 'nothing about us without us' becomes a rhetorical gesture.

Major players such as DPOs and NGOs are thus becoming disabling. For example, most of these players are located in capital cities, which are sites of political and economic power. Yet 80 per cent of disabled people in low-income countries are located in the rural areas (WHO and World Bank 2011). Furthermore, activism, DPOs and umbrella organizations become dominated by professionals and educated disabled men with particular types of physical impairments. It is these voices which often overshadow those from the margins, such as women, children and those with mental health needs.

Furthermore, Das and Addlakha (2001) argue that neoliberal political regimes situate disability discrimination within the realm of soft legal rights and not domestic spaces linked to sexuality or reproduction. They also illustrate how not all disabled voices make sense, nor can they contribute to debates conducted within political, economic or legal spheres. This means rethinking social justice and activism, to whom it applies and when. It also requires awareness of marginalized sites of disability activism and resistance.

Given the ignorance regarding big issues of discrimination and oppression and the espousal of soft rights linked to the CRPD, global institutions may not seriously engage with disability mainstreaming in Africa (Chataika and Mckenzie forthcoming). Other forms of social justice, such as how impairment and disability are created intergenerationally through poverty, violence and environmental degradation, receive scant attention (Meekosha and Soldatic 2011). The narrow or soft focus on 'disability' hides the creation of national and international conditions of inequality needing to be addressed. However, hard rights linked to political activism to ensure social change, new legislation or protests for greater democracy within an African context are rarely advocated by NGOs.[5]

While universal approaches like the CRPD are welcomed for their contribution to the realization of disability rights, the specific cultural settings and voices of African disabled people, activists and DPOs should be amplified. The question that comes to mind is: 'To what extent is the CRPD a product of neoliberalism, or of resistance to it, or a compromise between the two?' Gorman (2010) argues for an analysis of disability rights regimes as a form of neoliberal governance. The argument lies in the fact that the issue of 'inclusion' as the goal of the Western-focused disability rights movement emerged alongside ideologies of 'inclusion' expressed in European Union and World Bank policies in the bid to expand capitalist market relations and the reserve army of labour.

We believe that the answer lies somewhere in the compromise field, with both positives and negatives. We have illustrated that in low-income countries, the CRPD has become entangled with aid and development discourses on poverty. This is without acknowledgement of the neoliberal basis of historical situations of inequality that give rise to impairment (Barnes and Sheldon 2010), an investigation into why impairment is created in the global South (Meekosha and Soldatic 2011), or an expansion of the debate to ask, 'who profits?' Consequently, in-depth North/South reflections on questions and challenges surrounding relationships must be valued in order to promote African disability rights (Chataika 2012; Shava 2008). In this spirit, we want to examine some of the ways in which discourses linked to the CRPD, activism and empowerment are flouted and how to arrive at a 'win-win' situation.

If development is about liberating people from obstacles affecting their ability to lift their lives out of poverty (Chataika 2012), disabled people must express their own demands and seek their own solutions to their problems. In order to break the binary divides and imagine third spaces, it is necessary to promote 'productive exchanges and cross-fertilizations' of ideas while addressing the inequalities and silences that have long existed (Barker and Murray 2010: 219). Consequently, in-depth North/South reflections on questions and challenges surrounding relationships must be valued in order to promote African disability rights (Chataika 2012; Shava 2008). In this spirit, we examine some of the ways in which discourses linked to the CRPD, activism and empowerment are flouted.

Activism, emancipation and empowerment

In order for disabled people to express what they understand by rights, in their terms, they need to take centre stage. As such, African activists and DPOs must have the resources to establish links and partnerships in both African and international contexts (Charlton 1998; Shava 2008). This development of a 'global political economy of disability' or transnational disability activism (Thomas 2004) could promote a two-way information exchange and resource mobilization, both of which are key components of effective activism (Shava 2008). Fostering a more level playing field in terms of access to assistive devices, social media and resources would also allow African activists to discuss whether their priorities are in keeping with concepts created in the West, such as 'independent living', or to formulate their own issues, theories and slogans. This diversity would undoubtedly strengthen the capacity of the disability movement to collectively fight for disability rights (Teixeira and Menezes 2008), and dislocate it to where it is actually needed. Furthermore, Barnes (2014) argues that emancipation begins with accountability to the people for whom one works. A first step in ensuring a truly 'global political economy' would be to ensure external (legislative) accountability for the implementation of the CRPD, and internal accountability of DPOs to the people they represent. This would be the first step of empowerment defined as: 'The process by which individuals, groups and/or communities become able to take control of their circumstances and achieve goals, thereby being able to work towards maximizing the quality of their lives' (Baistow 1995: 35).

However, Barnes (2014: 39) warns, 'But empowerment is not something that can be given – it is something that people must do for themselves. The important point here is ownership. Within an emancipatory framework, it is organisations controlled by disabled people that devise and control ...'

Shava (2008: 60) argues, 'empowerment has an intuitive appeal because it essentially implies "independence" and "assertiveness", and is both a process and an outcome (Dempsey and Foreman, 1997)'. However, definitions of empowerment differ widely and some activists and academics espouse caution. For instance, Pease (2002: 137) argues that empowerment is too often 'done to others', who are seen as passive, and empowerment lies in the hands of outside NGO, health and legal professionals, etc. Hence, Dowson et al. (1998) note that when empowerment is imposed and the assumption is made that disabled people are not aware of or cannot adequately formulate their own issues in their own terms, marginalization and disempowerment occur. Pease (2002: 141–3) contends that while empowerment has meant the 'insurrection of subjugated knowledge', there needs to be a 'resurrection' of the 'subjugated knowledge' of marginalized communities.

Practically speaking, what would true empowerment look like for disabled people in an African context? Shava (2008) argues that the debate needs to be framed in terms of a 'liberational model of empowerment', where African DPOs, allies, activists and disabled people and their families work collaboratively at the micro level to define oppression and identify what they can do about it. This is consistent with the social model of disability, which is at the heart of the CRPD, but also calls for the creation of Southern theories and models to critique the CRPD or create something new. For Shava (ibid.), this is different from the neoliberal 'consumerist model of empowerment' that focuses on giving people false 'choices' within 'professionally defined services' in order to profit (Croft and Beresford 1995).

At the macro level, the disability movement in Africa will need to vigorously lobby national bodies and regional groups, such as the Economic Community of West African States and the Southern

African Development Community, as well as continental bodies such as the African Union, for practical and tangible recognition of the rights of disabled people, the drafting of national disability policies and anti-discrimination legislation across the continent. Yet, as stated above, the legislative route to social change is limited. Securing human and civil rights through existing legal frameworks requires resources people often do not have and has not always brought about equality, social protection or accountability for the overwhelming majority of disabled people or other oppressed groups (Barnes and Sheldon 2010). Thus, disability activism founded upon the wider politicization of grassroots disabled people is a fundamental antecedent to the realization of disability rights and freedoms.

Activism and its challenges in Africa

We understand activism as the ability of a particular group to collectively organize around issues that affect it. Issues can range from social and health-related ones (e.g. inclusion in HIV/AIDS activism) to economic and politically complex issues (e.g. implementation of the CRPD). In this section, we examine two different African contexts, Zimbabwe and Sierra Leone, to understand the challenges disability activism faces. Zimbabwe has a vibrant disability history, including the work of African philanthropists in setting up services (Devlieger 1995), disabled freedom fighters advocating rights, and later grassroots social consciousness movements of disabled activism at micro and macro political levels (Chimedza and Peters 1999).

Similarly, in post-conflict Sierra Leone, disabled activists mobilized people to protest for rights and came together in refugee camps to form DPOs based on earlier segregated disability histories (Berghs and Dos Santos-Zingale 2012; Dos Santos-Zingale and McColl 2006). People who became wounded during the war used the local and global press to raise their issues, protested their exploitation and refused to become involved in transitional justice until their needs were recognized (Berghs 2010, 2012). However, both contexts see a superficial allegiance to disability rights on the part of the political elite in order to ensure access to debt relief. Disability is included in PRSPs, disability bills are signed, and commissions are created, but there is a lack of political will to instigate real change in society. Above, we have discussed the lack of implementation and enforcement of the

CRPD and connected it to the dislocation of national funding streams and how policy is enforced through Western institutions instead. We now want to examine the micro level of activism. The disabled activist and lawyer Abraham Mateta has identified seven challenges to true inclusion and respect for disability rights in a Zimbabwean context.[6] We use this as a framework to explain disability rights in southern and West African practice.

Disability is becoming big business: elites as 'gatekeepers of charity'

In both Zimbabwe and Sierra Leone, DPOs are grossly under-resourced. In order to gain funding and survive, they must maintain relationships with religious organizations, charities, philanthropists, NGOs and international organizations based in capital cities. This gives the DPOs needed funding, but comes with strings linked to myriad global priorities, definitions of disability, and funding trends. For example, the current definition of disability ignores the sociocultural understandings and definitions of impairment in the different ethnic groups in both countries. In some cultures, 'disability' as a social category of identification may not even exist.

The people who can ensure these relationships or speak to their definitions in English become the 'gatekeepers of charity'. In Zimbabwe, they are sometimes placed in positions of power owing to ethnic and political links or even to NGO support. In such a way, true democracy or dissent with NGO or global policies is curtailed. As stated above, it is rare that these gatekeepers are women, children or come from marginalized positions, or have not been educated in segregated settings. Even when DPO leaders or activists advocate for their people, activism is curtailed, because it occurs within predetermined funding trends linked to institutional policies. When Mateta advocates for disability mainstreaming within youth policy, it is because this has been funded externally.[7] Likewise, if Chataika and Gandari are researching violence against disabled women, it is because it is now a part of the global disability agenda (Chataika and Gandari 2012). In post-conflict Sierra Leone, owing to the fact that aid funding became linked to impairments such as 'amputations', some people 'faked' identities or disabilities, or even set up false NGOs (Berghs 2012).

Yet being the head of a politically active DPO is not without risk as campaigning against government or international organizations can lead to both external and internal violence, as was the case with a community leader in Sierra Leone (Berghs 2011b). Gains made are often slow to materialize, so some leaders become disheartened and accept the system of corruption and dependency that trickles down to safeguard short-term or patrimonial gain. Also, there is often an umbrella organization or commission for which the heads of DPOs have been co-opted by the government, and in a context of poverty they will not bite the hand that feeds them. If they do, they are replaced.

However, while the heads and their supporters benefit, the majority of disabled people are disenfranchised and/or opt not to be members or part of a wider disability movement. At times, they are leaving one situation of vulnerability for another, where they are more marginalized, often aided by professionals, religious organizations and so-called philanthropists. This is also linked to ascriptions of different identities as activism becomes a condition or means of gaining resources. Thus, Mateta and Shava[8] note that one has to espouse an openly 'activist' identity to gain resources. At times, resistance and activism have to be secret because they may be politically dangerous, as in Zimbabwe, or even linked to secret societies, as in Sierra Leone.

Chataika et al. (2011) and Berghs (2012) also established that internalized negative stigma can be so great that disabled people do not feel they can take part in debates on politics or justice. They do not think they belong, or believe that these spheres are only for 'big men', and thus associated with corruption or other forms of exchange. There are also many grassroots organizers and women who are activists, but who do not call themselves 'activists', and hence receive limited attention and needed resources. As a result, the disability leadership can be characterized as disjointed, separated according to impairment, struggling to remain relevant, and just visible enough for the few leaders (at times disabled sharks) to continue exploiting matters for their own selfish ends. Meanwhile, leaders who are troublesome, not photogenic or do not say what NGOs or government want to hear are relegated.

Non-consultation, non-involvement and tokenism

Ideas of human welfare have been heavily influenced by the notion of the 'greatest good for the greatest number', a cliché that serves to obscure blatant exploitation and abuse of minorities within individual nation-states and globally (Shava 2008). The same is true within the disability movement and NGO development practices in general, and even in legal empowerment practices. Often, there is talk of respect for 'rights' and how they represent people with disabilities, but evidence of true consultation and inclusion is lacking (Berghs 2013). Governments and even the general public do not regard DPOs seriously and inevitably consider themselves as affording disabled people rights if they are provided with handouts, one-day training seminars and workshops, while expressing profound sympathy and publicly using the politically correct disability terminology of 'persons with disabilities'.

Access to justice for disabled people is an example. Human rights commissions in both Zimbabwe and Sierra Leone are overwhelmed by human rights abuses. However, the commissions work in conditions where the police and judiciary system are weak and allegations of corruption are rife. 'Disability' is also a relatively new issue and not a priority for them to investigate or highlight. They do not understand how it links into women's, children's or property rights, and instead focus on mainstreaming disability in educational settings through policy enforcement. Moreover, while legal activists try to guarantee legislative changes for greater social justice, institutional change and accountability, we find legal empowerment discourses applied to delimited settings, such as prisons, rather than larger structural issues such as accessibility or the marginal position of disabled people. Some paralegals will also demand compensation, which the poorest of the poor (often disabled people) do not have. We argue that legal empowerment must work on myriad levels, ensuring aid to specialist legal activists, access to justice for *all* people, and a truly consultative process with disabled people to ensure awareness of their legal needs.

NGO programming cycles rarely have needs assessments with disabled people or employ them, but often make tokenistic mention of work with DPOs or consultation with disabled 'stakeholders', who have sometimes been paid off (ibid.). Nationally, ministries are not involved in ensuring that disability mainstreaming is kept on national and international agendas, as this is not seen as a national priority. Most NGOs also view disability as a specialized or social welfare issue, rather than part of the work they do, thus affecting mainstreaming efforts. The message that people gain from this is of a disconnect between global and local discourses, enforced second-class citizenship, and hypocrisy associated with rights practices.

Lack of funding, training and understanding of resources needed and given

Disability is a global business and having able and professional national DPOs can constitute real competition for the global North. Consultation, inclusion of disabled people, and needs assessments to inform development policy and practice require resources, but there is general reluctance to seriously fund DPOs. When DPOs are funded, it is to offer assistance to a Western NGO, implement community-based rehabilitation (CBR), or even to accord legitimacy to superficial mainstreaming attempts. Often there is talk about grassroots DPO leaders' 'lack of capacity', because the skills needed in village or communal settings are different from skills in project proposal writing or fluency in the disability definitions that pander to the global North's NGO business. This is also linked to the lack of research and evidence base needed for disabled people to advocate and investigate their issues.

The onus of responsibility is placed on disabled people and not the NGOs to become more open and inclusive by rethinking the ways in which they fund programmes, the skill sets and resources they should fund, or how to ensure accessibility to programmes through the use of Braille or sign language. This is discrimination, but not recognized as such. Shava argues that, even as an educated activist, it requires asking and sometimes begging for resources, funding or information owing to the difficulties of working in resource-poor settings.[9] Mateta relates how lack of access to resources like electricity and the internet demands that activists use mobile phones, radio and community meetings to mobilize and educate on disability issues. This puts him at a disadvantage compared to foreign activists, who have access to more resources, a greater online presence, and opportunities to publish articles, but work less within communities.[10] In such subtle ways, discourses of dependency are substantiated and reinforced.

DPOs are constrained by the charity approach in that discourses of dependency accord them funding. The 'gatekeepers of charity' perpetuate the narratives and images of DPOs lacking capacity or living in poverty. Disabled people necessarily learn to use these 'scripts' to advocate their needs, thus hiding the strengths and successes of a community and people that should be celebrated. The heads of a DPO may lack certain professionalism or skills, but that does not mean that lack exists in the DPO's constituencies. The wealth of know-how and possibilities for inclusion and recognition in the fostering of long-term training and resources are never examined.

Additionally, there is unwillingness to make and learn from mistakes, so that programmes are cut off or are just short-term, with corruption often cited as a concern. However, many DPOs and activists lack business training or the managerial skills necessary to lead an organization and work in abject poverty, but this is hardly addressed (Mwendwa et al. 2009). Information about rights and resources is also a means of power and is curtailed by elites. It does not trickle down to the marginalized majority, and hence there is little accountability or transparency. When disabled people do hear about injustice, their ability to fight the status quo is constrained by 'lack of capacity' or an inability to go to an ombudsman or seek justice.

Disability as specialized charity

Historically, the disability business is seen as the purview of specialized charities with the technical expertise to implement programmes, such as rehabilitation (Chataika 2012). This is a colonial model, but international organizations and governments have inherited the charity approach, which views disability as a 'problem' needing specialized attention. Governments may think that having international NGOs deal with disability is easier than mainstreaming disability within government programmes, but the privatization of disability effectively panders to the biomedical, relief and charity business interests of neoliberalism and the global North. It also ignores informal CBR and indigenous healing systems that simultaneously exist in communities. CBR and even saving clubs have existed for centuries in African contexts, and yet now they need professionals to oversee them?

It is not surprising that Western donors send their own so-called technical experts to design and implement disability programmes in Africa without consultation with the would-be 'beneficiaries' of such programmes, and without due regard for the sociocultural contexts and actual needs of disabled people (ibid.). Even in cases where there are sufficiently educated disabled people, 'experts' from the global North pursue disability research with mostly non-disabled assistants. Ideas of true partnership are flouted, but control lies with the global North's research priorities and political agendas. NGOs that try to instigate true partnership in line with priorities of DPOs are ostracized and relegated. They lack the institutional sheen of true legitimacy of the big NGOs supposedly working for justice, and their evidence reports pandering to neoliberalism illustrate this.

In neoliberal Africa, disability is becoming a business linked to microcredit schemes, literacy programmes and skills training initiatives. Yet many of these programmes ignore the bigger structural issues of ensuring employment in unstable, patrimonial, corrupt and poorly resourced settings, or the micro issues, such as the extra costs associated with having an impairment or a disabled child. For example, in Zimbabwe, disabled people barely have safety nets to ensure their survival, thus driving them into perpetual begging. Likewise, these programmes are not cognisant of the fact that some disabled people may suffer stigma and discrimination. Others may never be able to work owing to severity of impairment, as is found in post-conflict environment (Berghs 2012), and may need welfare provisions instead. All too often, charities also ignore ownership and impose programmes. A good example is CBR, which already informally exists in many communities but is cheaper to implement for donors than ensuring rehabilitation clinics and services. The welfare of disabled people is borne by the family and caring work undertaken by female relatives or children. In this way, the possible activism of parents of disabled children, children or female relatives is curtailed. Their advocacy is never recognized as activism in decision-making processes by various agencies, which include organizations of disabled people. This ignores the vast experience accrued by parents, children and families and their work establishing DPOs and supporting CBR.

As the definition of 'disability' continues to grow, more specialized NGOs and researchers will be needed and new professionalisms will be created for experts from the global North, such as in mental health diagnoses with their requisite pharmaceuticals. Ultimately, these are new hegemonic and neoliberal business models to perpetuate charity models and research according to their needs. Cycles of dependency will not be broken, but again enforced.

Superficial CRPD mainstreaming in development aid

The CRPD has not been implemented nor mainstreamed in development aid, despite the fact that the images and voices of poor people, including disabled and war-wounded people, are usually used to highlight the need for humanitarian aid and peace (e.g. Berghs 2010, 2012). The flouting of the health, economic and social human rights of the poorest of the poor is the first step of any appeal or development discourse in Sierra Leone and Zimbabwe. Why has it been normal to 'use' those people, and deny how they benefit 'development'? Likewise, why is it now 'normal' to use a superficial disabled 'stakeholder' as evidence of CRPD mainstreaming?

Relief and development agencies have kept disabled people dependent, often pandering to empowerment through income-generating initiatives that are oversubscribed or irrelevant in communities (e.g. hairdressing, basket weaving, computer training), or micro-finance activities that create a profit, or are unsustainable in contexts of chronic poverty and discrimination. In Sierra Leone, Chataika et al. (2011) found that there was limited understanding of disability mainstreaming in poverty reduction work, which compromised inclusive development. Berghs (2012) found that real attitudinal change and non-discrimination in informal and formal employment linked to the CRPD was not understood. Despite great efforts in Zimbabwe and Sierra Leone to 'domesticate' the CRPD to local contexts, lack of information, understanding of the issues, transparency and resources limit progress.

In 2011, the Obama administration directed USAID not to fund any programme that did not demonstrate disability inclusion. Disability rights activists, such as Mateta, were ecstatic, thinking that this would mean a radical change in disability work. However, resistance is widespread and exclusion continues unabated. Likewise, DfID's 'twin track' approach cannot promote true inclusion for disabled people in an overall context of discrimination. Additionally, most organizations just incorporate disability into their proposals or workshops as tokenism to ensure access to funding, thus according themselves a false moral legitimacy and reinforcing the status quo.

In most cases, organizations do not employ, include or consult disabled people, but will use their photographs in evaluations and fund-raising reports. Disabled people and DPOs have very little say about how their images and stories are used, cannot request payment for those images, and cannot instigate research reports to be written on their issues. While some disabled people, DPOs and activists may use social media to represent themselves and their issues, they still have to ensure that they communicate in English, and that they use language that people will understand, such as disability rights slogans. In this way, development aid remains divorced from the real needs and realities of disabled people.

Rights divorced from local realities

When thinking about spaces of disability resistance ignored by global rights discourses, the divorce between rights and local realities of poverty and social histories of suffering stands out. For example, Mateta recounts being funded to work in communities to sensitize disabled people living in abject poverty, where no welfare system exists, on issues of good governance.[11] Similarly, Berghs (ibid.) was told to focus on 'survival' when she asked disabled people what their main concerns were in a post-conflict situation. Chataika and Shava note that, in settings of economic and political flux such as Zimbabwe, people's concerns are necessarily short-term, such as where their next meal is coming from. Hence, disabled people will support anyone who can assist with their immediate concerns.[12] As such, people are necessarily focused on meeting the basic needs of life, and this can cause human rights abuses, such as young girls unnecessarily engaging in sex work (Tsama 2014). Despite high-level discourses of rights, people still live with systems of patrimonial exchange and engage in night-time or illegal activities to survive, which are important yet ignored areas of activism and resistance. Activists too inhabit several worlds and must negotiate these dilemmas.

Chataika et al. (2011) found that there was limited understanding of 'rights' in Sierra Leone. Very few people knew how 'rights' could relate to disabled people or how poverty and impairment become linked. As such, rights are diffused concepts, sometimes pertaining to women, children and, to a limited extent, disabled people. Hence, one had to shop around to find the 'right' fitting one's issue. Programmes on disability rights linked to the right to reparations, social corporate responsibility and compensation are typically underfunded or ignored.

In Sierra Leone, imagery and discourses on rights were also relatively inaccessible (i.e. posters, radio or legislation) or focused on subsections within disabled communities, such as people with poliomyelitis, promoting charitable approaches and evoking ideas of burden (Berghs 2013). In terms of disability resistance, disabled people occupying public spaces, using drugs or alcohol, engaging in sex work, begging or who had been in accidents illustrated identities that were not dependent, but had negative moral ascriptions, falling outside of rights discourses. Yet in both Zimbabwe and Sierra Leone it is most important to engage with and understand why these people and spaces are created.

Greater attention to how people try to include themselves in society also requires a focus on economic and social rights, as well as why governments and the international community ignore them. Linking disability positively to those concerns may be a better approach to ensuring that the CRPD is truly enforced. At the moment, it feels like a burden or an imposition on governments and NGOs, since there is lack of understanding of how it will benefit society as a whole.

Lack of a regulatory and legislative framework: the quest for African disability rights

A proper regulatory and legislative framework to adequately prevent abuse of disability activism by those who use it for personal enrichment does not exist. In a context of poverty, disability activism becomes linked to resources and short-term gains. People may pay off 'supporters' or enrich themselves and, as stated above, there is no ombudsman or other justice-seeking mechanism that disabled people can go to if discrimination or exploitation happens within a DPO or is practised by activists.

In Sierra Leone, Berghs (2011b) relates how in one community leaders wanted payment before they would allow access to more vulnerable members of the community. In Zimbabwe, some disability rights activists side with elites and view other poor disabled people as 'troublesome'. These become outcasts who are ignored, thus stopping debates and dialogue on issues that affect them. In both contexts, disabled people are seen as victims and not human beings who can contribute to national development. The idea that disabled people can discriminate against, marginalize or even manipulate non-disabled people and NGOs is also part of an ignored discourse on activism and resistance. Ensuring some form of accountability internally and externally can only aid in dismantling imposed hegemonies and abuses.

In this section, we have shown where the current challenges of activism lie for disability rights. There are myriad forms of what disability rights could look like in keeping with the heterogeneity of Africa and disabled Africans. We do not want to impose any ideas, but rather suggest theories, possibilities and areas that need attention for true activism to occur. We want to show how disability rights, development theory and activism are connected, and how they need to change to ensure greater global and local equity.

Conclusion

In this chapter, we have illustrated how disability rights are framed within Western charitable and neocolonial approaches. We showed how rights are imposed from North to South, and are thus connected to neoliberal development discourses and debates. We noted what activism and empowerment could look like, and also what happens in both southern and West African contexts when rights are flouted, and the CRPD implemented in a superficial way. We noted seven areas where disability activism is being challenged and why. Disability rights challenge human rights precisely because, despite discourses of humanitarianism and the CRPD, disabled people are being oppressed (Sherry 2014).

We felt we needed to use our collective experiences to constructively open up debates about disability and human rights in Africa. We argue that there is a need to create spaces for African disability activists, understand how resistance occurs and what can be done to promote disability rights. At the same time, we want to challenge the African disability movements, activists and their allies to reclaim notions of rights in their own terminology in order to change policy and practice. We want to question why disability is a marginalized issue and illustrate how it is kept that way. Anybody who is truly serious about equality and rights cannot ignore issues of disability or the voices of disabled people.

Acknowledgements

We would like to acknowledge the guidance of Samantha Wehbi, who noted the importance of ensuring that these issues are framed from the perspective of disabled people from the global South. Thank you to Keren Yohannes for kindly inviting our contribution to this debate and aiding us with editing.

Notes

1 Corresponding author.

2 It is worth remembering that the Union of the Physically Impaired against Segregation (UPIAS), which developed the social of model of disability, was also formed with Vic Finkelstein (Barnes 2007). He was a disabled South African who was imprisoned, endured hard labour, was tortured and later deported to the United Kingdom (UK) for his anti-apartheid activism.

3 There are tensions in such an approach in that it still views disabled people as having separate needs but also tries to move away from a charity approach that segregates disability.

4 For a discussion on 'soft' and 'hard' law see Abbott and Snidal (2000).

5 This is no different from the global North where, for example, disability activism against cuts and austerity in the United Kingdom (i.e. DPAC, Black Triangle, WeAreSpartacus) receives no real political backing from the NGOs supposed to be working *for* and *with* disabled people.

6 E-mail communication.

7 E-mail communication.

8 E-mail communication.

9 E-mail communication.

10 E-mail communication.

11 E-mail communication.

12 E-mail communication.

References

Abbott, K. W. and D. Snidal (2000) 'Hard and soft law in international governance', *International Organization*, 54: 421–56.

Baistow, K. (1995) 'Liberation or regulation? Some paradoxes of empowerment', *Critical Social Policy*, 42: 34–46.

Barker, C. and S. Murray (2010) 'Disabling postcolonialism: global disability cultures and democratic criticism', *Journal of Literary and Cultural Disability Studies*, 4(3): 219–36.

Barnes, C. (2007) 'Disability activism and the struggle for change: disability, policy and politics in the UK', *Education Citizenship and Social Justice*, 2(3): 203–21.

— (2014) 'Reflections on doing emancipatory disability research', in J. Swain, S. French, C. Barnes and C. Thomas (eds), *Disabling Barriers, Enabling Environments*, London: Sage.

Barnes, C. and A. Sheldon (2010) 'Disability, politics, and poverty in a majority world context', *Disability and Society*, 25(7): 771–82.

Berghs, M. (2010) 'Coming to terms with inequality and exploitation in an African state: researching disability in Sierra Leone', *Disability and Society*, 25(7): 861–5.

— (2011a) 'Embodiment and emotion in

Sierra Leone', *Third World Quarterly*, 32(8): 1399–417.

— (2011b) 'Paying for stories of impairment – parasitic or ethical? Reflections undertaking anthropological research in post-conflict Sierra Leone', *Scandinavian Journal of Disability Research*, 13(4): 255–70.

— (2012) *War and Embodied Memory: Becoming Disabled in Sierra Leone*, Aldershot: Ashgate.

— (2013) 'Why does the personal need to be so political? PWDs, legal empowerment and self-advocacy in Sierra Leone', Presentation given at legal empowerment workshop, Centre for Applied Human Rights, 13 June.

Berghs, M. and M. Dos Santos-Zingale (2012) 'A comparative analysis: everyday understandings of disability in Sierra Leone', *Africa Today*, 58(2): 19–40.

Chambers, R. (1997) *Whose Reality Counts? Putting the First Last*, London: Intermediate Technology Publications.

Charlton, J. I. (1998) *Nothing about Us without Us: Disability, Oppression and Empowerment*, Berkeley: University of California Press.

— (2010) 'Peripheral everywhere', *Literary and Cultural Disability Studies*, 4(2): 195–200.

Chataika, T. (2012) 'Postcolonialism, disability and development', in D. Goodley and B. Hughes (eds), *Social Theories of Disability: New Developments and Directions*, London: Routledge.

Chataika, T. and E. Gandari (2012) 'Personal experiences of disabled women against violence in Zimbabwe and advocacy for change', Paper presented at the 8th Biannual International Disability Studies Conference, 11–13 September, Lancaster University.

Chataika, T. and J. A. Mckenzie (2013)

'Considerations for an African childhood disability studies', in T. Curran and K. Runswick-Cole (eds), *Disabled Children's Childhood Studies: Contemporary Thinking and Inquiry for Creative Policy and Practice*, London: Palgrave.

— (forthcoming) 'Global institutions and their engagement with disability mainstreaming in the South: development and disconnections', in S. Grech and K. Soldatic (eds), *Disability in the Global South: The Critical Reader*, London: Springer.

Chataika, T., F. Kallon, G. Mji and M. Maclachlan (2011) *Did What? Research Project in Brief A-PODD in Sierra Leone*, Stellenbosch and Dublin: A-PODD.

Chimedza, R. and S. Peters (1999) 'Disabled people's quest for social justice in Zimbabwe', in F. Armstrong and L. Barton (eds), *Human Rights and Education: Cross-Cultural Perspectives*, Buckingham: Open University Press.

Croft, S. and P. Beresford (1995) 'Whose empowerment? Equalizing the competing discourses in community care', in R. Jack (ed.), *Empowerment in Community Care*, London: Chapman and Hall.

Das, V. and R. Addlakha (2001) 'Disability and domestic citizenship: voice, gender and the making of the subject', *Public Culture*, 13(3): 511–31.

Dempsey, I. and P. Foreman (1997) 'Toward a clarification of empowerment as an outcome of disability service provision', *Journal of Intellectual Disability Research*, 44(4): 287–303.

Devlieger, P. (1995) 'From self-help to charity in disability service: the Jairos Jiri Association in Zimbabwe', *Disability and Society*, 10(1): 39–48.

DfID (Department for International Development) (2000) *Disability, Poverty and Development*, London: DfID.

Dos Santos-Zingale, M. and M. A. McColl

(2006) 'Disability and participation in post-conflict situations: the case of Sierra Leone', *Disability and Society*, 21(3): 243–57.

Dowson, S., E. Hersov, J. Hersov and J. Collins (1998) *Action Empowerment: A Method of Self-audit for Services for People with Learning Disabilities or Mental Health Support Needs*, Trafford: National Tenants Resource Centre.

Gorman, R. (2010) 'Empire of rights: the convergence of neoliberal governance, "states of exception", and the disability rights movement', Paper presented at 'Cripping neoliberalism: interdisciplinary perspectives on governing and imagining dis/ability and bodily difference', Charles University, Prague, 8 October.

Grech, S. (2009) 'Disability, poverty and development: critical reflections on the majority world debate', *Disability and Society*, 24(6): 771–84.

Hanlon, J. (2004) 'Do donors promote corruption? The case of Mozambique', *Third World Quarterly*, 25(4): 747–63.

Harpur, P. (2012) 'Embracing the new disability rights paradigm: the importance of the convention on the rights of persons with disabilities', *Disability and Society*, 27(1): 1–4.

Harrison, G. (2010) *Neoliberal Africa: The Impact of Global Social Engineering*, London: Zed Books.

Herald Reporter (2013) 'The blind cry foul', *Herald Reporter*, 21 February, www.herald.co.zw/the-blind-cry-foul/, accessed 5 January 2014.

Jain, S. and S. Jadhav (2008) 'A cultural critique of community psychiatry in India', *International Journal of Health Services*, 38: 561–84.

Kabbara, N. and J. Abou Khalil (2014) 'The forgotten people: persons with disability during the Israeli Lebanese War in 2006', in D. Mitchell and V. Karr (eds), *Crises, Conflict and Disability: Ensuing Equality*, London: Routledge.

Meekosha, H. (2008) 'Contextualizing disability: developing Southern/ global theory', Keynote paper given to the 4th Biennial Disability Studies Conference, Lancaster University, 2–4 September, wwda.org.au/meekosha2008.pdf, accessed 5 January 2014.

Meekosha, H. and K. Soldatic (2011) 'Human rights and the global South: the case of disability', *Third World Quarterly*, 32(8): 1383–97.

Mulumba, M. (2011) 'Mainstreaming disability into the poverty reduction processes in Uganda: the role of the human rights-based approach to the National Development Plan', MPhil thesis, Stellenbosch University.

Mwendwa, T. N., A. Murangira and R. Lang (2009) 'Mainstreaming the rights of persons with disabilities in national development frameworks', *Journal of International Development*, 21: 662–72.

Negash Gebrekidan, F. (2012) 'Disability rights activism: histories from below', *African Studies Review*, 55(3): 103–22.

Pease, B. (2002) 'Rethinking empowerment: a postmodern reappraisal for emancipatory practice', *British Journal of Social Work*, 32: 135–47.

Quinn, G. and T. Degener (2002) 'Human rights and disability: the current use and future potential of United Nations human rights instruments in the context of disability', Geneva: Office of the High Commission for Human Rights, 193.194.138.190/disability/study.htm, accessed 9 August 2014.

Rioux, M. and B. Heath (2014) 'Human rights in context: making rights count', in J. Swain, S. French, C. Barnes and C. Thomas (eds), *Disabling Barriers, Enabling Environments*, 3rd edn, London: Sage.

Scott, J. C. (1985) *Weapons of the Weak: Everyday Forms of Peasant Resistance*, New Haven, CT: Yale University Press.

Shakespeare, T. (1993) 'Disabled people's self-organization: a new social movement?', *Disability, Handicap and Society*, 8(3): 249–64.

Shava, K. (2008) 'How and in what ways can Western models of disability inform and promote empowerment of disabled people and their participation in mainstream Zimbabwean society', Master's thesis, University of Leeds, disability-studies.leeds.ac.uk/library/author/shava.kudzai.

Sherry, M. (2007) '(Post) colonising disability?', *Wagadu*, 4: 10–22.

— (2014) 'The promise of human rights for disabled people and the reality of neoliberalism', in M. Gill and C. J. Schlund-Vials (eds), *Disability, Human Rights and the Limits of Humanitarianism*, Aldershot: Ashgate.

Skelton, T. and G. Valentine (2003) 'Political participation, political action and political identities: young D/deaf people's perspectives', *Space and Polity*, 7(2): 117–34.

Spivak, G. C. and R. Guha (1988) *Selected Subaltern Studies*, New Delhi: Oxford University Press.

Stein, M. A. and J. E. Lord (2010) 'Monitoring the Convention on the Rights of Persons with Disabilities: innovations, lost opportunities and future potential', *Human Rights Quarterly*, 32(3): 689–728.

Stone, E. (1999) *Disability and Development: Learning from Action and Research on Disability in the Majority World*, Leeds: Disability Press.

Stubbs, S. (1999) 'Engaging with difference: soul-searching for a methodology in disability and development research', in E. Stone (ed.), *Disability and Development: Learning from Action and Research on Disability in*

the *Majority World*, Leeds: Disability Press, pp. 257–79.

Swartz, L. and M. MacLachlan (2009) 'From the local to the global: the many contexts of disability and international development', in M. MacLachlan and L. Swartz (eds), *Disability and International Development: Towards Inclusive Global Health*, New York: Springer.

Teixeira, P. M. and I. Menezes (2008) 'The promotion of active citizenship and empowerment of disabled people in Portugal: an organisational analysis', Paper presented at the International Society of Political Psychology 31st Annual Scientific Meeting.

Thomas, C. (2004) 'How is disability understood? An examination of sociological approaches', *Disability and Society*, 19(6): 569–83.

Tsama, M. (2014) 'Poverty ruining children, girl's futures', 22 January, www.zimeye.org/poverty-ruining-children-girls-future/, accessed 1 April 2014.

United Nations (2006) *Convention on the Rights of Persons with Disabilities*, www.un.org/disabilities/convention/convention.shtml, accessed 5 January 2014.

Wehbi, S. (2011) 'Crossing boundaries: foreign funding and disability rights activism in a context of war', *Disability and Society*, 26(5): 507–20.

— (2012) 'Advancing a disability rights agenda in a context of war: challenges and opportunities', *International Social Work*, 55(4): 522–37.

WHO and World Bank (2011) *World Report on Disability*, WHO and World Bank.

Yeo, R. and K. Moore (2000) 'Including disabled people in poverty reduction work: "nothing about us, without us"', *World Development*, 31(3): 571–90.

10 | ACTIVISM AND THE ARMS TRADE: EXPOSING THE SHADOW WORLD

Andrew Feinstein and Alex de Waal

Introduction

The international trade in weaponry should be a clear priority target for transnational activism. Guns kill, and illicitly acquired guns are even more likely to kill. Arms production and trade are systematically linked to secrecy, corruption, military rule and human rights violations. When weapons are used, they kill and maim, cause people to flee for their lives, destroy the environment and cultural heritage – and create demand for more purchases, which translate into profits for arms companies and their executives, and arms dealers. Yet, for eighty years, arms trade activism has been a small and fragmented affair. Single-issue campaigns, against particularly horrible armaments such as nuclear weapons (at one end of the scale) and anti-personnel landmines (at the other), have generated mass support. Building on the model of the International Campaign to Ban Landmines (ICBL), arms activism has led to the adoption of a slew of international documents, the most recent of which is the Arms Trade Treaty, adopted by the United Nations General Assembly in April 2013.

Today's dominant model of arms activism is a coalition among established NGOs that lobby Western governments to achieve international treaties. The metric of impact is the size and capacity of the coalition and the speed and comprehensiveness of the resulting convention. This approach privileges certain actors (Western 'advocacy superpowers') and tends to marginalize others (especially those from the global South). It prioritizes a legalistic framework that assumes, or hopes, that the business of manufacturing and selling weapons is legitimate and subject to effective regulation by states, and thus that conventions, treaties and agreements between states will translate into meaningful changes in behaviour.

In contrast to the more comprehensive disarmament campaigns of the first third of the twentieth century, some of the more structural evils of the arms business are meanwhile neglected. Paramount among these neglected issues is corruption. This ranges from outright bribery, to more sophisticated means of paying off decision-makers, to the more diffuse polluting of public discourse, guiding conventional wisdom and patterns of thinking so as to fence off certain key areas of national policy from public scrutiny. Corruption in these diverse forms lies at the heart of the continued malign influence of the weapons business over global politics.

This chapter investigates what has been learned from the successes and failures of past and ongoing activist efforts, why, despite small successes, the global arms trade as a whole has proved remarkably immune to effective critique and campaigning, and what experience suggests it may take to achieve more sweeping change.

The nature of the global arms business

The business of making and selling conventional weapons is unique in its functioning and consequences. The worldwide manufacture of weapons is a major global business, valued at $1,595 billion (SIPRI 2013) to $1,747 billion in 2013 (IISS 2014), or 2.4 per cent of global GDP. Forty per cent of this spending is by the US government. By way of comparison, global oil sales are valued at approximately $5 trillion (three times larger) and global pharmaceutical revenues are $800 billion (half the size). The international arms trade ranges from multibillion-dollar government-to-government deals for large-scale military equipment to informal deals for small numbers of light weapons. The officially measured international trade in conventional weapons was worth about $85 billion in 2011, of which the USA was responsible for over 70 per cent (Grimmett and Kerr 2012). Arms sales are, relatively speaking, a small element in global trade, but nonetheless one that has a disproportionate and malign influence. It is large enough, and has a political influence deep enough, to generate a parallel political economy that warrants the title 'shadow world' (Feinstein 2011).

Large, often publicly traded, weapons manufacturers and governments maintain that the sale of weapons between themselves is legal and clean, and bemoan the illicit trade as a regrettable but marginal affair which occurs among shady arms dealers, rogue leaders, non-state actors and organized crime. The reality is different: the arms business lies at the core of a shadow governmental system, centred in Washington, DC, London, Paris and other Western capitals, and with global reach.

The entire arms business is shrouded in secrecy, which makes it remarkably difficult for *any* arms procurement and trade decisions to be examined in a transparent manner. 'National security' is routinely used by all governments, democratic or authoritarian, to take decisions on military and security spending without meaningful parliamentary oversight or public scrutiny. Entire elements of national budgets are kept opaque. As well as rendering an important arena of public policy and spending extremely vulnerable to abuse – both to corruption for personal and party political gain, and to violations of citizens' rights by security and intelligence agencies – this makes it remarkably difficult to examine the logic behind defence and security decision-making.

National defence and security reviews for major countries, such as the USA and its NATO allies, typically and perennially observe that the world is a rapidly changing and more dangerous place. They identify new dangers from non-state actors and terrorists, and new systemic dangers such as the vulnerability of national infrastructure to cyber attack. Yet the procurement decisions of defence ministries remain dominated by weapons systems developed during the Cold War, such as tanks, aircraft carriers and fighter aircraft – not to mention nuclear submarines. Supply generates demand, in a self-reinforcing cycle. In the USA, the Department of Defense purchases enough weapons systems to keep the domestic industry fully serviced, but this is not the case for European manufacturers, for whom domestic contracts are simply not sufficiently large to enable them to operate with economies of scale or continuity of production lines. As a result, there is an incentive to use bribery for foreign sales – simply to lower unit costs and keep manufacturers busy. In turn this incentivizes cover-ups, because the business practices involved do not hold up to accepted standards.

Deals between governments and major manufacturers are riven with corruption. One study suggests, on the basis of figures up to the end of 2003, that the trade in weapons accounts for almost 40 per cent of all corruption in world trade (Roeber 2005). The US Department of Commerce claimed that 'the defense sector accounts for 50 percent of all bribery allegations in 1994–1999, despite accounting for less than 1 percent of world trade' (Trade Promotion Coordinating Committee 2000). The reality is that many of the arms dealers, agents and brokers engaged in the so-called illicit trade are used by the world's most powerful governments and defence contractors to facilitate the payment of bribes and other corruption on big deals. These same intermediaries are often used by governments for their own purposes. Perhaps the best-known example is the so-called 'Merchant of Death', Viktor Bout, who, while there was an Interpol warrant out for his arrest for arms trafficking into many of the world's conflicts, was being used by the US Department of Defense, and at least one major American defence contractor, to transport supplies and equipment into Iraq (Farah and Braun 2007). Weapons that, at one point, are bought 'legally' are often on-sold, 'stolen' or 'lost', thereby morphing into 'illegal' materiel.

The corruption that dominates the trade is not a case of a few renegade individuals sullying an otherwise exemplary activity – instead it is built into the very structure of the arms trade. In each year only a small number of major arms deals are concluded, usually worth billions of dollars each. The highly technical nature of the equipment tends to result in only a very small number of people making the procurement decisions. Crucially, almost every aspect of the deal takes place behind a national-security-imposed veil of secrecy, creating fertile conditions for corruption to flourish.

In addition, the participants in the weapons business are engaged in an almost perpetual revolving door, with people moving seamlessly and continuously between government, the military, intelligence agencies and the defence companies. Many arms trade intermediaries are used as intelligence assets by their own and other governments. These same intermediaries, and many of the corporate leaders of the manufacturers, are well connected to individual politicians and their political parties.

This insidious web, operating in secret, creates an environment in which those involved in the trade have significant impact and influence on key policy decisions – what materiel is bought and from whom, broad economic spending policies, and, of course, foreign and defence policies. The industry's insinuation into the

political and intelligence process at so many levels has also resulted in a situation in which the trade operates in something of
its own, parallel legal universe, where the breaking of laws, from
basic procurement regulations to the offering and acceptance of
multibillion-dollar bribes, goes largely unpunished. For example, of
502 recorded violations of United Nations' arms embargoes, only two
have resulted in any legal action (Feinstein 2011). Cases of illegality
against major weapons manufacturers are rarely investigated, even
less regularly brought to court, and almost never result in criminal
sanction and punishment.

But perhaps the trade's most malign influence is in the dominance of war-making over diplomacy as the default tool of dispute
resolution. This is reflected in the constant scaremongering of the
defence companies, their lobbyists and governments, aided by the
entertainment industry, in what has been referred to as the military-
industrial-media-entertainment network (Der Derian 2009). The
consequence is the significant tilt in spending from departments
of foreign affairs to the military, to the extent that today there are
more personnel running and maintaining one aircraft carrier in the
US Navy than there are US diplomats throughout the world. The USA
has ten aircraft carriers with three under construction (Gates 2007).
Vast spending on equipment is justified by the invocation of remote,
even fantastical threats. The Lockheed-Martin F35 stealth fighter
will – at current estimates – consume $1 trillion of US taxpayers'
money, for a machine of unproven usefulness.

Who suffers the consequences of the arms trade?

The impact of the trade is felt both deeply and widely. Most
obvious, and often fatally, are those in conflict situations – most
conflicts are not caused by the arms trade, but are elongated and
intensified by the easy availability of weapons. The massive build-up
of weaponry, aided by among others the French and South African
governments, in the lead-up to the Rwandan genocide is perhaps
one of the more tragic exemplars (Feinstein 2011).

But in addition to the victims in conflict zones, there are many
who suffer other consequences of the arms trade in both buying and
selling countries. The purchase of weapons, especially unnecessary
and overpriced systems, comes at significant socio-economic oppor-

tunity costs. For instance, in immediate post-apartheid South Africa, the ANC government, together with members of the old military order, decided to spend around $6–7 billion on weapons that the country did not need and barely uses. It has been alleged that millions of dollars in bribes were paid to senior politicians, officials and even the ruling ANC itself. This was at the time that President Thabo Mbeki was claiming the country lacked the fiscal resources to provide antiretroviral medication to the almost six million South Africans living with HIV or AIDS. A study at Harvard's School for Public Health suggests that 365,000 people died avoidable deaths as a consequence of this decision (Feinstein 2009). With the money spent on its arms deal, the South African government could have built almost two million houses or created 100,000 low-entry-level jobs a year for ten years in an economy with a formal unemployment rate of between 25 and 30 per cent (Holden and Van Vuuren 2011).

The bribes themselves are often added on to the purchase price of weapons, and so are paid for by taxpayers in the purchasing country. In addition, citizens in the producing countries fund the significant amounts of public money that are invested in the companies building weaponry. And in almost all countries of the world, taxpayers and citizens are expected to accept spiralling defence budgets almost regardless of the real threats facing them.

Governments in buying and selling countries also go to great lengths to hide the corruption implicit in their arms dealing. In the case of South Africa this included undermining the accountability role of parliament and closing down the two main anti-corruption bodies, as well as fatally politicizing their prosecutorial and investigative agencies. In the United Kingdom, Tony Blair ordered the shutting down of an investigation into the country's largest defence company, BAE Systems, in relation to bribes of £6 billion that were allegedly paid to facilitate a massive arms deal with Saudi Arabia (Feinstein 2011).

A key question for activists concerns the roots and measurement of corruption. The global media feeds on stories of corrupt politicians and others in countries of the South, but seldom focuses the spotlight on the corporations – often publicly traded entities in the North – and their enabling and benefiting politicians. In fact, it is likely that the amount of corruption emanating in many countries of the North – some of which circulates back to corporate executives, officials, politicians and political parties in those countries – often far outstrips corruption by ruling elites in the South.

The global arms business, with its deep and well-concealed connections to the world's intelligence and military establishments, with its corrupt dealings providing political funds, both overt and clandestine, pollutes democracy and the rule of law. In the aftermath of the First World War, campaigners identified these connections and challenged the entire political economy of armaments. Today, efforts to expose, confront and limit this shadow world are fragmented and modest.

Anti-arms-trade activism from the First World War to Vietnam

The high point of activism against the arms trade came in the period following the Great War of 1914–18. The war itself was a profound shock to Western civilization, confounding the optimism of those who argued that any war between great powers would be irrational because its destructive impact would be so greatly in excess of any advantage that a belligerent could gain (Angell 1910). The logic was impeccable, and was borne out by events, but those same events demonstrated that enlightened self-interest did not guide the affairs of nations. One common response was to blame the pre-war arms race, especially the British–German competition to build dreadnought battleships, and in turn to scrutinize those who had a material interest in war and the preparation for war.

Arms-makers were seen to have made a financial killing out of the bloodbath. Opposition to them was led by pacifist or anti-war groups, but gained wider public support. The views of the time were summarized by British prime minister David Lloyd George, who declaimed that 'If you want to preserve peace in the world you must eliminate the idea of profit of great and powerful interests in the manufacture of armaments' (Royal Commission 1936: 544). US president Woodrow Wilson went so far as to enshrine in the Covenant of the League of Nations a paragraph which agreed 'that the manufacture by private enterprise of munitions and implements of war is open to grave objections' (Sampson 1977).

These sentiments, expressed by opinion-formers and ordinary people in the press, led to the creation of a Commission to Reduce

Arms. Its 1921 report accused the arms companies of 'fomenting war scares, bribing government officials, disseminating false reports concerning the military programmes of countries and organising international armaments rings to accentuate the arms race by playing one country off against another' (ibid.).

Between the two world wars, the companies endured an unparalleled slump in orders and profits. This did not stop them agitating against disarmament. Revelations of arms companies employing lobbyists to argue against disarmament at the Geneva Disarmament Conference of 1927 coincided with a wave of pacifism and an underlying distrust of big corporations, made more intense by the Wall Street Crash of 1929. The petition circulated by women's international organizations calling for disarmament, with 8 million signatures from fifty-six countries, is the largest in history (Davies 2011: 39). Pacifists used this confluence of events to push for a Senate Committee in 1934, chaired by an outspoken Republican senator, Gerald P. Nye. Best-selling books and numerous press articles supported the campaign against the companies earning 'cold cash profits on smashed brains and smothered legs'.[1]

Nye's report was a devastating critique of the companies and their supporters in government. It led to the creation of a Munitions Control Board in the USA and had significant influence in the UK, where over 90 per cent of adults believed that there should be an international agreement prohibiting 'the manufacture and sale of arms for private profit' (Sampson 1977). The government was forced to set up a Royal Commission, which provided a wide-ranging, if muted, critique of the British arms trade.

However, by the time the Commission reported, public opinion had started to shift in response to the aggressive behaviour of Hitler's Germany. The resultant massive rearmament saved the arms companies financially and put an end to criticism of them. Concurrently, the response of the European left to the Spanish Civil War was disarray – many mobilized to fight for the Republicans, and to condemn the timidity of democratic governments that failed to join the battle. As Europe slid towards general conflagration, patriotic enthusiasm for weaponry in democratic countries drowned out the critique of the role of arms corporations in driving the expansion of fascism, for example by the French leftist Daniel Guérin (1936).

Among the many tragedies of the 1930s was the rise of democratic militarism, and the historic eclipse of disarmament as a mainstream political agenda.

By the time of the outbreak of the Second World War, disarmament became linked in the public mind to appeasement – a status it has never quite managed to lose. Arms manufacturers became heroic names, along with their products and the men who fought using them. No sooner had the war finished than the Iron Curtain fell across Europe and the USA, Britain and France began updating their inventories for what they feared would be a Third World War against the Soviet Union.

The post-Second World War environment saw significant new arms production and sales in the nascent Cold War. It is surprising, especially with the reaction to the First World War in mind, that there was not more public concern about these sales in the aftermath of the most destructive war in the history of mankind. Disarmament was discussed as never before, but it was nuclear disarmament which understandably dominated the arguments and conferences. Compared to the new danger of a nuclear holocaust, the problem of the export of conventional weapons seemed relatively harmless, and inevitable as a by-product of the growing Cold War. During the Berlin Airlift and then the Korean War, the prospect of nuclear escalation was real.

Possibly the least expected advocate for arms control was President Dwight Eisenhower, former Supreme Commander of Allied Forces in Europe, who in his farewell address in January 1961 warned,

> We must guard against the acquisition of unwarranted influence, whether sought or unsought, by the military–industrial complex. The potential for the disastrous rise of misplaced power exists, and will persist. We must never let the weight of this combination endanger our liberties or democratic processes. We should take nothing for granted. Only an alert and knowledgeable citizenry can compel the proper meshing of the huge industrial and military machinery of defense with our peaceful methods and goals so that security and liberty may prosper together.

There is debate among Eisenhower's biographers as to whether he contemplated, in a draft of the speech, using the term 'military–

industrial–*congressional* complex', in reference to the way in which manufacturers had co-opted Congress (Thomas 2011). Eisenhower's key point, about the close meshing of special interests in the arms business and the culture and conduct of politics, resonates fifty years on.

It was not until the Vietnam War that a broad-based anti-war movement flourished once again in the United States. This movement did not target the arms manufacturers in any organized manner, despite Eisenhower's identification of the dangers of an untrammelled military–industrial complex and Bob Dylan's accusatory song 'The Masters of War'. Only Dow Chemical, the manufacturer of napalm, which was used in the conflict, became the focus of student and other activist groups.

In the 1970s, in response to Vietnam and war in the Middle East, peace groups in some countries, especially in Europe, created organizations committed to the abolition of the global arms trade. For instance, in the UK in 1974, in response specifically to the Middle East war of the previous year, when the UK had armed both sides, a number of organizations (Quakers, the Campaign for Nuclear Disarmament, Pax Christi, the United Nations Association and others) found themselves working on arms export issues and came together to form what was intended to be a joint campaign of limited duration, Campaign Against Arms Trade (CAAT). By 1984 there were enough groups in Europe working on the issue for the European Network Against Arms Trade to be formed. Its composite groups operate differently in different countries – for example, the arms trade is one campaign of several run by the general-purpose peace organization the Swedish Peace and Arbitration Society (SPAS). CAAT in the UK and many of the network's organizations, which still vary in size and modus operandi – remain crucial players in anti-arms trade work today. They tend to focus on campaigning against their own companies' and governments' participation in the trade, often with the support of individuals and/or organizations in the countries to whom the weapons are sold, or against whom the weapons are used. In many instances they situate the arms trade and its consequences within a broader political critique of militarism and corporate power.

This is in contrast to most arms trade campaigning – see 'The

Arms Trade Treaty' below – which is largely uncritical of the political and militarist context in which the trade occurs. As Anna Stavrianakis (2010) argues, arms trade campaigners, by focusing on abuses at the margins of the arms production and trade business, endorse a global normative framework that regards the arms business as legitimate, requiring only better regulation.

Whether directly or indirectly, antipathy towards anti-arms-trade activism and a lack of funding for work on broad research and campaigning around the global arms trade led to a focus on specific-issue campaigns. A number of specific issues were candidates for this focused activism, including biological weapons, fuel-air explosives, pain weapons and depleted uranium. The entry point for activism was not ending war, but limiting weapons: the impulse was to tighten the laws of war, inherently a paradoxical exercise.

The landmines campaign

The issue that unexpectedly emerged around 1990 was a campaign against anti-personnel landmines. This campaign has a broader signi-ficance in the modern history of activism because its successes have strongly influenced other international campaigns and it is widely held out as a model by international campaigners on social issues. It has inspired a number of follow-on campaigns, such as the cam-paign against cluster munitions and that against the proliferation of small arms.

Following three years of parallel and loosely coordinated cam-paigning, six organizations, three in Europe and three in the USA, came together to formally launch the ICBL in 1993. The ICBL con-tained many elements of a classic single-issue campaign – that is, a campaign with a narrow focus that deliberately disregards the wider context. Landmines are a visible, arguably unique (or at least somehow 'different') weapon of uncertain military utility. The injuries produced by landmines, many of them to civilians including children, are conspicuously gruesome. The majority of landmine victims are adult men, many of them soldiers, but most photographs of amputees show women and children. Landmines are particularly ugly because they are so inherently indiscriminate and continue to claim casualties years after the end of hostilities. Following the precedent of chemical weapons, the solution – a ban – is simple and attractive (perhaps misleadingly so – chemical weapons do not need to be dug out of the ground one by one).

Writing on the campaign has stressed its innovative use of the internet and other ways of networking and raising issues, and the role of leading personalities and their strategies of cooperating with governments and/or confronting them (Don 2000; Scott 2001). Links between two campaign goals – a global ban and a global fund for demining activities – have been less explored. In retrospect, the meteoric rise of the campaign seems inevitable, but at the time the prospects of success appeared remote. The very first publications on landmines as a campaigning issue date from 1990 and 1991 and were published in the teeth of considerable scepticism (McGrath 1990; Asia Watch 1991).

Within five years of its official launch in 1993, the campaign won the attention of Princess Diana, achieved the Ottawa Convention on the Prohibition of the Use, Stockpiling, Production and Transfer of Anti-Personnel Mines, and was awarded the Nobel Peace Prize. But was it really that simple or wonderful?

The ICBL was a hybrid of organizational models. The US section recruited Jody Williams, who had spent the previous decade campaigning to reform US policy towards Central American dictatorships. Williams focused on lobbying policy-makers, especially in Washington, DC, to support an international treaty. There was little mobilization of the grass roots. Williams' best-known innovation was her use of the internet. In Europe, Asia and Africa, the goals and strategy were different from the outset. The vision was to generate a social consensus that so stigmatized the production and use of landmines that there would be a revulsion against them comparable to that against chemical weapons. From this change in moral sensibility, it was hoped, a number of key actions would emerge, including an international treaty to ban landmines and a fund to ensure that landmines could be cleared. This was a much larger and more complex campaign, which engaged grassroots organization and dealt directly with the trade unions in the manufacturing sector. Notably, one of its successes was challenging the Italian government and Valsella Meccanotecnica, the principal Italian landmine manufacturer (in Brescia), leading to the Italian government deciding that Italy should cease mine production in 1994.

The triumphs of the campaign – Princess Diana's advocacy, the Ottawa treaty and the Nobel Prize – helped shape Western public attitudes and governmental policies. With the notable exception of the USA, almost all Western countries signed the Ottawa Convention. A princess's patronage, a treaty and a prize came to define the success of the landmines campaign in the popular mind. But there are important shortcomings and unlearned lessons. In the countries where most landmines are actually laid – mostly poor countries in Africa and Asia – the campaign did not reach the critical threshold of establishing a moral consensus that absolutely prohibits the production and laying of mines. For many front-line commanders in the wars of Africa, Asia and the Caucasus, anti-personnel mines are still seen as a useful weapon. In fact, more mines were laid in the decade following the Ottawa Convention than were removed from the ground (though huge stockpiles were destroyed).

In addition there is the problem of the legacy of the past. Landmine clearance is slow, and the public triumph at Ottawa had the unfortunate effect of demobilizing many of the campaign supporters, who believed prematurely that the key problem had been solved. At current rates of clearance it will take many decades to remove landmines from many countries. Casualties from landmines have reduced but are still high. The landmines campaign still has to do the hardest task of maintaining the momentum of international public policy to remove these devices.

The campaign included a number of organizations that were not natural campaigners on the issue. Their remit was mostly material assistance directly relevant to the issue at hand – clearing landmines and treating people injured in landmine explosions. Often, international charity is diametrically opposed to political campaigning, or at least insidiously undermines it. And indeed initially some mine clearance charities (e.g. Halo Trust in Britain) criticized the campaign for directing attention and resources away from the task of clearance. Other charities such as Oxfam joined the campaign rather late (it was only in 1994 that Oxfam decided that it could support a ban, and the British Red Cross was belatedly corralled into the campaign in 1997 after Princess Diana visited Angola and spoke out in favour of a ban). But from the outset, the leading charities involved (Mines Advisory Group and Handicap International) were stimulated to campaign for the abolition of mines on the grounds that their charitable activities were meaningless unless there was a long-term solution to the problem, i.e. banning landmines altogether. A vital aspect of the campaign was its technical mastery of the issue, which was established right at the outset of the campaign. The practical experience of demining, including the removal of cluster munitions and other kinds of weapons, meant that the mines campaign was never at a disadvantage when dealing with its adversaries. One of the weaknesses of the campaign was that some advocates either used (imprecise) numbers freely and haphazardly, or became too focused on numbers of mines. These metrics were misleading and usually irrelevant, and they laid the campaign open to the occasional critique that it was exaggerating (Maslen 2004).

In retrospect, it is clear that the Ottawa Convention and the Nobel Prize were gained too fast, before substantive progress had been made. Pressure from the Canadian government and the US campaign for a quick triumph meant that fateful compromises were made. Most notably, the definition of an anti-personnel landmine was not a weapon that had the effect of an anti-personnel landmine, but rather a weapon that was designed by the manufacturer to have that effect. Thus entire categories of weapons, such as air-delivered cluster munitions, which have a high rate of non-explosion on initial impact and lie in or on the ground acting in a manner identical to anti-personnel landmines, were excluded. Implementation provisions and penalties for non-compliance are all but non-existent.

Moreover, the Convention was adopted and the Nobel Prize awarded before the campaign had really begun in many affected countries. This worried many campaigners at the time. As soon as the Nobel Committee announced the award, jointly to Jody Williams and the ICBL, there was a vigorous debate among members of the coalition as to whether to accept their part, and if so, on what terms. The debate was resolved in favour of acceptance, on the precondition that the award would be extended beyond the six founder members of the campaign to include partners from the South. While Jody Williams was made a celebrity by the international media, the award to the larger campaign was received by Rae McGrath, founder of the Mines Advisory Group and one of the originators of the campaign, who stressed in his speech that he was accepting it on behalf of the wider global effort. Quickly thereafter, those who had been cautious about the prize were vindicated. As soon as the criterion for compliance shifted from taking practical action to stop using landmines and increasing efforts to take them out of the ground, to signing an international convention, real effort and impact were dissipated.

For example, many African governments enthusiastically signed up to the Ottawa Convention and then did little to make their obligations real. Some of the Ottawa signatories, such as Sudan and Angola, continued to use anti-personnel mines without any evident pause. Other signatories, such as Ethiopia, resumed the use of mines as soon as they faced a military threat a few months later. Only a few countries, such as Egypt and Eritrea, took the course of openly opposing the treaty and insisting that they would continue to use these weapons. Some members of the campaign have argued that allowing Angola and Sudan to accede to the treaty, while it was clear that they had no intention of respecting it, undermined its credibility. In these countries, there has been no significant public pressure for governments to meet the requirements of the Convention, because freedom of association and expression are very limited. On the other hand, South Africa led the way in destroying its stockpiles of mines, reflecting its government's high international public moral standing on a range of issues as well as pressure from a domestic advocacy campaign (Stott 1998).

The landmines campaign illustrates the evolution of ethical standards. When a campaign was first discussed in 1990, the existing standard was no more than a provision in an obscure annexe to a little-known convention.[2] Less than a decade later the use of anti-personnel landmines was widely condemned as an abuse, and non-use of landmines became an international norm. This change was brought about by the initiative and energy of rights entrepreneurs: individuals whose vision and passion succeeded in creating new moral standards. However, the campaign rushed quickly to its triumphs, and this success demobilized many campaign supporters before some of the key goals, such as a global fund for mine eradication and real policy changes in developing countries, could be achieved.

The cluster munitions campaign

For activists in Western capitals, the landmines campaign was one of the most rapidly successful international movements of modern times: it achieved a major triumph in a few years and showed the possibilities of partnership between a coalition of NGOs, some of them specialists and others with tangential interest in the issue, and small and medium states (notably Canada), circumventing the traditional fora for establishing new multilateral norms (Cameron et al. 1998). The campaign caught the military establishment by surprise, leading the US Department of Defense to pay new attention to the threat posed by activists to its weapons systems, and consider direct monitoring of NGO activities, especially when sponsored by liberal governments in smaller Western states (Deam 2001). But perhaps the most important lesson from the landmines campaign is that success at the level of international leadership has not yet translated into the effective prevention of landmine use in conflicts, especially in poor countries.

For an activist community desperate for success, and keen to engage with issues around weapons, the ICBL was an inspiration. It was quickly followed by attempts at similar coalition-building. An immediate successor was the attempt to mobilize against cluster munitions. This partly arose from the transatlantic division within the landmines campaign, as many European campaigners had wanted to include cluster munitions within the definition of anti-personnel landmines.

The Cluster Munition Coalition (CMC) was set up in 2003 on the precise model of the ICBL – and indeed advertises itself as a 'sister campaign'. It was launched by European NGOs with sympathetic support from smaller European countries and culminated in the Convention on Cluster Munitions, signed in Oslo in 2008, which bans the stockpiling, use and transfer of virtually all existing cluster bombs and attempts to provide for the clearing up of unexploded munitions.

The cluster munitions campaign resembles the landmines campaign in many respects. However, to date it has been an even more heavily qualified success story. The differences in initial conditions, the CMC's approach and the outcome are instructive.

Cluster munitions – bombs which release a large number of sub-munitions, often called 'bomblets', upon delivery – share many of the characteristics that made it possible to create general public revulsion towards the use of landmines. The overwhelming majority of their victims are civilians, many injured by unexploded bomblets long after a conflict has ended, including occasionally children who confuse brightly coloured bomblets for toys (Handicap International 2007). However, unlike landmines, cluster munitions were and are still a significant part of the actively employed arsenal of major military powers. The USA used them in both Iraq and Afghanistan before 2003, and has declared that 'they are integral to every Army or Marine manoeuvre element and in some cases constitute up to 50 percent of tactical indirect fire support. U.S. forces simply cannot fight by design or by doctrine without holding out at least the possibility of using cluster munitions' (Kidd 2008).

Thus it was clear early in the cluster munitions campaign that the USA and other major militaries would not sign up easily or quickly. The CMC chose to use the existing momentum from the landmine success to move forward to the 2008 Convention anyway. Some of those involved in the CMC have explained that this was because the cluster munitions campaign was more heavily focused on prevention – as Matthew Bolton and Thomas Nash (2010) recount, stockpiles of cluster munitions '... reach into billions of sub-munitions. Many states, including those in Africa and Latin America, noted during the negotiations that it was important to act now ... Indeed, many participants in the process noted that it would prevent the problem from reaching a global scale that could eclipse the landmine problem.'

It was also an advantageous moment to make progress with 'persuadable' countries. Lebanese civilian casualties from Israel's 2006 use of cluster munitions became an international scandal, and the USA had stopped using cluster munitions in Iraq and Afghanistan in 2003 in large part because of civilian casualties (McGrath 2004).

This approach yielded some notable successes. The smaller group of signatories yielded a fairly comprehensive treaty, which bans production, stockpiling, transfer and use of almost all varieties of cluster munitions. CMC organizers argue that a comprehensive ban, rather than a compromise version that might have attracted more support, is 'a critical element in promoting the stigmatisation of the weapon and the norm-building power of the Convention' (Bolton and Nash 2010).

As of September 2013, 108 states had signed the Convention while 84 have ratified, as compared to 140 signatories and 118 ratifiers of the decade-older landmine ban (Cluster Munition Monitor 2013). Perhaps more significantly, forty-two of the Convention's signatories were previous users, producers and/or stockpilers of cluster munitions, several more former users have signed in recent years (Chad, Iraq and Peru), and there have been 'no confirmed reports or allegations of new use of cluster munitions by any State Party' since adoption in 2008 (ibid.). Of the four state parties to have used them – Syria, Myanmar, Libya and Thailand – most are such frequent violators of the laws of war that they can hardly be said to be reinforcing a norm that use is acceptable.

However, it has become increasingly clear over time that the Convention's 'race to the finish line' left the larger, long-term campaign with some serious deficiencies. Early in the CMC organizing process, Rae McGrath identified extensive public education and encouraging public debate as essential elements in changing the norm on cluster munitions use (McGrath 2004). As previously noted, the norm-shifting success of the European branches of the landmine campaign had come largely from grassroots mobilization and inculcating anti-landmine revulsion across the broadest possible spectrum of the population and among opinion-formers.

Education, debate and publicity regarding cluster munitions have never taken place on a comparable scale. There has been no high-exposure, Princess Diana-esque spokesperson, and the resulting lack of a 'public opinion' check has made it much easier for signatories to reinterpret their obligations more leniently, and for non-signatories to claim they have made (or are about to make) technical progress that makes signing unnecessary, with activist counter-claims attracting little attention.

For example, then UK foreign secretary David Miliband faced only minor political blowback for exploiting a legal loophole that allows the USA to continue to stockpile cluster munitions in Britain, despite its status as a Convention signatory (Evans and Leigh 2010). The same can be said of state signatories Afghanistan, Germany, Italy, Japan and Spain, all of which Wikileaks cables identified as having allowed (and as possibly still allowing) US storage of cluster munitions on their territory.

The Convention appears to have had some impact on shifting US policy, but only incrementally, and not as a result of much public and/or electoral pressure. The Cluster Munitions Convention was a complete non-issue in the hotly contested 2008 Democratic Party primary, even among the 'peace activist' constituency, owing largely to lack of awareness. The same year the Convention was signed, the USA pledged to bring failure rates among its cluster munitions stockpiles down to 1 per cent by 2018 (Secretary of Defense 2008), but continues to export these munitions to dubious end-users such as Saudi Arabia with, once again, no real domestic political consequences (Jones 2013). Current bills in the US Congress to further restrict cluster munitions use have garnered little publicity and appear unlikely to pass.

The lessons of the cluster munitions effort reinforce the critical lessons of the landmine campaign – whether a formal treaty is signed early or late in a process, activists cannot view it as an end point, or even the primary goal of their efforts. The work of creating a lasting public moral consensus against particular weapons is indispensable – the less that such work is done, the easier it will be for governments to find ways around their obligations and pledges at very little cost.

Other attempts to emulate the ICBL

Campaigners against gun violence were energized by the model of the ICBL, and activism against illicit transfers of small arms and light weapons (SALW) followed. A large number of small organizations – 250 full members and almost 600 associate organizations, with different approaches and agendas – came together under the umbrella of the International Action Network on Small Arms (IANSA). IANSA's biggest effort was to push for a special UN conference on the illicit trade in small arms, and a plan of action to combat that trade. However, the network has withered, having run out of funding. Its existence, such as it currently is, depends on the work of a small group of volunteers.

According to Aaron Karp, academic and consultant to the Small Arms Survey, small arms activism has reshaped the international agenda and created an institutional legacy that will guarantee that the issue remains on the international agenda for the long term. He cites the Programme of Action to Prevent, Combat and Eradicate the Illicit Trade in Small and Light Weapons (PoA), adopted by the UN in 2001, as well as a number of Security Council embargoes on specific countries as significant, but concedes that progress since then has been slow. The movement, he suggests, was threatened by its inability to articulate clear goals, poor coordination between groups and the success of governments in transforming the campaign into something that was safe for them, posing no threat to their key policies on gun control (Karp 2006). One critique of the movement stresses 'the failure of NGOs to develop an independent voice, the result of a Faustian bargain with sympathetic governments' (ibid.: 17). The reliance on funding from mostly European governments has, according to Karp, resulted in NGOs and research institutes 'losing the independence they require to press for dramatic change. For [them] government recognition and financing also means government influence.'

If IANSA was too large and dispersed to mount an effective challenge to the arms industry and its government protectors, the 'killer robots' campaign illustrates the other extreme – a well-organized campaign run by a small elite of well-connected activists. While IANSA's members lost their independence because of the financial and organizational constraints of running a campaign, the organizations behind the 'killer robots' campaign were already sufficiently intimate with their adversaries in government that they knew precisely how to design a campaign so that it would have precise impacts – effects within defined limits.

The campaign against autonomous weapons systems (defined as weapons that can select and fire upon targets on their own, without human intervention, popularized as 'killer robots') that suddenly surfaced in 2012 shows how a group of professional advocacy organizations in the USA seized upon a hitherto obscure issue and made it the centrepiece of a new campaign. It is the focus of a fascinating case study of the operation of the 'human security network' by Charli Carpenter (2014). This network is primarily North American and secondarily European.

Carpenter describes how, from about 2007, the humanitarian and human rights specialists who had been engaged with law and advocacy around weapons systems were increasingly concerned about the moral implications of the shift in military technology towards robots. Some lawyers and activists were concerned with whether automated weapons – 'taking the man out of the loop' – can make ethical targeting decisions. Related issues included who should be held accountable for errors, and whether the automation of combat altered the political incentives for war-making. On the other side of the debate were techno-optimists, experts who argued that technological advances can lessen the lethality of war, and specifically that autonomous weapons can make decisions with consistency, proportionality and restraint, which human beings too often lack. However, what Carpenter calls the key 'advocacy superpowers' – the International Committee of the Red Cross (ICRC) and Human Rights Watch (HRW) – were sceptical about fully autonomous weapons, seeing them as a 'science fiction' issue remote from reality. Another difficulty was that the leading organization, the International Committee on Robot Arms Control (ICRAC), was seen as a left-leaning anti-war organization, with which the gatekeepers of legitimized activism, such as HRW, were not ready to associate.

This began to change as the issue of weaponized drones attracted media attention and public concern. Several elements then came together to make the automated weapons issue salient. The emergence of drones as the US weapon of choice in low-intensity counter-terrorist operations generated a sense of urgency, that robotic conflict is the future of warfare.[3] Concern with drones' humanitarian impact shifted the question to one of international humanitarian law and brought in new, and newly energized, humanitarian actors. And equally significantly, the advocacy networks were reshaped in 2011, when Richard Moyes and Thomas Nash, two veterans of the landmines and the cluster munitions campaigns, established a new organization, Article36, for humanitarian control of weapons technology.[4] Article36 reconfigured many members of the former ICRAC group as a less radical and more mainstream initiative. Moyes and Nash, already well connected throughout the Washington advocacy arena, had their impact amplified when Steve Goose, head of the HRW Arms Unit, decided to take on the issue – partly at the prompting of his wife, Jody Williams, 'who possesses perhaps the widest social network of any individual in the humanitarian disarmament network' (Carpenter 2014: 118). With the tacit support of the ICRC, this elite advocacy network was able to mobilize a high-profile campaign against 'killer robots'.[5]

The 2012 launch of the campaign against autonomous weapons systems illustrates both the strength and the weakness of the highly specialized professional advocacy networks in North America. The leaders of these groups have enormous power and discretion over which issues are adopted and how they are framed, and – by extension – which remain as 'lost causes'. These individuals share a social milieu that closely overlaps with that of Washington, DC policy-makers, skill in legalistic framing of issues, and an acute sensibility to how a cause can best gain traction in order to achieve the goals of changing US laws and winning an international convention. But in doing so, they also trim the cause to fit the policy audience, and as such it is sometimes hard to tell whether they are leading US policy change or responding to the discreet openings signalled by their colleagues in government. Insofar as they are radical, it is establishment radicalism.

The Arms Trade Treaty

A signal attempt to break out of the narrow confines of single-issue campaigning, and to energize a truly transnational activist coalition, was made by the Control Arms Campaign. But in doing so, it also failed to break out of a conservative legalistic campaigning paradigm. In 2003, a number of the IANSA constituent groups, together with large NGOs such as Amnesty International, Oxfam, Saferworld and myriad smaller organizations from across the world, formed the Control Arms Campaign to push for the adoption of an international Arms Trade Treaty (ATT) at the United Nations. A decade later, on 2 April 2013, an Arms Trade Treaty was adopted by the UN.

While at some levels the campaign was extremely important, it was by no means unproblematic. It effectively brought together numerous organizations from all corners of the world to focus on the impact of the arms trade. It linked the obvious deadly consequences of weapons to the relative lack of regulation of their buying and selling. However, the campaign enunciated a moderate view of the arms trade, distinguishing between legal and illegal arms sales without paying sufficient attention to the murky nexus of the two, underplaying the extent and governance impact of corruption in the trade and failing to point fingers at governments and corporations which often break their own existing laws and regulations in their arms dealing. The crucial and deeply troubling role of intermediaries, and their links to governments, politicians and political parties, was also soft-pedalled.

It was, therefore, not particularly surprising that the treaty eventually passed in the UN is extremely weak. It barely deals with the issues of corruption and intermediation and contains no enforcement mechanisms whatsoever. Countries could adopt the treaty and do absolutely nothing to enforce its basic tenets. As a consequence many of the more confrontational organizations working on the trade, such as CAAT and International Physicians for the Prevention of Nuclear War (IPPNW), have been dismissive of the ATT.

The campaign, which has consumed significant NGO time and resources, has been symbolically important for raising the issue of the arms trade, but it is possible that the very weak treaty actually creates more problems than it solves. Many campaigners, as well as members of the general public, may believe that the signing of the treaty is, in itself, a massive victory and that the issue of arms can be ticked off as dealt with. However, the treaty itself could see some countries actually weaken their arms export controls. For instance, the government of Japan announced that it will effectively do away with many of its restrictions on the export of arms, and, according to an activist in the country, the ATT is being used to legitimize the decision (Natsuki 2014). Arms companies do not envisage the treaty changing the way they operate at all, as confirmed by the chairman of BAE Systems at the company's AGM in May 2014 (CAAT 2014).

The campaign around the ATT obfuscates the systemic issues that underpin the global arms trade: the collusion between governments, weapons manufacturers, intelligence agencies, the military and political parties to distort policy, undermine the rule of law and facilitate widespread corruption, while actively opposing any meaningful measure of transparency and accountability for their actions. The campaign and the ATT itself therefore replicate similar shortcomings to those of the Ottawa Convention: they assume that the treaty is *in itself* an achievement, rather than a tool towards a further goal. A number of active participants in the ATT process are considering whether their focus on the UN has perhaps been misplaced, positing a greater focus on national and regional interventions (Mack 2014).

However, the campaign has brought into sharp focus the distinction between those working on the issue who accept the legitimacy of current state and corporate arrangements, and those who focus on power structures and their attendant secrecy, centralization of power and inherent injustice. This distinction has become more accentuated in the post-9/11 world, in which a simplistic national security discourse, with obvious similarities to the Cold War era, went unchallenged for many years, enabling defence contractors to reap enormous financial gains, while delivering little of value. In this they resemble the war profiteers who were so severely maligned in the aftermath of the First World War and whose influence so disturbed President Eisenhower.

A progressive agenda for anti-arms trade activism

Since the eclipse of the broad-based peace movement with its focus on disarmament in the 1930s, the most successful examples of activism on arms have been single-issue campaigns, framed as humanitarian issues, notably the ICBL. The Control Arms Campaign was wider in its mandate but not deeper in its agenda. This chapter has posed the question: do these campaigns distract attention from the bigger picture and indeed end up legitimizing the global military–commercial complex? Or do they serve as an educational tool for the general public and an apprenticeship for campaigners, who thereby become aware of the more profound and sinister structural issues? But if they do the latter, then a campaign on global arms needs a framework into which these graduates of constituent campaigns can insert themselves.

The main structural features of the global trade in arms remain firmly in place. The flow of weapons around the world appears inexorable, leaving death, displacement, corruption and poverty in its wake. The major arms manufacturers are unworried by the major thrusts of arms trade activism, which focus either on weapons systems that (for them) are minor or redundant (such as anti-personnel landmines) or which generate international conventions that can easily be worked around (such as the Convention on Cluster Munitions and the Arms Trade Treaty). Arms activism has not threatened the business model itself, which is protected by political, security and commercial interests at the secret heart of political establishments in Washington, DC and European capitals.

This raises the question of whether it is feasible to create a global campaign to tackle the basic structure of the business. This would need to target the centre of gravity of the problem itself: the unaccountable nexus between industry, politics and the military and security establishments. It would need to expose the shadow world of arms manufacture and trade. The campaign would address the global problem of excessive armaments not solely as a humanitarian issue, not solely as an issue of waste and corruption, and not solely as an invitation to warmongering. It would seek to encompass all the constituencies that are driven by outrage against humanitarian tragedies, corruption, waste and destruction, and war, but in addition would explore common ground in a shared agenda of democratic scrutiny of decisions over what instruments of destruction to design, build and sell, and why.

Given the political interests inherent in the current functioning of the trade, the difficulty of open and vigorous debate on matters pertaining to national security, the concomitant difficulty in raising funds for work on the issue that might challenge state and corporate interests, and the complexity of some of the issues, the challenge remains how to develop a focused campaign that speaks simply and persuasively to large numbers of people, that links people who are affected by the trade in areas of conflict as well as producing, selling and buying countries. A broad-based movement to change the conversation around the arms trade would need to involve those who engage with the structures of interlocked power as well as those who challenge that power itself.

Such a movement would need to link the global dimensions of the trade to local activism that has, for instance, kept the South African arms deal alive as a major political issue in the country for over fourteen years; or which resulted in a recent Swiss referendum rejecting the purchase of Gripen jet fighters by the country's government.

While these preliminary thoughts reflect the paucity of engagement with the structural issues of the arms business, one thing is certain: if the manufacture and trade in weapons are allowed to continue to function in the way they do, they will continue to make the world a poorer, more corrupt, less democratic and less safe place for us all.

Notes

1 *Chicago Daily News*, 3–5 August 1933.

2 The 1980 Convention on Prohibitions or Restrictions on the Use of Certain Conventional Weapons Which May Be Deemed to Be Excessively Injurious or to Have Indiscriminate Effects, commonly referred to as the Convention on Conventional Weapons (CCW).

3 Drones are not in fact fully automated, but are remotely operated by a human being, but they share technologies with autonomous weapons systems.

4 The name refers to the article in the 1977 Additional Protocol of the Geneva Convention that requires governments to consider the legality of new weapons and methods of warfare.

5 www.hrw.org/topic/arms/killer-robots.

References

Angell, N. (1910) *The Great Illusion: A study of the relation of military power to national advantage*, London.

Asia Watch (1991) *The Cowards' War: Landmines in Cambodia*, New York: Human Rights Watch, September.

Bolton, M. and T. Nash (2010) 'The role of middle power–NGO coalitions in global policy: the case of the cluster munitions ban', *Global Policy*, 1(2): 172–84.

CAAT (2014) 'Campaigners dominate "memorable" BAE Systems AGM', CAAT press release, 7 May.

Cameron, M. A., R. J. Lawson and B. W. Tomlin (eds) (1998) *To Walk without Fear: The Global Movement to Ban Landmines*, Toronto: Oxford University Press.

Carpenter, C. (2014) *'Lost' Causes: Agenda vetting in global issue networks and the shaping of human security*, Ithaca, NY: Cornell University Press.

Cluster Munition Monitor (2013) 'Cluster Munition Monitor Report 2013' and 'Landmine Monitor Report 2013', *Landmine & Cluster Munition Monitor*, www.the-monitor.org/index.php/publications/display?url=cmm/2013/.

Davies, T. R. (2011) 'The rise and fall of transnational civil society: the evolution of international non-governmental organizations since the mid-nineteenth century', in L. Reydams (ed.), *Global Activism Reader*, New York: Continuum.

Deam, S. R. (2001) 'The Antipersonnel Landmines Convention and the evolving politics of arms control', Unpublished thesis, Master's in Public Policy, Harvard University.

Der Derian, J. (2009) *Virtuous Wars: Mapping the Military-Industrial-Media-Entertainment-Network*, New York: Routledge.

Don, H. (2000) 'The landmine ban: a case study in humanitarian advocacy', Occasional Paper no. 42, Thomas J. Watson Jnr Institute for International Studies.

Evans, R. and D. Leigh (2010) 'WikiLeaks cables: secret deal let Americans sidestep cluster bomb ban', *Guardian*, 1 December, www.theguardian.com/world/2010/dec/01/wikileaks-cables-cluster-bombs-britain.

Farah, D. and S. Braun (2007) *Merchant of Death: Money, guns, planes and the man who makes war possible*, London: John Wiley & Sons.

Feinstein, A. (2009) *After the Party: Cor-ruption, the ANC and South Africa's Uncertain Future*, London: Verso.

— (2011) *The Shadow World: Inside the global arms trade*, London: Hamish Hamilton.

Gates, R. (2007) Landon Lecture, Kansas State University, 26 November, www.k-state.edu/media/news releases/landonlect/gatestext1107.html.

Grimmett, R. and P. Kerr (2012) 'Conventional arms transfers to developing nations 2004–2011', Washington, DC: Congressional Research Service, August.

Guérin, D. (1936) *Fascisme et grand capital. Italie–Allemagne*, Paris: Éditions de la révolution prolétarienne.

Handicap International (2007) 'Circle of impact: the fatal footprint of cluster munitions on people and communities', Brussels: Handicap International.

Holden, P. and H. van Vuuren (2011) *The Devil in the Detail: How the Arms Deal Changed Everything*, Johannesburg: Jonathan Ball Publishers.

IISS (International Institute for Strategic Studies) (2014) *Military Balance 2014*, London: IISS.

Jones, B. (2013) 'Defying international concerns, US to sell cluster bombs to Saudi Arabia', *Business Insider*, 27 August, www.businessinsider.com/us-to-sell-cluster-bombs-to-saudi-arabia-2013-8.

Karp, A. (2006) 'Escaping Reuterswärd's shadow', *Contemporary Security Policy*, 27(1): 12–28.

Kidd, R. (2008) 'Is there a strategy for responsible U.S. engagement on cluster munitions?', Office of Weapons Removal and Abatement, US Department of State, 28 April.

Mack, D. (2014) 'What next? Thoughts for global civil society working on arms control and armed violence reduction', São Paolo: Instituto SoudaPaz, April.

Maslen, S. (2004) *Mine Action after Diana: Progress in the Struggle against Landmines*, London: Pluto.

McGrath, R. (1990) *Landmines: An aid issue*, Refugee Participation Network, Oxford: Refugee Studies Programme, August.

— (2004) 'Campaigning against cluster munitions – strategic issues: a discussion paper', www.academia.edu/3102654/Campaigning_against_Cluster_Munitions_-_Strategic_Issues.

Natsuki, M. (2014) 'ATT should not be used as a legitimization to weaken national policies on arms transfers: Japan's ratification and its abandonment of the ban on arms exports', *Control Arms Blog*, 9 May.

Roeber, J. (2005) 'Hard-wired for corruption', *Prospect*, 28 August.

Royal Commission on the Private Manufacture and Trading in Arms, 1935–36 (1936) Minutes, London: HMSO, Q3989.

Sampson, A. (1977) *The Arms Bazaar*, London: Hodder & Stoughton.

Scott, M. (2001) 'Danger – landmines! NGO–government collaboration in the Ottawa Process', in M. Edwards and J. Gaventa (eds), *Global Citizen Action*, Boulder, CO: Lynne Rienner.

Secretary of Defense (2008) 'Memorandum for the Secretaries of the Military Departments, Subject: DOD Policy on Cluster Munitions and Unintended Harm to Civilians', 19 June, www.defense.gov/news/d20080709cmpolicy.pdf.

SIPRI (Stockholm International Peace Research Institute) (2013) 'Military expenditure database', milexdata.sipri.org/files/?file=SIPRI+milex+data+1988-2011.xls.

Stavrianakis, A. (2010) *Taking Aim at the Arms Trade: NGOs, Global Civil Society and the World Military Order*, London: Zed Books.

Stott, N. (1998) 'The South African

campaign', in M. A. Cameron, R. J. Lawson and B. W. Tomlin (eds), *To Walk without Fear: The Global Movement to Ban Landmines*, Toronto: Oxford University Press.

Thomas, E. (2011) *Ike's Bluff: President Eisenhower's secret battle to save the world*, New York: Little, Brown.

Trade Promotion Coordinating Committee (2000) *National Export Strategy: Working for America*, Washington, DC, March.

11 | A RIGHT TO LAND? ACTIVISM AGAINST LAND GRABBING IN AFRICA[1]

Rachel Ibreck

Introduction

Land retains a spiritual value in Africa. In the words of Al Haji, a Sierra Leonean farmer: 'If we sell that bush we have sold our life ... We don't admire anything more than the land we live in'.[2] In practice, many rural people treat their land as a material asset and seek to extract value from it, but they continue to associate land with identity, community and heritage. They accord it profound sacred and historical meanings, while they rely on it as a primary means of subsistence and social security.

African land has recently become an attractive investment for global corporations and local elites, resulting in a 'great African land grab' (Cotula 2013). We might imagine that this process will establish land markets and erode reverent conceptions of land which treat it as integral to social relations, but the association between land and community is a norm which has proved resilient over generations. This sensibility is not regressive – on the contrary, it holds out a promise of social solidarity to counter the worst predations of the market and the negative impacts of globalization; it informs those who seek to uphold rights and it animates resistance to inequalities and injustices. The idea of land as a social or common good is also spreading from south to north, resonating globally, and is a resource for transnational activists who define land grabbing as a human rights violation.

Transnational networks of human rights activists, scholars and peasants are constructing norms and knowledge about land grabbing: they classify it as an urgent concern – a global threat to rural communities. They have succeeded in redefining 'large-scale land acquisitions', a technocratic and morally neutral term, as 'land grabs' and documenting and sharing information about the exponential growth in such investments, especially in Africa.

This surge in land-grab activism dates back to 2008, when activists revealed that foreign investors were acquiring large tracts of the world's richest agricultural land for plantation farming, biofuels and land-banking, and linked this to a spike in global food prices in the preceding years.[3] They warned of dangers and demanded interventions (GRAIN 2008). Land grabbing has since become the subject of numerous studies by advocates and researchers. The groups concerned with land are diverse, including NGOs and individuals concerned with rural development, environmental issues, minority rights, anti-corruption and human rights. The land rush has produced a corresponding 'literature rush' (Oya 2013) with responses from critical agrarian scholars, anthropologists, political scientists and legal experts, feeding into a Land Deal Politics Initiative (LDPI). The range of the advocates and the establishment of networks have been invaluable in foregrounding the issue – and a mix of different skills, locales, relationships and access[4] promotes internal debates and more robust positions.[5] But it has also led to diverse and sometimes contradictory agendas and made it a complicated task to develop a common language and platform. Nonetheless, this has happened, and is an instance of activists creating new issues and meanings through 'framing' to persuade and gain leverage over more powerful organizations and governments (Keck and Sikkink 1999: 89).

The land grab is complicated. Strong local constituencies support, and benefit from, the consolidation of landownership. The documentation of deals is patchy and confusing, there may be delays between land acquisition and development,[6] and some large-scale farms are failing, leading to reforms.[7] But there is a clear case for activism: investments in agricultural projects, water and mineral resources, tourism and environmental schemes have increased; smallholder farmers and pastoralists are losing jurisdiction over land they have held for generations and they are receiving, at best, minimal compensation.[8] Even the potential of investment creates uncertainty and contestation and the rural poor who lack land rights and political voice are vulnerable.[9]

There is good case-study evidence that the new land deals limit local communities' access to water and livelihoods, and have costs for the environment (Anseeuw et al. 2012: 34–46). Plantation farming elsewhere in the global South has contributed to rural poverty and unemployment (Li 2011: 281) and it poses a threat to food security (De Schutter 2011). Yet large-scale investments are being promoted as part of development strategies; they have the backing of governments and international donors, and they are generally pursued within the terms of existing national and international legislation. As such, local efforts to expose and challenge land grabbing are bound to connect to transnational activism and to launch broader appeals to human rights principles.[10]

All the same, land rights advocates face scepticism about whether their case is a legitimate human rights concern. Land confiscation was the basis for economic development in many modern states, and the discipline of development economics was founded on the premise that a strong state could decide what was best for the people, overriding concerns for human rights, including some forms of property rights (Easterly 2014). This logic of agricultural revolution undermines a view of land rights as a fundamental human right. Indeed, international human rights law has yet to specify a right to land, and the issue was rarely taken up by mainstream human rights organizations until recently. Economists have written of the benefits of industrial farming and portrayed its critics as misguided romantics (Collier 2010) – the implication is that the problem is not land alienation as such, but the violations that sometimes accompany it. These and other factors impede human rights advocacy on land issues.

This chapter reviews how the problem of land grabbing and the concept of a right to land are defined in public discourse and policy arenas. It then reflects on the process of knowledge construction by activists: how do different groups, with their distinct interests, commitments and experiences, articulate the problem and relate to one another in their efforts to publicize the issue? Whose voices have been heard and represented? To what extent do the experiences and views of African peasants and pastoralists influence the discourse? The rationale for the investigation is that defining a human rights issue is essentially a political endeavour, and certain views and actors gain prominence.[11] Activists must critically reflect upon their aims, processes and relationships, learning from past mistakes and adapting to the contemporary globalizing context. In particular, they must be informed by the ideas and experiences of the most directly affected people.[12]

Land-grab advocacy has already had some impact – there is a critical discourse on large-scale land acquisition, and it is making a difference to the extent that corporations and policy-makers are reviewing their strategies. However, it has not stopped the process of commodification: there have been modifications rather than moratoria on land deals and ongoing land grabs by local elites. Activists present the problem from different perspectives – some emphasize the need to improve the governance of land and the acquisition process, while others demand radical agrarian reforms and alternatives to commodification. Meanwhile, local responses to investments depict land grabs as a human rights violation, a breach of norms relating to community rights to land, as suggested by field research in Ethiopia, Sierra Leone and South Sudan. Combating land grabs may depend on a revival (and reinvention) of these local norms and their promotion in the international sphere.

Narrating the land grab

A conception of the global land grab has circulated and become established in international media reports. As Lorenzo Cotula observes, these often appear to be weaving a 'simplistic' narrative: 'pitching greedy global capitalists – the "land grabbers" – against poor communities' (2013: 7). Foreign corporations are said to be taking over huge swathes of land for the production of exports, and displacing or otherwise trampling on the rights of local populations, mainly small farmers. Some media reports also aired the claims that Africa's rural hinterlands are underused and ripe for commercial exploitation and that land deals present development opportunities. But the prevailing common sense is that large-scale investments are problematic and that only 'responsible investment' is acceptable.[13]

Land seizures in Africa captured the interest of the world's media with the farm invasions of 2000 in Zimbabwe; at this point 'land grabs' referred to state-sponsored and often violent seizures of white-owned farmland for redistribution.[14] Since 2008, the issue has been reframed and has attracted much more coverage.[15] The problem is summed up as a new global land rush 'triggered by food riots, a series of harvest failures following major droughts and the western investors moving out of the US property market in 2008' and as 'driven by the expansion of sugar cane and oil palm for biofuel production' (Guardian Unlimited 2011). 'Foreign investors', including 'Chinese and Middle Eastern firms', are often blamed (Guardian 2011: 19).[16] Headlines typically cite the negative impacts on local access to food; for instance: 'Biofuel project funded by UK leaves Africans without food' (Independent 2013); 'Greed for land boosts hunger' (Deutsche Welle 2014). Journalists refer to 'a second scramble for Africa' in which investors from 'cash rich but land poor states ... are trying to guarantee their own long-term access to food by buying up land in poorer countries', while African governments promise that 'revenue would go to infrastructure and development' (Guardian 2008). The promises of development are seen to be hollow: local communities are identified as victims, losing access to their land and their 'right to food' as irresponsible corporations sweep through. The deals are 'widely condemned by both western non-government groups and nationals as "new colonialism", driving people off the land and taking scarce resources away' (ibid.).

Initially the discourse in favour of agricultural investment was also visible and robust: investors have 'promised to create jobs'; 'Agricultural development is not only sustainable, it is our future. If we do not pay great care and attention now to increase food production by over 50% before 2050, we will face serious food shortages globally'; 'The farmers ... can find land elsewhere and, besides, they get compensation' (ibid.). But, over time, this has been supplanted by a more sophisticated policy discourse.

Significantly, the World Bank made an important concession in 2010, with a report on 'Rising global interest in farmland'. It concluded: 'an unprecedented number of large-scale land acquisitions took place in 2009, involving some 56 million hectares, more than 70% of them in Africa' (World Bank 2010: xiv). The report was silent on the World Bank's own part in financing land deals,[17] and openly critical of 'media reports', accusing them of some misleading claims; it was not comprehensive.[18] Nevertheless, it was an important high-level acknowledgement that land grabbing is ongoing, and a matter for human rights concern. Although the World Bank did not pursue a rights-based analysis,[19] it exposed a range of violations, including mass displacements. It demonstrated that investments were frequently detrimental to rural livelihoods and environments or simply unproductive. It detailed failures to compensate communities for the loss of land rights, as well as flaws in the technical and economic viability of the projects and in the feasibility of implementing environmental and social safeguards (ibid.: xiv).

And yet, seemingly regardless, the World Bank's 2010 report argued that foreign investment in large-scale agriculture can deliver real opportunities, when properly pursued, and that it has 'a place' as part of strategies for sustainable rural development alongside smallholders (ibid.: xiii). It argued for the potential social benefits, such as good roads, commercial opportunities and the promise of jobs and compensation.

The conviction that large-scale agriculture has a role to play in development continues to be shared by influential global policymakers. They express concern about corporate excesses in large-scale land acquisitions, stating their opposition to land grabbing. Their positions differ according to agency priorities, but most acknowledge the problem while gearing their narratives and actions towards promoting responsible investment through voluntary guidelines.[20] The Principles for Responsible Investment in Agriculture that Respects Rights Livelihoods and Resources (PRAI), backed by the FAO, IFAD, the UNCTAD Secretariat and the World Bank Group (World Bank et al. 2013), are an exemplar. The guidelines seek to promote food security and environmental sustainability and to generate positive social and distributional impacts (ibid.), and they insist upon consultation with local communities. They also call for respect for 'existing' land rights and the rule of law. In reporting of the issue since, proponents of land investment reference the 'desire for investments to benefit locals' (Daily Telegraph 2012).

This 'win-win narrative' has taken root in the media. Although there are regular references to the threat posed by land grabs to the 'right to food', most reports do not explicitly contradict the need for private investment, and do not discuss alternative approaches to agricultural development, such as those that demand radical agrarian reforms.[21] As it stands, the dominant account of land grabbing demonstrates that human rights are under threat, while also stressing the need for agricultural investment and modernization, with the policy implication that governments need only place restrictions on investors and demand responsible deals based on consultation (Cotula 2013: 7). Current international policy frameworks and media discourses acknowledge 'existing use or ownership rights to land' (World Bank et al. 2013) – which are limited customary rights – but fall short of articulating a fundamental 'right to land'.

Land grab advocacy: networks and frames

We can attribute the media attention given to the land-grab issue, and the policy shift to 'responsible investment', largely to the efforts of human rights advocates.[22] Here as elsewhere, they have strategically framed human rights issues to promote a shared understanding and to provide a rationale for collective action; they have also established transnational networks (Keck and Sikkink 1998). Groups and individual activists participate in these networks motivated by shared values, including, in this instance, concern for the welfare of the rural poor in Africa. But they have diverse political persuasions and allegiances and differ in their approach, 'framing' of the issue, and relationships to each other.

Land-grab activists position themselves on a spectrum of views ranging from a commitment to 'food sovereignty' to 'responsible investment'. Some demand radical agrarian reforms – principally the international peasant movement La Via Campesina and its allies – while others align themselves with agribusiness and encourage transformations in land tenure systems aimed at economic growth. This leads to distinct strategies in engagements with policy-makers and investors. Radical activists, seeking an end to land deals, may advance a 'regulate to stop and roll back land grabbing' argument. Less controversially, mainstream groups tend to demand fairer processes: 'regulate to mitigate negative impacts'. There are even activists who promote land deals, following a 'regulate to facilitate land deals' approach favoured by leading international institutions (Borras Jr et al. 2013). These approaches are not fixed and activists tend to straddle or shift between them depending on the specifics of cases (Borras Jr and Franco 2012b: 3), but there are also polarized debates, tensions and different degrees of influence. Advocates for the 'stop' perspective criticize the 'overly tactical' approaches of those who seek to mitigate the effects on communities by winning specific concrete concessions, arguing that this can undermine principled opposition to land grabs.

The 'stop' strategy has gained coverage and brought groups together, but it remains marginal to policy (Borras Jr et al. 2013).

Early international campaigns against land grabbing were supported by human rights 'entrepreneurs' newly focusing on the 'right to food' and environmental concerns.[23] They vigorously employed information politics to reveal the problem of land grabbing. At the forefront of these was GRAIN, a small non-profit advocacy organization. In 2008, GRAIN published *Seized*, an influential report. It also established a website (www.grain.org) and the collaborative Farmland grab.org website,[24] which became a central point for information-sharing, archiving hundreds of relevant reports, now averaging a hundred per month.[25] Another source regularly cited is the Oakland Institute, which took a firm stand against large-scale farming and in favour of commitment to the environment and undertook a series of investigations into the issue after 2008. Its 2009 report echoed GRAIN and emphasized a fear of negative impacts on 'food security for the world's most vulnerable' (Shepard and Mittal 2009: 18). Since then, the Oakland Institute has steadfastly documented deals in Africa and elsewhere, producing over forty relevant investigations including the 'World Bank bad business' and the 'Understanding land investment deals' series. Further information on and support for this approach came from the FoodFirst Information and Action Network, now known as FIAN (founded to champion the right to food), which is now calling for 'a stop to and a rolling back of land grabbing' (FIAN 2014). Other like-minded groups include World Rainforest Movement (WRM), Friends of the Earth International, Bread for the World, Bread for All, and Le comité catholique contre le faim et pour le développement (CCFD Terre Solidaire). These campaigners have strong links to communities and social movements in the South.[26]

A 'Global Alliance Against Land Grabbing' was forged in meetings between groups concerned about the impacts of neoliberalism and global capital. In 2007, 500 representatives, mainly food producers but also landless people, gathered in Senegal to expose the problem and to appeal for 'food sovereignty', specifically 'food, farming, pastoral and fisheries systems determined by local producers and users' (Forum for Food Sovereignty 2007). Some of these groups later raised the 'land grab' issue directly at the 2011 World Social Forum in Dakar, drafting a collective statement, the 'Dakar appeal against the land grab' (Petition online 2011), demanding a halt to large-scale land investments, support for small-scale farming as a means to 'food sovereignty' and a rejection of the World Bank-led PRAI. It asked states and regional and international institutions to 'guarantee people's right to land and support family farming and agro-ecology'. The Nyéléni conference of 2011 built on this position (Reisenberger and Suárez 2011).

The supporters of 'food sovereignty' in Africa seek greater control for local producers and echo some of the critiques of corporate food regimes associated with the international peasant movement La Via Campesina. The rural movement, which formed in Nicaragua in 1992, coalesced around opposition to market-led agrarian reform[27] (Borras Jr 2008) in Latin America and Asia, and has since built a coalition of local, national and international groups of 'diverse ideological orientations' seeking to influence global (and hence national) policy on land and food (ibid.: 277; McKeon 2013). This has an estimated two hundred million members in seventy-three countries and identifies land as 'the key struggle in the world' (Vidal 2013). Only fifteen of La Via Campesina's current membership of 164 organizations are based in Africa, and its original five African members did not all share a radical perspective (Borras Jr 2008: 279), but they did call upon the movement to take up the issue of the privatization of public land (ibid.: 281), and membership has grown since the movement began its campaign against land grabs. An Alliance for Food Sovereignty in Africa has also been established, linked to La Via Campesina, to 'champion small African family farming' (AFSA 2011) and to challenge the G8's New Alliance for Food Security and Nutrition Initiative, established in 2012 to promote 'jobs and market opportunities for small and large farms in African agriculture' (New Alliance n.d.). Such groups perceive land grabs as 'colonialism' and perceive corporate interests in land (and seeds) as a drive for profit and a threat to household food security (War on Want 2013). They view land in historical and social terms: in the words of one of the Malian organizers of the Nyéléni conference, 'People may not have legal titles, but they have been there for generations, even centuries, whereas the Malian state was first founded in 1960' (Coulibaly, cited in Reisenberger and Suárez 2011).

In contrast, the 'responsible investment' strand of activism accepts the commodification of land, in line with the dominant neoliberal paradigm, but demands improved tenure security and better codes of corporate behaviour, while also raising the issue of food security. This is exemplified in the 'Kathmandu Declaration' of 2009 from members and partners of the International Land Coalition (ILC), which calls for the 'centrality of land tenure security to poverty reduction' and for 'transparency, disclosure and ... consultation of all stakeholders' (ILC 2009).[28] Participating organizations have collaborated to share information and to establish land-grab documentation bases, the Land Matrix (www.landmatrix.org) and Land Observatory (www. landobservatory.org).[29]

Notably, several ILC members have a long-standing commitment to promoting land titling as part of creating land markets, perceiving that the registration of individual property rights is essential to realize the potential of land as an economic asset which can be exploited to promote growth. Their commitment to promoting small farming preceded debates about land grabbing (see Manji 2006) and their aim has been to actively promote some form of privatization to encourage investment. This means that most ILC members favour 'responsible investment', albeit to promote small farming and food security. For instance, one ILC member, Oxfam, runs an energetic campaign to identify land grabs as a threat to the right to food, a home and livelihood (Oxfam 2014) and demands 'food justice', but concedes that 'responsible investment is an important part of fighting poverty' (ibid.). The organization is a member of the leadership council of the New Alliance for Food Security and Nutrition. While it has been critical of the New Alliance's investment activities and policy reforms, and particularly of its failure to uplift small-scale producers, it holds that: 'private investment in the agriculture sector of developing countries ... is critical to driving inclusive growth' (Oxfam 2013: 2). Oxfam demands a 'stop' to land grabbing but does not consider land deals to be 'land grabs' by default, nor does it insist that small farming is the only means to achieve the right to food. This perspective moves away from a principled argument against investments, focusing instead on improving practice and 'corporate social responsibility'.

Divergent frames of 'food sovereignty' and 'land governance' dominate advocacy on land grabbing,[30] but they share some common ground. Proponents of both visions contributed to and broadly support the FAO-initiated 'Voluntary Guidelines on the Responsible

Governance of Tenure of Land, Fisheries and Forests in the Context of National Food Security', endorsed by the Committee on World Food Security (CFS) in May 2012 (hereafter CFS Voluntary Guidelines), which specify duties upon states, such as the protection of 'legitimate tenure rights to the ancestral lands' of indigenous communities (CFS 2012: 15, 9.5) and the consideration of 'redistributive reforms'.

Similarly, radical criticisms have influenced mainstream arguments for responsible investment to promote the 'right to food' and the interests of 'small farmers', such as in the Antigua Declaration of ILC members (2013), which calls for 'people-centred land governance', advocating for small-scale farming and redistributive agrarian reform; strengthening of land rights, including those 'not recognized by law'; and empowerment of local land users to manage ecosystems. These shifts are important to note, even if the declaration ultimately reverts to the 'regulate' perspective on large-scale land deals, suggesting that land grabbing can be prevented and remedied by ensuring that 'all large-scale initiatives that involve the use of land, water and other natural resources comply with human rights and environmental obligations and are based on: the free, prior and informed consent of existing land users' (ILC 2003).

We might conclude that 'land governance' arguments have won out against the 'food sovereignty' critique in advocacy, as indeed in media and policy discourses on land grabbing (explored above). There is broad acceptance of the premise of food security and regulation, despite the strong backing for the food sovereignty alternative from La Via Campesina and its allies. Radical opponents have managed to gain recognition for customary rights and the need to consider land redistribution and restitution, but overall the concept of 'responsible investment' has held firm (Borras Jr and Franco 2012a).

However, African activists have thus far been the least prominent and well-resourced actors in this (and other) transnational advocacy movements, although they are increasingly vocal and organized (see War on Want 2013).[31] They are opposing land grabs and making their voices heard – in certain countries they are campaigning vigorously at the national level[32] – but they are not setting agendas either for 'food sovereignty' or 'responsible investment', and this may be one reason why the current advocacy frames do not bring to the fore some crucial aspects of the problem.

The idea of 'responsible investment' is flawed in ways that both the 'food sovereignty' advocates and supporters of land titling hint at, but do not entirely expose, perhaps because of their central commitments to small farmers and food producers, albeit from different perspectives. First, it does not confront the role of domestic elites (among them local farmers) who are involved in land grabs, for diverse purposes, including but not limited to agriculture. Secondly, and most importantly, the 'responsible investment' approach cannot fully address the fact that rural communities are highly differentiated and any form of consultation is subject to local power relations and manipulation. Indeed, the identification and formulation of customary rights are also likely to be selective and to work to the advantage of local big men.[33]

Development experts present strong arguments for the benefits of individual land titling (De Soto 1989); for some it provides the best protection against land grabbing (see Manji 2006). However, land titling and the associated individualization of tenure may entrench the commodification of land, which typically benefits local elites – they are best placed to take advantage of a land market, while the poorest land users lose usufruct rights that are less easy to formalize. Olivier de Schutter, UN Special Rapporteur on the Right to Food, argues that small-scale farmers, pastoralists and forest dwellers risk being 'fenced off' from livelihoods and argues for the registration of use rights based on customary forms of tenure (De Schutter 2011: 269–71).[34] Also, where such registration has taken place, it has not been sufficient to protect peasants and pastoralists from the current land rush.[35] As Borras Jr and Franco (2010: 10) write, 'legal recognition of poor people's land rights has never alone guaranteed that they will actually be respected and protected in the courts or on the ground'.

One way forward for governments and 'responsible investors' is to ensure citizen participation in land titling processes and in decisions regarding land investment. However, they must proceed with caution – issuing an invitation to participate itself constitutes an 'act of power' and the terms and spaces of engagement radically affect outcomes (see Cornwall 2002); previous consultations by 'responsible investors' amply illustrate their limitations.[36] Land, power and 'voice' are unevenly distributed in communities; existing land rights reflect power and limit the potential for participation to deliver equitable outcomes. As such, there is a need to openly confront the dual fictions perpetuated by policy discourses on 'consent based on consultation' and 'legitimate existing rights'. If implemented these might mitigate the most extreme corporate land grabs, but they cannot prevent some form of land grabbing in practice, because of entrenched inequalities at the local level.

This issue is already being confronted from a gender perspective. Women rarely have equal access to land, in either legal or customary systems, and land rights advocates have argued that this should be addressed through redistribution. For instance, the CFS Voluntary Guidelines state: 'States should ensure that women and girls have equal tenure rights and access to land, fisheries and forests independent of their civil and marital rights' (2012: 5). Implicitly, women are seen to have a right to access land as part of upholding equality and combating discrimination.

Aside from the progress in the CFS Voluntary Guidelines, for the most part land grab activists do not foreground the problem of existing inequalities in access to land, nor do they attempt to define the scope and meaning of land rights as a basis for action. The concept of a right to land is generally implied by activists, but not articulated. This may soon change, as its potential is being explored in scholarly debates, both from a legal perspective (Gilbert 2013) and as part of an argument for 'land sovereignty' – defined as 'the realisation of the working people's human right to land' (Borras and Franco 2012b: 6).[37] Transnational activists have yet to take up these arguments with any force, but there are good reasons to move towards such approaches.

Significantly, the frames of 'land governance' and 'food sovereignty' do not evoke the familiar language of struggle in Africa, where resistance to colonialism and revolutionary politics have mobilized around a demand for land to be returned to the people. This despite the contemporary example from South Africa, where landless people call for a 'right to land' and have made this a key issue in debates about welfare provision (James 2002: 19).[38] Such rural movements are unusual in Africa at present, but historical and comparative examples of resistance to land alienation suggest that as commercial agriculture spreads, so too will the discourse of 'land rights as human rights'.[39] This concept rests on an 'untheorised consensus' and is therefore all the more powerful as an appeal to action (see Taylor 1999). If and when the negative impacts of land grabs spread, we may expect the demand for a right to land to become a call to arms if it is not taken up in civil protest.

Defining the right to land

A 'right to land' is neither codified in international human rights law nor recognized as a norm internationally.[40] There is a non-binding commitment to protect property rights (UDHR, 1948, Article 17), ensuring that that which has already been accorded to a person is retained by them, which applies to land which is indisputably owned or officially 'titled'.[41] But there is no requirement upon states to guarantee or provide access to land on the basis of need or principle. Thus, from the perspective of international human rights norms, duty-bearers must protect landowners' property, but need not protect or accord access to land for existing or potential land users.

However, international human rights norms are the outcomes of social struggles and reflect historical and political relations. They should not be seen as a prescribed 'universal' doctrine but rather as an evolving process. If they are to represent the local in the global, to evolve as 'emancipatory script', they must embrace a practice of cross-cultural dialogue, producing both 'global competence and local legitimacy' (De Sousa Santos 2002). A specific right to land may be missing from this system, despite, or perhaps because of, its place at the 'heart of social justice' (Gilbert 2013: 116).

The right to land is already implied in various human rights instruments and decisions. At the international level, women are deemed to have equal rights to land under the law (see Wickeri and Kalhan 2010: 19), although this does not require active initiatives to provide or 'equalize' their access to land. There is the right to housing, which offers a more robust specification of a fundamental right to be provided with access to land, even if it is only sufficient for 'adequate housing' – it may be vague on the relationship between land and housing, but it provides a basis to contest evictions.[42] Additionally, the International Convention on Economic, Social and Cultural Rights (ICESCR) requires states to provide for the 'right to adequate food' and to ensure that natural resources are used effectively to deliver this (ICESCR, 1976, Article 11, 2), which may be interpreted as a requirement to provide access to land under certain conditions. For indigenous peoples, there is a further obligation: that states must guarantee them access to land 'which they have traditionally owned, occupied or otherwise used or acquired' as part of protecting their right to self-determination.[43]

The claim for an indigenous right to land is specified in the African Charter for Human & Peoples' Rights (ACHPR). Article 22 specifies group rights, including the right of peoples to 'economic, social and cultural development' with due regard to their freedom and identity (African Charter 1981: Art. 22). In 2010, the African Commission on Human & Peoples' Rights found the Kenyan government guilty of failing to protect the Endorois' rights as an indigenous people to 'property, health, culture, religion and natural resources', following the loss of their ancestral land dating to the 1970s. This decision set an important precedent in international law relating to land rights (HRW 2010) and paved the way for further claims, such as that of the Ogiek community in Kenya (see MRG 2013). Importantly, the ACHPR contains a broad definition of indigeneity: an advisory note indicates that self-identification and attachment to 'traditional land' are key criteria, such that 'any African can legitimately consider him/herself indigene to the continent' (ACHPR 2007: 4).

We can identify, then, at a minimum, an emerging regional norm relating to the right to land, and implicit references to this concept within the frameworks of international human rights law, and in particular the ICESCR. In certain circumstances, the provision of land may be necessary to fulfil the right to food, cultural and indigenous rights, the right to adequate housing, and indeed the rights to water and work. Even some civil and political rights (freedom from discrimination, the right to privacy, and equality before the law) depend upon access to land in some instances. These established rights constitute 'political opportunity structures' (Keck and Sikkink 1998), which activists can exploit in their struggles. They represent established international norms even if they are not all legally binding.[44] More than this, taken together, this bundle of rights might be seen to provide the moral foundation for a fundamental right to land. They indicate that land is not merely an economic resource, or a utility (a means towards other rights); rather it is a social good.

This understanding is shared by rural activists articulating opposition to land grabs in Africa.

Land and people: learning from African activists

'They want the land but they don't want the people,' observed an Anuak opposed to the land leases in his native Gambella, Ethiopia.[45] In the process of commodification, land is conceptualized as an economic good and is thus severed from its social and cultural meanings; this applies to land titles for small farmers, which register individual private property, as well as to commercial land acquisitions. One achievement of land-grab advocacy has been to gain recognition for customary land rights as a component of 'responsible investment', but efforts to discern such existing rights are open to political manipulation (as noted above). Moreover, both formal and customary land rights reflect the deep relations between land and people only in fragmented forms. They are outcomes of long-term processes of political and economic contestation, of unequal power relations and sometimes of violence, through pre-colonial processes of migration and conquest, colonization, post-colonial interventions and the era of neoliberal globalization. As such, these are not 'rights' in the sense of idealized precepts or norms, but are attenuated expressions of these in the same way that, for instance, freedom of speech becomes a limited 'right' in actuality.

In contrast, relations between land and people are tightly bound in the memories and moralities of Africans. The principle of a right to land is nurtured in many African cultures, despite processes of commodification. Corporate investments are resisted primarily because of the negative social and economic impacts, as well as failures of consultation, but they are resented also because they intensify processes of land commodification which typically breach moral norms and which have been associated with violence in the past. The notion of a 'right to land' does not in essence rule out commercial farming, practised in diverse forms in different contexts. But the idea that there must also be land for people is ingrained in many rural societies in Africa. Insofar as they violate this principle, the land deals are felt as assaults upon dignity and identity, and as a source of social disturbance.

The idea of land as heritage, identity and the basis of rights and social relations remains strong even in contexts in which the social fabric is torn, as Betty Okot finds in her study of the trajectory of Acholi relations with the land in Uganda. Land is integral to the Acholi philosophy of identity and their social security. Their displacement into camps, forced by decades of insurgency in northern Uganda, followed by the introduction of new land tenure policies upon their return, is at the heart of their social crisis. She concludes that their struggle for a return to the land is concerned with social reparation: 'the attempt to define or redefine, express and uphold their communal land rights' is not driven by a desire to return to the past but 'correlates with their desire to rebuild and recover from the ravages of war and grow wealth again but all within a culture and social system that remains anchored in the land' (Okot 2013).[46]

This ideal of a 'right to land' has animated historical struggles and can be found in present political discourse. Ethiopia's violent revolution of 1974/75 was waged under the slogan of 'land to the tiller'. Its current constitution holds all land as common property, vested in 'the state and the peoples of Ethiopia', and specifies that 'any Ethiopian who wants to earn a living by farming has a right ... to obtain without payment, the use of land', while pastoralists 'have a right to free land'. These rights are not adequately protected in existing law and practice (see Witten 2007) and are regularly breached, including during the recent villagization programme and large-scale land investments (HRW 2012). Nevertheless, it is apparent that land is recognized as a social good at the highest level.

An idealized relationship between land and people is embedded in many customary systems. It is recounted in stories of the past – 'this land was given to our forefathers' – and employed to make sense of the present, rousing either fear or solidarity. When people are threatened, then land too is felt to be at risk, and vice versa. An Anuak from Gambella, Ethiopia, recalled the threat felt during the massacre of December 2003: 'If I am killed for my land, I will die on my land.' A decade later, the Anuak community described the displacements induced by a government villagization scheme, foreign investors and domestic investors as a second attempt at genocide: 'they are extinguishing us'; 'it is indirect killing'; 'it is to kill the indigenous people of Gambella'. This perception stems also from direct experience of assaults, imprisonment without charge, torture and a series of other violations of civil and political rights associated with forced displacements in Gambella.[47] Land is at the root of a simmering conflict between the Anuak and the state, and recent land investments have exacerbated this: 'if ever the government needed peace it would not give land to those investors'.[48] At the same time, among the Anuak, as in communities elsewhere in Africa, a willingness to share land with newcomers exemplifies morality: 'when the Nuer came through Anuak land, we protected them ... when Dinkas and Nuers came to Ethiopia to settle we shared the land (but they turned against the Anuak)'.

In practice, the terms on which land is shared are bound to be conditional and constrained; customary practices are often opaque and riven with gender and other inequalities and dynamics – so we should be wary of generalizations.[49] There is also a practical dimension: it is viable to share where there is a lack of 'land hunger'. For instance, historically in Sierra Leone, local land tenure systems are flexible so that even if 'strangers' are not accorded similar rights to own land, land was shared for their use: 'migrants are nearly always welcomed and encouraged to stay by being given land on which to farm ... without rent' (Richards 1996: 121). In contexts of scarcity, such norms inevitably come under threat. Yet the beliefs that land belongs to and represents communities, and that it ought to be treasured and shared, continue to be expressed and promoted across the continent.

The relationship between people and land in Sierra Leone has been shaken up by a succession of land grabs for mining and agribusiness since 2008. As one local official in Pujehun explained, there had been so many recent investments in his area that even he could not keep track of which corporations had leased land and why.[50] The existing system of customary tenure is now under assault as paramount chiefs, deemed to be custodians, have made agreements with investors which will prevent them from honouring their duty to protect land for 'ancestors, living community members, and unborn family members' (USAID n.d.: 6) and to distribute it in accordance with familial ties and need.

Change has ever been a violent process in Sierra Leone, and shaped by external influences, including the historical violence of slavery and a decade of civil war from 1991 to 2002. But Sierra Leoneans do not dwell on the past; even in the most remote areas, communities are characterized by a dynamic 'cultural creolization' (Richards 1996: 37) in their farming techniques and social relations. Some communities integrate new ideas and people to the extent that even oral histories may be redrafted to accommodate newcomers; there is a 'heritage of cultural compromise' (ibid.: 69). Yet the story of the SOCFIN oil palm plantation, established in Malen, Pujehun district, in 2011, illustrates that the idea of a deep relationship between people and their farmland has endured, and is employed in current discourses of resistance.

SOCFIN Agricultural Company is among several foreign corporations which have recently established themselves in Pujehun and have begun to transform the district, in this case through plantation agriculture, improvements to the road and the construction of new homes and offices. However, local opponents charge that the oil palm plantation, established in March 2011, has had destructive impacts. They describe a flawed acquisition process, suggesting the company obtained the 'consent' of the residents of Malen through opaque contracts and payoffs: piles of the local currency, leones, were placed on the table, landowners were pressured to 'thumbprint' a contract which was barely explained to them, and the paramount chief's decision to award the company a fifty-year lease was rapidly approved. Those who challenged the deal were ignored and their land was generally included in the concession against their will: 'We never dreamt of selling our land. That was our stance. It was forcibly taken. It was all vandalised and it used to be our livelihood but now it is all gone.'[51]

Opposition to the investment spread as the significance of the contract began to be understood. The compensation barely covered home improvements – in some cases, residents said they bought zinc roofs to protect their homes from the rain but did not even have enough left to pay workmen to erect them. They identified 'economic trees' which had been cut down and explained that food security, nutrition and even education have suffered: 'We used to eat three times a day and now you hardly see two meals every day ... Some people can hardly eat.' Since then, they claim, 'brown envelopes' have been offered to buy off opponents of the deal.[52]

In response, a group of community activists united to form the Malen Affected Land Owners and Users Association demanding the return of their land and compensation; since 2011, several community members have been subject to arrest or intimidation. As part of their efforts to challenge the investment, they promote a residual belief that land constitutes social security and identity. Their struggle is primarily driven by hardship and necessity, but their sense of anger and trauma is also informed by a sentiment that the loss of their land means the profound destruction of their community. 'The land is inhabited for generations to come, we don't know what the impact of destroying this will be. It is not only economic, the land is a bank for all villagers. It is for educating children and for them to be proud that they have a home ... it is for history and for tomorrow.'[53]

The norm of the right to land is not recognized in a common manner across the continent, or even within communities. Rural dwellers are a differentiated group, with varying degrees of attachment to and dependency upon the land and integration into local cultures. Some may already have 'one foot in town' (Scoones 2014) or have gained and treated their farm as a commercial enterprise, while for others the land is the nexus of their social, economic and cultural life and the foundation of their identity. And not all African activists reference such a norm in their opposition to land grabs. They must weigh up short-term and long-term priorities to make decisions in conditions of scarcity and flux, and they look outwards and to the future, as well as to historical and local connections.[54] But the notion of a 'right to land' is still frequently expressed by activists in affected communities in Africa and animates their struggles against land grabbing.

The moral economy (see Scott 1976) of the African peasant, characterized as 'a right to subsistence and norm of reciprocity', has sometimes been seen as an obstacle to capitalist progress; its 'economy of affection' is blamed for underdevelopment (Hyden 2005). Yet such commitments might also be resources for development (Sugimura 2007), sources of social solidarity and moderating forces against the excesses of neoliberal globalization and its production of 'outcasts and wasted lives' (Bauman 2004). Long before the recent land rush, processes of modernization, land alienation and associated conflicts destabilized rural communities, dispossessed Africans, and led to poverty and migration. Where land issues are concerned, Africans have long been engaged in various forms of resistance; the cultivation of the idea of a right to land has been part of these struggles and is an idea that transnational advocacy can 'learn from the South' (De Sousa Santos 2002), ensuring that local histories and principles define global struggles.

Conclusion

There are plural discourses and practices of resistance to land grabbing and these are evolving. Although the 'regulate to mitigate' approach currently holds sway, its limitations are already apparent – regulating the terms of corporations' land acquisitions cannot address the entrenched historical global inequalities that underpin the practice. In contrast, the notion of a 'human right' to land animates struggles at the local level, and is emerging as a potentially firm position from which to launch transnational challenges to ongoing 'legal' dispossessions.

A right to land is implicit in international human rights law but explicit in some constitutions, national legislation or customary law in Africa. It has also been nurtured and respected in local norms and has informed people's relationships with land and with each other over generations. This norm offers a counter-discourse to challenge the commodification of land – at a minimum implying a slowdown of the process and the promotion of more equitable distributions of resources. Given the profound challenges posed by the prospects of further climate change and population growth (and corresponding land shortage), it also necessarily implies a rethinking of the paradigm of large-scale industrial farming and leads towards consideration of whether and how concepts such as 'land sovereignty' or 'food sovereignty' might be relevant in practice in specific contexts, as a challenge to the neoliberal development model. Moreover, land is one of the few resources that states in Africa can secure for the people and distribute based on need. In economies where growth is matched by rising inequality and where large populations remain dependent on some form of aid – irregularly supplied and shared – such commitments would not be new, but could revive the best of those inherited from communal tenure, while introducing reforms in governance and equity. A right to land approach offers a platform to rural people to determine development models in their locality, rather than presenting them with prescribed solutions.

Looking beyond the substance of land-grab campaigns, there are also lessons to be derived from their methods. Many campaigners have sought to build strong relationships with the peasantry and with scholars, contrasting with the more cavalier tendencies identified in other chapters in this volume. As such, land-grab activists may have their own part in reclaiming human rights advocacy. Their approach is innovative partly because such campaigns require the active, detailed and repeated construction of the problem to reveal both the specific forms and impacts of land grabs in particular contexts. They require research, openness regarding both the costs and benefits for affected communities, and information-sharing, not just transnationally but locally – in affected communities. Ultimately they require the mobilization of affected communities to articulate their historical conception of land rights and demand that these are recognized and secured.

The authenticity and legitimacy of transnational human rights activism depend upon engaging closely with local communities, and attending to complexities of their experiences; it must foreground the voices and opinions of individuals and groups whose rights are threatened or violated. In efforts to combat land grabbing and associated violations, solidarity is not only an ethical good, it is a core principle for success. What is at stake here is not simply the need to challenge egregious corporate land grabs, but the need to revive local norms regarding a right to land and to link these to the promotion of a new international norm.

Notes

1 I am grateful to the Irish Research Council and the Conflict Resolution Unit of the Irish Department of Foreign Affairs for their generous support for the research. Thanks are also due to all the participants in the seminar on 'Resistance to land grabbing' at the University of Limerick, 4/5 June 2013, in particular to Lansana Hassan Sowa of SiLNoRF, Joseph Rahall of Green Scenery, Karol Balfe of Christian Aid and Professor Tom Lodge for all their contributions and insights. I am enormously grateful to the participants in my research in Pujehun, Tonkolili and Freetown, Sierra Leone, in Addis Ababa and Gambella in Ethiopia, in Nairobi, Kenya, and in Juba and Nimule, South Sudan, for sharing their ideas and experiences with generosity and courage.

2 Interviewed in Pujehun, Sierra Leone, February 2013.

3 The food price rise was attributed to rising global population, falling yields and environmental threats (see OECD 2008: 4).

4 For instance, in Ethiopia, where there is limited scope for human rights

NGOs to operate, Ethiopian scholars have delivered significant insights; see Rahmato (2011).

5 For instance, Christian Aid is developing its position carefully, opposing the G8's New Alliance (Guardian 2014), supporting networking for local human rights organizations opposing land grabs and commissioning research to inform its approach to the issues. See ALLAT (2013).

6 See Cotula (2013: 39–46) for a critical analysis of the estimates of land acquired (ranging from 50 million hectares worldwide over ten years to up to 63 million in Africa in 2008–10) and for indications of delayed impacts on the ground.

7 For example, the poor performance of the Karituri investment in Gambella, Ethiopia, prompted a review of policy (Sethi 2013).

8 See Cotula (2013), which identifies many of these complexities. I am also basing this assessment upon observations on the ground in Sierra Leone, Ethiopia and South Sudan. It is worth noting that the urban poor who still rely on familial access to land for social security also lose out, a problem raised in a focus group discussion with young men originally from Pujehun district and living in Freetown, Sierra Leone, February 2013. Cotula (ibid.: 181) notes that farming has often been a source of funds for education. This issue needs further investigation.

9 This assertion is based on the academic and activist sources discussed below as well as on field research at biofuel plantations established by Addax Bioenergy (Bombali district) and SOCFIN (Pujehun district) in Sierra Leone in February 2013 and in the Gambella region of Ethiopia, June 2013.

10 See Wisborg (2013) for a review of the ways in which campaigners have connected to human rights discourse and for counter-arguments against advocating for a right to land.

11 This is based on a social-constructivist position that discourse reflects and reinforces existing power relations: discourses associated with powerful institutions including the media can be said to reflect dominant views which shape popular identities, beliefs and actions.

12 This chapter aims to contribute to such critical reflection.

13 This section is based on an analysis of UK newspapers as a leading English-language source of international news about Africa which will reflect common understandings of the term land grabbing. I used the Lexis Nexis database to identify, sort and analyse stories on land grabbing over a thirty-year period between 1984 and 2014.

14 These were part of the ruling party's campaign to shore up dwindling support (Alexander 2006: 183) and were associated with state-led political violence, although the need for land redistribution was well established.

15 For instance, in the UK print and online newspapers on the Lexis Nexis database there were 757 references to land grabs in Africa between September 1994 and September 2014. After 2008, there were 470 stories; overwhelmingly these focused on the new global land rush (many were published in the *Guardian*). After 2008, there were rare references to the previous conception of domestic land grabs in Africa, e.g. 'South Africa firebrand calls for Mugabe-style land grabs' (The Times 2013). In contrast, between 1994 and 2008, there were 468 stories on land grabs, of which 363 focused on the Zimbabwe case. The global land grab first came to the attention of the press in 2007/08, with nine related stories appearing in this period.

16 Closer examination suggests that the majority of land deals are by

Western companies (Cotula 2013: 67).

However, it is important to bear in mind that rising powers such as India and China, which are less accessible for civil society engagement, present particular challenges for transnational activists (Borras Jr et al. 2013: 4).

17 The World Bank has, through its International Finance Corporation (IFC), directly encouraged and supported African states to open their markets to foreign investors, providing technical assistance and advice on the legal and regulatory environment (see Da Vià 2011: 16–17 and fn 14).

18 Indeed, the report relied heavily on the material on an activist website farmlandgrab.org (see below for further information). As GRAIN put it: 'the Bank ... sent out teams of consultants to see if they were real or not. Is this the best that the World Bank could do?' (GRAIN 2010).

19 As a subsequent critique from the EU working group on land issues (2010) noted, the report lacked reference to human rights issues and ignored the extent to which the land grab was also a 'water grab'.

20 See Borras Jr and Franco (2010) for an overview and critique of this 'win-win' narrative.

21 It is worth noting that food sovereignty was mentioned in ten of the articles reviewed while land sovereignty was mentioned only once (see below for a discussion of these concepts).

22 Each of the above-cited newspaper articles on land grabbing and many more reviewed from the Lexis Nexis database cited one or more human rights groups. The exceptions were those that referred to the southern African land grabs in Zimbabwe or a potential 'land grab' in South Africa, which principally cite politicians.

23 They exemplify the more radical voices among the 'new rights advocates'

(Nelson and Dorsey 2008): blending rights and development concerns and expressing demands for social, economic and environmental rights.

24 This website was launched by GRAIN in 2008 as an open forum to host reports on land grabbing.

25 With one earlier exception the reports archive as far back as 2003. Most of the reporting is from 2008, when the site was launched, and the numbers are growing; for instance, in January 2009 the monthly archive included eighty-two reports while in January 2014 the total was 121 (Farmlandgrab.org 2014). It is worth noting that the reports are in various languages (although mostly Spanish, French and English) and that they include several references to the same cases. The site welcomes contributions from the public, which can be uploaded directly.

26 Indeed, Farmlandgrab has become a platform for the peasant organization La Via Campesina, featuring regular news and statements from it. A search of the website on 9 May 2014 revealed 177 statements relating to the peasant movement.

27 A process to create land markets as a mechanism for redistribution (and an alternative to state-led agrarian reform). For instance, Brazil introduced a World Bank-funded rural poverty reduction programme, the PCT, to replace its existing method of redistribution.

28 The ILC embraces a diverse range of 152 organizations, among them NGOs, such as Namati and Land Net Malawi; leading research institutes, such as the International Food Policy Research Institute (IFPRI); and intergovernmental organizations, including the World Bank Group and the Food and Agriculture Organization (FAO).

29 These may be used by diverse groups concerned about land acquisitions and grabs.

30 There are other approaches from human rights organizations which frame the issue as forced displacement (Amnesty International, Human Rights Watch), but these tend to focus on civil and political rights violations which are commonly associated with the problem but not inherent to it.

31 My research in Sierra Leone demonstrates the prominent role played by local activists and networks in documenting, advocacy and support for local communities; this was also apparent at the University of Limerick and Christian Aid seminar on 'Resistance to land grabbing' (June 2013).

32 In Sierra Leone, for instance, there have been vigorous efforts by community activists and NGOs including SiLNoRF and Green Scenery and the formation of a national network to combat land grabs.

33 This is apparent from field research, particularly in the Gambella region of Ethiopia and in Eastern Equatoria in South Sudan. See also Cotula (2013).

34 Customary tenure is still the dominant form of landholding in Africa (Alden Wily 2011: 2).

35 See Alden Wily (2011) for a review of the steps made towards security of tenure for customary landholdings in a range of African countries and their limitations. She regards Tanzania as 'most advanced'; in this regard, however, Manji critiques Tanzanian policy, illustrating that there are different views on precisely how to deliver security of tenure outside of the individual titling/land market model.

36 The Addax Bioenergy investment in Sierra Leone is a case in point, as demonstrated by SiLNoRF's work.

37 Christian Aid, for instance, has opposed the G8's New Alliance (Guardian 2014) and supported partner organizations engaged in resistance to land grabs in Sierra Leone, but has commissioned research into both impacts and strategies in order to inform its approach.

38 This struggle is pursued in the context of a failure of the market-led approach to land reform which has hindered land redistribution and restitution, privileged 'commercial' farming over family-sized farms with poor outcomes (Lahiff 2010) and prevented any reversals of the economic and social legacies of apartheid.

39 For instance, such calls already underpin activism in other countries such as Brazil and India.

40 Note that I shall argue that it does meet the criteria of a human rights norm in two senses, as an actual norm in some African contexts and as a justified norm supported by strong reasons, bearing in mind that 'a human rights norm might exist as (a) a shared norm of actual human moralities, (b) a justified moral norm supported by strong reasons, (c) a legal right at the national level (where it might be referred to as a "civil" or "constitutional" right), or (d) a legal right within international law' (Stanford Encyclopedia of Philosophy 2013).

41 Either through a private contract or through legal or customary rules that specify clearly the relationship between the person and the thing.

42 For instance, states are required to provide remedies where evictions do not comply with international law (Wickeri and Kalhan 2010: 22).

43 This is specified in the binding ILO Convention 169 (ratified by twenty countries, none of them in Africa) and in the non-binding UN Declaration on the Rights of Indigenous Peoples (see Wickeri and Kalhan 2010: 18–19).

44 Since the optional protocol of 2008 which would make these rights legally binding has yet to be widely ratified.

45 Interview in Addis Ababa, June 2013.

46 Similar understandings can be found in South Sudan, based on my interviews with Madi people in Nimule (April 2014).

47 See Oakland Institute (2013), HRW (2012).

48 Interviews with Anuak in Gambella and Addis Ababa and Anuak refugees in Ruiru, Kenya, June 2013.

49 As Gabbert points out, 'cultural rules are constantly being re-evaluated and changed' even among the pastoralist communities of southern Ethiopia, depicted as 'closed' (2014: 27).

50 Interview, Pujehun, 8 February 2013.

51 Interview, young man, Banaleh, 6 February 2013. For further information on the land deal and the responses of the community see www.greenscenery. org. Green Scenery has been at the forefront of highlighting the impacts of the investment and the views of affected landowners and users. For instance, its first report on this issue was in May 2011 (Green Scenery 2011).

52 Interviews in Pujehun, 6/7 February 2013. These findings are supported by ALLAT (2013).

53 Interview, MALUA member, Bassaleh, 6 February 2013.

54 And some are vulnerable to co-option.

References

ACHPR (African Commission on Human & Peoples' Rights) (2007) Advisory Opinion of the African Commission on Human & Peoples' Rights on the United Nations Declaration on the Rights of Indigenous Peoples, Adopted by the African Commission on Human & Peoples' Rights at its 41st Ordinary Session held in May 2007 in Accra, Ghana, www. achpr.org/files/special-mechanisms/ indigenous-populations/un_ advisory_opinion_idp_eng.pdf, accessed 18 December 2014, www. achpr.org/files/special-mechanisms/ indigenous-populations/un_advisory _opinion_idp_eng.pdf, accessed 25 June 2014.

African Charter (1981) African [Banjul] Charter on Human & Peoples' Rights, Adopted 27 June 1981, OAU Doc. CAB/ LEG/67/3 rev. 5, 21 I.L.M. 58 (1982), entered into force 21 October 1986.

AFSA (2011) 'Alliance for Food Sovereignty in Africa', www.african biodiversity.org/content/alliance_ food_sovereignty_afsa, accessed 20 June 2014.

Alden Wily, L. (2011) 'The law is to blame: taking a hard look at the vulnerable status of customary land rights', *Africa Development and Change*, (2)3: 733–57.

Alexander, J. (2006) *The Unsettled Land, State-making and the Politics of Land in Zimbabwe 1893–2003*, Oxford: James Currey.

ALLAT (Action for Large-Scale Land Acquisition Transparency) (2013) *Who is Benefiting: The Social and Economic Impact of Three Large Scale Land Investments in Sierra Leone: A Cost Benefit Analysis*, July, www. christianaid.org.uk/images/who-is-benefitting-Sierra-Leone-report.pdf, accessed 28 August 2014.

Anseeuw, W., L. Alden Wily, L. Cotula and M. Taylor (2012) 'Land rights and the rush for land: findings of the Global Commercial Pressures on Land Research Project', Rome: ILC.

Bauman, Z. (2004) *Wasted Lives, Modernity and Its Outcasts*, Cambridge: Polity.

Borras Jr, S. M. (2008) 'La Vía Campesina and its global campaign for agrarian reform', *Journal of Agrarian Change*, 8: 258–89, doi: 10.1111/j.1471-0366.2008.00170.x.

— (2013) 'Towards a better understanding of the market-led agrarian reform in theory and practice: focusing on the Brazilian case', FAO, www.fao.org/docrep/004/y3568t/y3568t05.htm, accessed 4 June 2014.

Borras Jr, S. M. and J. Franco (2010) 'Towards a broader view of the politics of global land grab: rethinking land issues, reframing resistance', ICAS Working Paper Series no. 001, May.

— (2012a) 'Global land grabbing and trajectories of agrarian change: a preliminary analysis', *Journal of Agrarian Change*, 12(1): 34–59.

— (2012b) 'A "land sovereignty" alternative? Towards a people's counter-enclosure', TNI Agrarian Programme Discussion Paper, July, www.tni.org/sites/www.tni.org/files/a_land_sovereignty_alternative_.pdf, accessed 31 August 2014.

— (2013) 'Global land grabbing and political reactions "from below"', *Third World Quarterly*, 34(9): 1723–47.

Borras Jr, S. M., J. Franco and C. Wang (2013) 'Governing the global land grab: competing political tendencies', Land and Sovereignty in the Americas Series, no. 2, Oakland, CA: Food First/Institute for Food and Development Policy and Transnational Institute.

Borras Jr, S. M., P. McMichael and I. Scoones (2010) 'The politics of biofuels, land and agrarian change: editors' introduction', *Journal of Peasant Studies*, 37(4): 575–92.

Borras Jr., S. M., R. Hall, I. Scoones, B. White and W. Wolford (2011) 'Towards a better understanding of global land grabbing: an editorial introduction', *Journal of Peasant Studies*, 38(2): 209–16.

CFS (Committee on World Food Security) (2012) 'Voluntary Guidelines on the Responsible Governance of Tenure of Land, Fisheries and Forests in the Context of National Food Security', www.fao.org/docrep/016/i2801e/i2801e.pdf, accessed 11 February 2014.

Collier, P. (2010) *The Plundered Planet: Why we must – and how we can – manage nature for global prosperity*, London: Penguin.

Cornwall, A. (2002) 'Locating citizen participation', *IDS Bulletin*, 33: i–x, doi: 10.1111/j.1759-5436.2002.tb00016.x.

Cotula, L. (2013) *The Great African Land Grab: Agricultural Investments and the Global Food System*, London: Zed Books.

Da Vià, E. (2011) 'The politics of "win-win" narratives: land grabs as development opportunity?', Paper presented at the international conference on 'Global land grabbing', IDS, University of Sussex, 6–8 April.

Daily Telegraph (2012) 'Protest at the great African land grab', Damien McElroy, 4 October, p. 20.

De Schutter, O. (2011) 'How not to think of land-grabbing: three critiques of large-scale investments in farmland', *Journal of Peasant Studies*, 38(2): 249–79.

De Soto, H. (1989) *The Other Path: The Invisible Revolution in the Third World*, New York: HarperCollins.

De Sousa Santos, B. (2002) 'Towards a multicultural conception of human rights', *Beyond Law*, 9(25), June, Bogotá: ILSA.

Deutsche Welle (2014) 'Greed for land boosts hunger', 27 March, farmlandgrab.org/23327, accessed 29 March 2014.

Easterly, W. (2014) *The Tyranny of Experts: Economists, dictators, and the forgotten rights of the poor*, New York: Basic Books.

EU Working Group (2010) 'Comments by the EU Working Group

on land issues', ediscussion. donorplatform.org/wp-content/uploads/2010/09/10-09-24_Common-position_EU-WG.pdf, accessed 9 May 2014.

Farmlandgrab.org (2014) www.farmland grab.org/, accessed 9 May 2014.

FIAN (2014) 'FIAN International, for the right to adequate food', www. fian.org/what-we-do/issues/land-grabbing/, accessed 20 June 2014.

Forum for Food Sovereignty (2007) 'Declaration of Nyéléni', 27 February, Sélingué, Mali, www.world-govern-ance.org/IMG/pdf_0072_Declara-tion_of_Nyeleni_-_ENG.pdf.

Gabbert, C. E. (2014) 'The global neighbourhood concept: a chance for cooperative development or Festina Lente', in M. G. Berhe (ed.), A Delicate Balance. Land Use, Minority Rights and Social Stability in the Horn of Africa, Addis Ababa: Institute for Peace and Security Studies, Addis Ababa University.

Gilbert, J. (2013) 'Land rights as human rights, the case for a specific right to land', Sur: International Journal on Human Rights, 10(18): 115–34.

GRAIN (2008) 'Seized: the 2008 land grab for food and financial security', Barcelona: GRAIN, 24 October, www. grain.org/article/entries/93-seized-the-2008-landgrab-for-food-and-financial-security, accessed 4 June 2014.

— (2010) 'World Bank report on land grabbing: Beyond the smoke and mirrors', 19 September, www. globalpolicy.org/globalization/globalization-of-the-economy-2-1/world-bank-2-10/49506.html, accessed 8 May 2014.

Green Scenery (2011) 'Report on fact finding mission to Malen Chiefdom, Pujehun District. 22nd–24th April 2011', file:///C:/Users/justice%20africa/Downloads/201105_Socfin_

Pujehun_report%20EDITED%20(1). pdf, accessed 20 June 2014.

— (2012) 'Launching Action for Large scale Land Acquisition Transparency (ALLAT)', press release.

Guardian (2008) 'Special report: Agriculture: rich countries launch great land grab to safeguard food supply', 22 November, p. 30.

— (2011) 'US universities in Africa land grab: institutions use endowment funds to make deals that may force thousands from land', John Vidal, Claire Provost, 9 June, p. 19.

— (2014) 'G8 New Alliance condemned as new wave of colonialism in Africa', www.theguardian.com/ global-development/2014/feb/18/g8-new-alliance-condemned-new-colonialism, accessed 4 June 2014.

Guardian Unlimited (2011) 'Oxfam warns of spiralling land grab in developing countries', John Vidal, 22 September.

HRW (Human Rights Watch) (2010) 'Kenya landmark ruling on indigenous land rights', 4 February, www. hrw.org/news/2010/02/04/kenya-landmark-ruling-indigenous-land-rights, accessed 10 June 2014.

— (2012) Waiting for Death: Forced Displacement and Villagisation in Ethiopia, www.hrw.org/fr/node/104284, accessed 1 June 2014.

Hyden, G. (2005) African Politics in Comparative Perspective, Cambridge: Cambridge University Press.

ILC (International Land Coalition) (2003) 'Antigua Declaration', www. landcoalition.org/sites/default/files/news-files/AntiguaDeclaration_1.pdf, accessed 10 February 2014.

— (2009) 'Kathmandu Declaration: securing rights to land for peace and food security', www.landcoalition. org/en/publications/kathmandu-declaration, accessed 18 June 2014.

Independent (2013) 'Biofuel project funded by UK "leaves Africans without food"', 1 September, www. independent.co.uk.

International Covenant on Economic, Social and Cultural Rights (1966) General Assembly resolution 2200A (XXI), entry into force 3 January 1976, in accordance with article 27, www. ohchr.org/EN/ProfessionalInterest/ Pages/CESCR.aspx, accessed 8 May 2014.

James, D. (2002) '"Human rights" or "property"? State, society, and the landless in South Africa', London: LSE Research Online, eprints.lse.ac.uk/ archive/00001028, accessed 3 June 2014.

Keck, M. E. and K. Sikkink (1998) *Activists beyond Borders: Advocacy Networks in International Politics*, Ithaca, New York: Cornell University Press.

— (1999) 'Transnational advocacy networks in international and regional politics', *International Social Science Journal*, 51: 89–101.

Lahiff, E. (2010) 'Q&A: Land reform in South Africa', www.pbs.org/pov/ promisedland/land_reform.php, accessed 3 June 2014.

Li, T. M. (2011) 'Centering labor in the land grab debate', *Journal of Peasant Studies*, 38(2): 281–99.

Manji, A. (2006) *The Politics of Land Reform in Africa: From Communal Tenure to Free Markets*, London: Zed Books.

McKeon, N. (2013) '"One does not sell the land upon which the people walk": land grabbing, transnational rural social movements, and global governance', *Globalizations*, 10(1): 105–22.

MRG (Minority Rights Group) (2013) 'African court issues historic ruling protecting rights of Kenya's Ogiek community', www.minorityrights. org/11822/press-releases/ african-court-issues-historic-ruling- protecting-rights-of-kenyas-ogiek-

community.html, accessed 10 June 2014.

Nelson, P. J. and E. Dorsey (2008) *New Rights Advocacy: Changing strategies of development and human rights NGOs*, Washington, DC: Georgetown University Press.

New Alliance (n.d.) www.gov.uk/govern- ment/uploads/system/uploads/ attachment_data/file/205883/new- alliance-factsheet.pdf.

Oakland Institute (2011a) *Understanding Land Investment Deals in Africa. Country report: Ethiopia*, Oakland, CA: Oakland Institute, www.oakland institute.org/sites/oaklandinstitute. org/files/OI_Ethiopa_Land_ Investment_report.pdf, accessed 30 May 2014.

— (2011b) *Understanding Land Invest- ment Deals in Africa. Country report: Sierra Leone*, Oakland, CA: Oakland Institute.

— (2013) *Lives for Land in Gambella*, 1 August, media.oaklandinstitute. org/ethiopia-lives-land-gambella, accessed 30 May 2014.

Observer (1990) 'White farmers furious at land grab by Mugabe', 9 December, p. 12.

OECD (2008) *Rising Food Prices: Causes and Consequences*, www.oecd.org/ trade/agricultural-trade/40847088. pdf, accessed 21 April 2014.

Okot, B. (2013) 'Uganda, breaking the links between the land and the people', www.iied.org/uganda- breaking-links-between-land-people.

Oxfam (2013) 'The New Alliance: a new direction needed, reforming the G8's public–private partnership on agriculture and food security', www. oxfam.org/sites/www.oxfam.org/ files/bn-new-alliance-new-direction- agriculture-250913-en.pdf, accessed 11 February 2014.

— (2014) 'Guide to land grabs', www.oxfam.org.uk/get-involved/

campaign-with-us/our-campaigns/
grow/guide-to-land-grabs, accessed
11 February 2014.

Oya, C. (2013) 'Methodological
reflections on "land grab" data-
bases and the "land grab" literature
"rush"', *Journal of Peasant Studies*,
40(3): 503–20.

Petition online (2011) 'Dakar appeal
against the land grab', www.
petitiononline.com/petitions/dakar/
signatures?page=5, accessed 2 June
2014.

Rahmato, D. (2011) *Land to Investors:
Large-scale Land Transfers in Ethiopia*,
Addis Ababa: Forum for Social
Studies.

Reisenberger, B. and S. M. Suárez (2011)
'Nyéléni, Mali: A Global Alliance
Against Land Grabbing', www.fian.at/
assets/Nyeleni-MaliGlobal-Alliance-
Against-Land-Grabbing.pdf, accessed
4 June 2014.

Richards, P. (1996) *Fighting for the Rainforest: War, youth and resources in
Sierra Leone*, London: James Currey.

Scoones, I. (2014) 'Missing politics and
food sovereignty', *Future Agricultures
Blog*, 27 January, www.future-
agricultures.org/blog/entry/missing-
politics-and-food-sovereignty#.
U6yq4fldVMI, accessed 3 June 2014.

Scott, J. C. (1976) *The Moral Economy of
the Peasant: Rebellion and Subsistence
in Southeast Asia*, New Haven, CT:
Yale University Press.

Sethi, A. (2013) 'Karituri debacle prompts
Ethiopia to review land policy', *The
Hindu*, 1 June, www.thehindu.com/
news/international/world/karuturi-
debacle-prompts-ethiopia-to-review-
land-policy/article4772306.ece,
accessed 20 June 2014.

Shepard, D. with A. Mittal (2009) *The
Great Land Grab; Rush for World's
Farmland Threatens Food Security
for the Poor*, Oakland, CA: Oakland
Institute.

Stanford Encyclopedia of Philosophy
(2013) 'Human rights', plato.stanford.
edu/entries/rights-human/, accessed
7 May 2014.

Sugimura, K. (2007) 'African peasants
and moral economy', *PEKEA News-
letter*, 9: 1–6, www.pekea-fr.org/
PubliSurNLetter/Sugimura-NL9.pdf,
accessed 2 June 2014.

Taylor, C. (1999) 'Conditions of an un-
forced consensus on human rights',
in J. Bauer and D. A. Bell (eds), *The
East Asian Challenge for Human
Rights*, Cambridge: Cambridge
University Press.

The Times (2013) 'South Africa firebrand
calls for Mugabe-style land grabs',
12 July, p. 30.

UNICEF (n.d.) 'At a glance: Sierra Leone
statistics', www.unicef.org/infoby
country/sierraleone_statistics.html,
accessed 3 July 2013.

USAID (n.d.) 'Sierra Leone – property
rights and governance profile', usaid-
landtenure.net/sites/default/files/
country-profiles/full-reports/USAID_
Land_Tenure_Sierra_Leone_Profile.
pdf, accessed 3 June 2014.

Vidal, J. (2013) 'La Via Campesina's
Saragih: "We have no choice but
to change the system"', *Guardian*,
17 June, www.theguardian.com/
global-development/2013/jun/17/
la-via-campesina-henry-saragih,
accessed 5 June 2014.

War on Want (2013) 'African groups
reject G8 corporate food plan as
"colonialism"', www.waronwant.
org/news/press-releases/17907-
african-groups-reject-g8-corporate-
food-plan-as-colonialism, accessed
4 May 2014.

Wickeri, E. and A. Kalhan (2010)
'Land rights issues in international
human rights law', *Malaysian Journal
on Human Rights*, 4(10).

Wisborg, P. (2013) 'Human rights against
land grabbing? A reflection on

norms, policies, and power', *Journal of Agricultural Environmental Ethics*, 26: 1199–222.

Witten, M. W. (2007) 'The protection of land rights in Ethiopia', *Afrika Focus*, 20(1/2): 153–84.

World Bank (2010) 'Rising global interest in farmland. Can it yield sustainable and equitable benefits?', Washington, DC: World Bank.

World Bank, UNCTAD, FAO, IFAD (2013) 'Principles for responsible agricultural investment that respects livelihoods and resources (PRAI)', unctad.org/en/Pages/DIAE/G-20/PRAI.aspx.

World Bank Group (n.d.) 'Rebuilding business and investment in post-conflict Sierra Leone', Washington, DC: World Bank.

12 | CONCLUSION: RECLAIMING ACTIVISM

*Casey Hogle, Trisha Taneja, Keren Yohannes
and Jennifer Ambrose*

Introduction

As can be seen from the diverse nature of the included case studies, the goal of this volume is not to provide a standard universal solution regarding what 'good' activism should be. Rather, this volume recognizes the diversity of activist campaigns and the need for local or regional variation. While we cannot offer a gold standard that should be lauded as a definitive case study, we can reflect on how certain elements of various campaigns can be replicated to implement the 'nothing for us without us' adage, and offer suggestions to better understand how to identify and emulate the most ethically sound and effective elements of transnational solidarity movements that De Waal outlines in Chapter 2. Ultimately, 'reclaimed' activism is activism that prioritizes the empowerment of people (rather than media impact) as the basis for transformational change, and that is accountable to the people most affected by an issue. Hence, instead of offering a unique formula for activism to follow, this volume proposes a few general themes that should underlie transnational activist movements and which can be adapted according to need and context. Four common themes emerge from the assortment of cases in this volume which serve as essential components of reclaiming activism.

First and foremost, responsible activism empowers local actors to define and lead any efforts on their behalf, including identifying the advocacy targets, methods, narratives and definitions of success. The tendency of Western actors to co-opt any of those key pieces to frame their own narratives dilutes the legitimacy of such activist campaigns as they are no longer in solidarity with or accountable to the local people.

Second, activism that addresses only specific occurrences or news events without addressing the broader context – i.e. the underlying and structural problems that have led to that event – is superficial. Recognizing the complexity of conflict and/or human rights violations is a prerequisite to responding effectively to it.

Third, reclaimed activism accepts a wide swathe of actors and encourages them to participate in its campaigns and movements. Inclusivity itself is a tenet of responsible advocacy; excluding stakeholders from a movement that affects them cannot render a movement successful. Inclusivity is also indispensable to ensure that multiple perspectives are heard and to allow opportunities for working across groups to find common ground.

Finally, responsible campaigns and movements accept and promote diverse voices and understandings of an issue. Activism should reject singular narratives, especially those crafted from the outside that tend to highlight one aspect of a conflict or perpetuate one stereotype of the country. While having a single story to tell may be the most simplified way to spread a message, it is by no means the most accurate. Misdiagnosing a problem through simplification invariably leads to incorrect application of a proposed solution.

In the rest of this concluding chapter, we offer a further elaboration of these themes, with specific references to the cases in the book from which they were drawn. Additionally, we also define the key audiences, and how they can use these themes to craft or participate in responsible advocacy.

(I) Empower local actors to define advocacy targets, methods, narratives and success

A key theme that emerges from the variety of case studies in this volume is also pointed out by De Waal's historical-theoretical chapter – the importance of empowering local actors to craft the mission and direction of any activism of which they are targets. As De Waal notes, this empowerment often takes place through allowing space for solidarity between transnational activist campaigns and existing local ones, where the resources and reach of Western or transnational campaigns should support the direction and mission of local ones. In his case study of advocacy in Latin America, Brett illustrates a failure of the solidarity model and its consequences. He points out how several thriving movements in Latin America were co-opted by Western advocates, who created their own parallel but contentious

advocacy campaigns with competing goals, methods and narratives
- in this case, specifically framed by the Liberal Peace agenda.

This volume contends that a two-way dialogue and information
exchange is more purposeful and more impactful because it provides
space for empowering local advocates to identify their own goals and
lead their own struggles. Two case studies from the book illustrate
the necessity of addressing the structural inequalities that are inherent between international and localized advocacy movements,
which risk disempowering local actors.

The case of disability rights in the African context offers a primary example of how an international advocacy movement can not
only fail to support domestic movements but also use methods and
structures that necessarily exclude the affected audience. Chataika,
Berghs, Mateta and Shava discuss how the profound connection
between disability and poverty results in many disabled people being marginalized in society. They argue that when disabled people's
organizations are primarily located in capital cities or the global
North, the very people these movements seek to represent cannot
access the activist space. As a result, exclusion occurs on both the
national and international levels through the creation of structures
that not only fail to empower local actors, but necessarily disempower
them. Chataika et al. go on to offer a solution: a purposeful recognition of these structural inequalities by the activists. By reflecting on
the problems, third spaces of inclusion and idea exchange can be
created, thus providing the affected audience and local actors with
control over the methods and goals of activism that targets them.

Ibreck's chapter on land rights illustrates a similar tale of contested exclusion, but with a different outcome. Ibreck shows how local
land rights activism has historically been challenged on its categorization of the struggle for land rights as a human rights issue. Western
academics, policy-makers and activists have spent a great deal of
time debating the movement's place within a precarious structural
hierarchy of activism, thereby neglecting the local ownership of the
land rights struggle and the deeper issues driving it. This debate
resulted in the exclusion of local actors from what became primarily
an academic space. Ibreck argues, however, that land rights activism
has more recently experienced a process of consensus through the
creation of a consistent international platform that also allows the

space for local actors to identify their own goals and methods of advocacy in response to localized land grabs. Although land rights activism is not without challenges, this case forms a positive example of how an international, consensually built platform can empower and engage local actors.

(II) Recognize complexity of cases and target underlying issues

In many cases, both those addressed in this volume and others, activism focuses on one particular issue or problematic event but ignores the broader context and underlying issues that contribute to the problem. This type of activism, which addresses only the most visible symptom and not the root of the problem at hand, is too superficial to have a meaningful impact. Furthermore, these campaigns oversimplify the issues they seek to address and focus on one narrative at the expense of others, often focusing on the one that is the simplest, most catchy or most immediately relevant to Westerners. By ignoring the true complexity of the problems it wants to solve, oversimplified advocacy results in the promotion of solutions that are not appropriate or would be ineffective.

Perhaps the most obvious examples of this kind of superficial activism in this volume are found in Seay's chapter on the Democratic Republic of Congo (DRC) and Schomerus's chapter on the Lord's Resistance Army (LRA) in Uganda and its neighbours. With regard to the DRC, Western advocacy campaigns have emphasized the narrative of conflict minerals and focused on actions to regulate the mineral trade. In Uganda, advocacy primarily revolves around the effort to locate LRA leader Joseph Kony in order to capture or kill him. In both cases, however, advocacy organizations have largely ignored the root causes of conflict – the presence of structural violence, issues of governance and the impact of poverty – which underlie the one-dimensional problems of conflict minerals and the LRA presented by Western advocacy.

Consequently, campaigns that ignore critical underlying issues often make inappropriate 'asks' of policy-makers. Since the advocacy goals are based on a simplistic understanding of the context and on one of many narratives, the problem is presented as solvable by (a usually ineffective) ask. In the case of the DRC and the LRA, these asks are to domestically legislate against American trade in conflict minerals and to use American troops to 'catch' Joseph Kony. However, given the multilayered nature of these conflicts, single propositions are unlikely to be impactful. A deeper, more structural analysis of Uganda and DRC might discuss the widespread militarization and struggle with peace and democratization, respectively, thus raising the prospect of longer-term, locally focused solutions that address these ingrained issues. The current, dominant kind of superficial activism and its asks might address the symptoms of a problem, but it can reinforce its underlying causes because it envisions an international solution to a local complexity and is uncritical about the use of US or other Western force. Similarly, Feinstein and de Waal's analysis of activism around the arms trade highlights multiple campaigns' failure to address the deep-seated corruption and noxious military–industrial complex that are connected to the arms trade. Advocacy has instead focused on single weapon types with limited asks (e.g. UN treaties) that proved ineffective at cementing lasting change.

Interestingly enough, one campaign that has been successful in emphasizing the underlying causes of a problem (despite its other shortcomings) is the Occupy Movement. Occupy began in New York City in 2011 and spread to other US cities, with similar localized protests occurring around the world. One thing that differentiates Occupy from the DRC and LRA campaigns described in this volume is that it addresses the problem of unemployment and the financial crisis by focusing on the broad structural issues systematically re-inforcing inequality. Occupy activists protest against this entrenched inequality and advocate for less hierarchical structures for distribution of money and power. It is worth noting, however, that the broad focus of the Occupy Movement makes it less able to focus on specific, detailed policy change. This trade-off between complex narratives and detailed policy asks need not be inevitable, and a process of refining and prioritizing desired change can still emerge from a complex understanding of the many layers of an advocacy issue.

Using Occupy as a positive example is not a call to limit Western activist campaigns to broad issues such as inequality or poverty. Understandably, addressing inequality as a structural issue is prob-ably easier for the Occupy Movement since inequality is a widely understood issue worldwide. As such, Occupy activists are not re-quired to explain or simplify a remote context or esoteric issue to their audience. The salient point is that Western activist campaigns should always take broader, underlying causes of issues into consideration. The lack of instant recognition or resonance of a concept – as Occupy has with 'inequality' – should not preclude Western activism centred on the LRA and DRC from addressing the causal issues; if anything it necessitates this contextual grounding even more. Instead of starting with a solution – regulating the mineral trade or hunting down Kony – and making that their goal, advocates should start by considering the larger context and how it is driving the problem.

(III) Inclusivity: engage a wide swathe of actors

Recognizing *who* is a member in a campaign or movement, and, essentially, who has the actual power to define and alter it, is a basic starting point for analysing the accountability of activism. Including a diversity of stakeholders is crucial to fairly represent the target communities, while those cases that allow single groups to dominate a campaign are often incapable of incorporating the full complexity of an issue. Inclusivity should be considered on at least three different levels and should recognize the importance of the following: (1) engaging a range of key transnational stakeholders, such as academics, policy-makers, activists, development actors, human rights advocates, peace-building communities, political actors and marginalized communities; (2) including those stakeholders at local, national and international levels; and (3) being cognizant of the diversity within stakeholder groups across key demographic markers such as gender, ethnicity and socio-economic status. Reclaimed activism does not need to check each of these boxes, but it should consider the full range of actors and at least be cognizant of whom the campaign excludes and which stakeholders it privileges.

Diversity necessitates compromise; it brings together different narratives, opinions and interests that demand a process of working across difference to find common ground. Activists should encourage opportunities for more inclusive movements and celebrate the processes needed to bring in new and diverse perspectives. This is not easy, and while campaigns that bring together multiple voices can provide a forum for a constructive debate about the key elements of activism, often the interaction results in 'winners' and 'losers' among actors based on power imbalances.

One evident case that lacks transnational diversity is described in Schomerus's Chapter 7 on the LRA of Uganda. Invisible Children chose to engage American youth as the primarily stakeholder, ignoring key actors who had a deeper and more relevant understanding of the underlying issues. In Chapter 4, Brett described how transnational inclusivity of stakeholders allowed for amplified messaging and important financial and capacity-building support for the local actors. As positive as this inclusivity was, a lack of dialogue and solidarity led to the promotion of the Liberal Peace agenda at the expense of the local priorities of emancipation.

A case that illustrates the dangers of a lack of ethnic diversity among local stakeholders is Zarni and Taneja's chapter on Burma. They point out that by clustering around a single democratic icon, Aung San Suu Kyi, the Burmese campaign became exclusionary and in no way represented the ethnic struggles of and violence against the Muslim Rohingya population. In fact, by not including diverse ethnic stakeholders, Burma's campaign became trapped in a self-inflicted single narrative advocating democracy, while ignoring decades-old underlying ethnic tensions, the consequences of which are discussed in the next section.

Similarly, in Chapter 11, Ibreck identifies the tensions between local and transnational academics, policy-makers and activists in defining and advocating around land-grab issues. She notes some key successes in developing a common framework to gain international attention for the notion of the right to land. At the same time, divergent policy and development theories among key actors continue to hinder collective action. Ibreck recommends greater connectivity among the key stakeholders – scholars, human rights activists and the rural communities most affected by land grabs – in order to understand each specific case within its social and economic context.

(IV) Accept diverse voices and reject singular narratives

Closely related to inclusion of diverse stakeholders is inclusion of diverse narratives; reclaimed activism should recognize complexity, doubt and multiple voices. Chimamanda Ngozi Adichie's famous TED talk in 2009 outlines the 'dangers of a single story'. We quote at length, as she eloquently identifies the power dynamics inherent in the authorship of narratives:

It is impossible to talk about the single story without talking about power. There is a word, an Igbo word, that I think about whenever I think about the power structures of the world, and it is 'nkali.' It's a noun that loosely translates to 'to be greater than another.' Like our economic and political worlds, stories too are defined by the principle of nkali: How they are told, who tells them, when they're told, how many stories are told, are really dependent on power. Power is the ability not just to tell the story of another person, but to make it the definitive story of that person. The Palestinian poet Mourid Barghouti writes that if you want to dispossess a people, the simplest way to do it is to tell their story and to start with, 'secondly.' Start the story with the arrows of the Native Americans, and not with the arrival of the British, and you have an entirely different story. Start the story with the failure of the African state, and not with the colonial creation of the African state, and you have an entirely different story.

Activism in conflict is especially wrought with the dangers of a single story. While competing narratives may not be the proximate cause of most violent conflict, the tensions, escalation and entrenching of that conflict are inevitably aided by competing narratives between warring sides. Narratives are addressed throughout this volume, and the power to define a campaign or movement's narratives – and the amount of diversity and nuance that is allowed within narratives – has huge ramifications for the level of solidarity that activism espouses.

The most problematic campaigns tend to be those that disregard Adichie's warning and fasten on to a single narrative, ignoring alternative descriptions of an issue. As Seay writes in Chapter 6, describing the crises in the DRC as solely a story about so-called 'conflict minerals' is an example of a single narrative that misidentifies the drivers of conflict. Somewhat similarly, as Zarni and Taneja explain in Chapter 3, the privileging of one narrative in Burma, which is defined primarily by one individual, silences alternative narratives regarding conflict drivers, actors and potential solutions to the complex Burmese political struggle. In this instance, the unquestionability of Suu Kyi's definition of the Burmese context prevents Burmese activism from addressing the full range of social and political issues facing the country. A single story is just as dangerous when accepted unquestionably from a local or international actor. Similarly, De Waal's description of the Western campaign for South Sudan, described in Chapter 8, shows how its demonization of one actor (the government in Khartoum) contributed to systematically overlooking the shortcomings and dangers represented by the Sudan People's Liberation Army.

Defining the conflict narrative is a key theme of Biletzki's description of activism directed at Gaza, with Israeli and Palestinian communities both advancing a narrative of victimhood. The power imbalance between the two, and the asymmetry in their ability to mobilize resources and leverage international (and particularly American) support for their narrative, has thus far resulted in a failure to create mass support for the pro-Gazan narrative. Biletzki's stance does not support both narratives, but rather advocates the deconstruction of the conception that both are equally valid. Allowing room for multiple narratives and for complexity does not mean the activist must privilege all sides or stories equally. Rather, recognizing the complexity allows the space for conversation about narrative construction, and in this case understanding how the Israeli refrain that 'all Gazans are terrorists' can be used to drown out alternative narratives in this conflict.

(V) Key audiences

We turn now to the key audiences for whom this book was written and draw out the main lessons and guidance we find most relevant for each group. First, we hoped to encourage practitioners to be more aware of the contestation and power relations embedded in the process of defining issues for campaigning and the methods of campaigning. In particular, Western activists need to consider more carefully the impacts of transnational activism on the people they aim to help, to find ways to represent their agency and capacity respectfully, and to present an accurate view of the situation they wish to address. International NGOs have long struggled with the question of appropriate representation, and many now accept a set of practices in fund-raising and advocacy that portray their participants as actors rather than helpless recipients, as dignified rather than supplicant. The principle of 'do no harm', extended from medical practice to humanitarian action and conflict transformation, is also relevant to the field of activism.

As advocacy movements have spread across high school and college campuses, students have become a key target audience, with the Kony2012 and STAND (Students Taking Action Now: Darfur) campaigns among the most obvious examples. Before engaging in such campaigns, however, students and general consumers of advocacy campaigns should think critically about the appropriateness of their involvement. How inclusive is the campaign of a range of stakeholders? Who are the decision-makers in the campaign and who holds power? Where are the voices of those most affected by the conflict or the issue? Reflecting on these and similar questions can help determine whether the students are acting in solidarity with and supporting local actors, or whether they are promoting solutions developed externally and marketed with single narratives. Students should invest time in understanding how the campaign was developed before rushing to buy bracelets and posters or participating blindly with the assumption that good intentions are good enough.

Academics have increasingly taken the issues of advocacy and activism as the subject of research, with a slew of books and articles analysing both the issues and the practices of campaigning. Academics have long been advocates themselves. In many of the cases discussed in this volume, however, there has been a disconnect between academics and practitioners and a reluctance on the part of both to engage in open dialogue. This disconnect extends to the nuances of individual campaigns, in which academics are rarely sought out as sources of knowledge for advocacy campaigns regarding issues of their area of expertise. This has been particularly obvious in the cases of the LRA and the Democratic Republic of Congo, where prevailing academic opinion on the facts of the conflicts differs greatly from the narratives presented by American advocacy organizations. On the other hand, there are some issues, particularly land rights, in which academics have taken a leading role in defining the problem and setting the advocacy agenda. At the same time, the professional demands of academia do not value the types of communication that might lend themselves to broader audiences, which affects academics' ability to engage with and influence transnational activism.

This phenomenon is common in all cases in which academics study areas of public policy and practice. But it becomes particularly acute in the study of advocacy practices, in which practitioners are driven by a sense of urgency and ethical righteousness and may interpret critiques of their methods and representations as attacks on their entire projects. For practitioners, research is often an instrumental activity to garner useful facts in support of their campaigns; for academics, the simplification of issues for public consumption is too often seen as ignorance or carelessness. The two need to be sensitive to one another, recognizing the constraints of each field while being willing to engage in constructive conversations that can strengthen responsible advocacy.

Academics also have the opportunity to educate their students about responsible activism. Though they are still fairly uncommon, there has been a rise in experiential education courses on activism in US colleges and universities. Professors in the USA and abroad have also used case studies of advocacy, such as the International Campaign to Ban Landmines, in courses on civic engagement, transnational contention, leadership and diplomacy. Since mass advocacy campaigns often target young people, it is essential that teachers and professors push their students to critically engage with the methods, impacts and ethical foundations of such campaigns. The classroom offers a valuable space in which to expose students to criticisms of advocacy and to encourage them to consider the unintended negative effects that good intentions can sometimes have.

The media are also essential in mass advocacy campaigns. Journalists, columnists and editorial writers often take part in advocacy, either through their efforts to raise awareness, their reporting on advocacy campaigns, or their editorials. In their efforts to participate in activism themselves, media professionals can heed all recommendations outlined above by reporting the perspectives of local actors, investigating the full causes of conflicts and abuses, and including a range of voices and narratives in their pieces. Furthermore, this volume aims to encourage the media to take a more balanced approach in their *coverage* of advocacy campaigns, reporting not only on Westerners' efforts to raise awareness but also on criticism of these efforts, objective information about their impacts, responses from people affected and existing local movements. These recommendations are not aimed solely at Western media professionals; we also encourage more active and critical media coverage from the affected countries themselves.

Finally, the national or local public in affected countries, and their social movements, political parties, media and NGOs, are the most important stakeholders in advocacy campaigns. Too rarely do local actors have the opportunity to define an issue and thereby become masters of the agenda for tackling it. They are instead often obliged to accept a definition of the problem, and consequently a political agenda, established elsewhere. This book hopes to be relevant to indigenous movements and strengthen them by illustrating the lessons local activists can learn from similar groups' interactions with transnational activism.

This volume serves as our modest contribution to encouraging greater introspection on the part of transnational activists. We aim to reclaim activism for those who act in true solidarity with the individuals who are most affected by a conflict or suffer most from human rights abuses. Activists should always be true to the complexity and diversity of the world, especially in their efforts to change it. We hope we've pushed the field of advocacy one step closer to achieving the goal: 'nothing for us without us'.

ABOUT THE CONTRIBUTORS

Jennifer Ambrose currently works as a research analyst at AidGrade, where she conducts meta-analyses on evaluations of development projects, with the aim of understanding how to improve foreign aid. She is also the editor-in-chief at WhyDev, a blog dedicated to promoting critical discussion on development. Jennifer served for two years as a Peace Corps Volunteer in Rwanda, where she taught English and implemented a variety of health and community development projects. She holds an MA from the Fletcher School of Law and Diplomacy at Tufts University and a BA from Claremont McKenna College.

Maria Berghs is currently a research fellow in Health Sciences at the University of York. Her research interests include gender, models of disability, humanitarianism and West Africa.

Anat Biletzki is the Schweitzer Professor of Philosophy at Quinnipiac University and Professor of Philosophy at Tel Aviv University. For over thirty years, she has been active in the peace movement and in human rights work in Israel. During the first intifada, Biletzki was one of the founders of a peace movement called 'The Twenty-First Year', which was devoted to promoting civil objection to the Occupation. Later, she helped establish the movement called 'Open Doors', which worked to liberate Palestinian administrative detainees in Israel. From 2001 to 2006 she was chairperson of B'Tselem – the Israeli Information Centre for Human Rights in the Occupied Territories – and was nominated among the '1,000 Women for the Nobel Peace Prize 2005'. Biletzki is the author of *What is Logic?* and *Talking Wolves: Thomas Hobbes on the Language of Politics and the Politics of Language.*

Roddy Brett is a lecturer with the School of International Relations, University of St Andrews, and co-coordinator of the MLitt in Peace and Conflict Studies. He lived for over a decade in Latin America, principally in Guatemala and Colombia, working as a scholar-practitioner, in the fields of conflict and peace studies, political and other forms of violence, social movements, indigenous rights and transitions. He has published and co-edited eight books on these subjects and a series of articles in international journals. He has acted as adviser to the United Nations in Latin America and worked with the Centre for Human Rights Legal Action in Guatemala, initially as field investigator, and subsequently as coordinator of the Department for Justice and Reconciliation (DEJURE). In this capacity, he was a member of the original team that prepared the evidence for and political strategy of the legal case filed against three former presidents of Guatemala and their military high commands of the 1980s for genocide, war crimes and crimes against humanity. This led to the conviction by a Guatemalan court of former dictator General Efraín Ríos Montt in May 2013 and a sentence of eighty years for genocide and crimes against humanity.

Tsitsi Chataika is a senior lecturer in the department of Educational Foundations in the Faculty of Education at the University of Zimbabwe. She is a disability mainstreaming advocate and researcher with an international reputation and she serves on various international editorial boards. Dr Chataika has conducted work in several African countries, Malaysia and the United Kingdom. She recently developed a gender and disability mainstreaming manual and she is also contributing to the Southern African Development Community Inclusive Education Strategy.

Andrew Feinstein was a Member of Parliament for the African National Congress in South Africa from 1994 to 2001. He is the author of *After the Party: Corruption, the ANC and South Africa's Uncertain Future* (2007) and *The Shadow World: Inside the Global Arms Trade* (2011), a full-length documentary feature of which will be released in 2015. He is the director of Corruption Watch UK and chairs the Friends of the Treatment Action Campaign.

Casey Hogle currently works for Search for Common Ground, managing their peace-building programmes across the Middle East and

North Africa. She previously worked for human rights and women, peace and security organizations in the USA and in the Middle East and North Africa (MENA) region. She has lived in Jordan, Libya and Syria. Casey holds an MA from the Fletcher School of Law and Diplomacy at Tufts University and a BA from Carleton College.

Rachel Ibreck is a Fellow in International Development at the London School of Economics and Political Science and an associate of the Human Rights Consortium, University of London. Her research focuses on the themes of memory politics, transitional justice, social movements and human rights struggles in Africa. She examined the political significance of genocide memorialization in Rwanda, during PhD research at the University of Bristol, 2009. She has since published in journals such as *African Affairs, Journal of Intervention and Statebuilding, Journal of Contemporary African Studies* and *Memory Studies*. She formerly worked for African Rights and Justice Africa.

Abraham Mateta is a lawyer by training and a disability rights activist by calling. After graduation, he worked for the government of Zimbabwe in the Office of the Public Protector for two years. He left in 2009 to join civic society, where he has been a disability rights and advocacy officer for the Zimbabwe national league of the blind for the past five years. He also sits on the Zimbabwe Youth Council board, where, in addition to providing general legal advice, he also advises on disability inclusion. Currently, Abraham is taking an LLM postgraduate course on Human Rights at Leeds University.

Mareike Schomerus from the London School of Economics and Political Science is a researcher on the dynamics of violent conflict and its resolution, the violence of democratization, civilian security, and the impact of living in militarized situations on personal lives. Her publications on the LRA include 'The Lord's Resistance Army in Sudan: a history and overview', HSBA Working Paper 8 (2007) and the two chapters 'Chasing the Kony story' and 'A terrorist is not a person like me: an interview with Joseph Kony' in *The Lord's Resistance Army: Myth and Reality* (2010).

Laura Seay is Assistant Professor of Government at Colby College in Maine, USA. Her research focuses on non-state actors and governance in Central Africa's fragile states and the effects of Western advocacy movements on conflict outcomes in Africa.

Kudzai Shava is a lecturer at the Reformed Church in Zimbabwe and a disability rights activist. He holds a master's degree in Disability Studies from the University of Leeds.

Trisha Taneja has a background in global health and humanitarian research and is an alumna of the University of British Columbia, the Harvard Humanitarian Initiative, and the Fletcher School of Law and Diplomacy at Tufts University. She has previously worked with Médecins Sans Frontières, Femmes et Villes International/Women in Cities International, and Catholic Relief Services on projects relating to microfinance and women's empowerment, gender inclusion and urban planning, and access to essential medicines.

Keren Yohannes is a Foreign Service Officer with the US Department of State. She previously worked in refugee resettlement in the USA and as a Watson research fellow on disability rights for refugees in Sierra Leone, Uganda, Jordan, Sri Lanka and Nepal. She holds an MA from the Fletcher School of Law and Diplomacy and a BA from Macalester College.

Maung Zarni is a lecturer in the Department of Global Health and Social Medicine, Harvard Medical School, specializing in the political economy of racism, violence and genocide. He is a fiercely independent Burmese exile with more than twenty-five years of deep involvement in Burmese politics and policy activism. Zarni founded the Free Burma Coalition in 1995, having advocated Western economic sanctions and diplomatic isolation of Burma. Disillusioned with Western Burma policies, Zarni shifted tack and worked with three successive heads of Burma's military intelligence services, pushing for home-grown reconciliation among the Burmese and Western re-engagement with the military government. As a scholar, Zarni has taught and/or held research appointments at National Louis University (in Chicago), the University of London

Institute of Education, the University of Oxford, the London School of Economics and Political Science, Chulalongkorn University and the University of Malaya. He was a member of the Georgetown Leadership Seminar (2004) and a Fellow in the Rockefeller Foundation Next Generation Leadership Program (2001–03). Educated at the universities of Mandalay, California, Washington and Wisconsin, Zarni blogs at maungzarni.net and tweets at @drzarni.

INDEX